EXPLORING PHILEMON

Society of Biblical Literature

Rhetoric of Religious Antiquity

Vernon K. Robbins, General Editor
Duane F. Watson, General Editor
David B. Gowler, Associate Editor
L. Gregory Bloomquist
Rosemary Canavan
Alexandra Gruca-Macaulay
Roy R. Jeal
Harry O. Maier
Walter T. Wilson

Number 2

EXPLORING PHILEMON

Freedom, Brotherhood, and Partnership in the New Society

Roy R. Jeal

for Terry and Myrna
in friendship

[signature]

4 JANUARY 2016

SBL Press
Atlanta

Copyright © 2015 by SBL Press

Publication of this volume was made possible by the generous support of the Pierce Program in Religion of Oxford College of Emory University.

The editors of this volume express their sincere gratitude to David E. Orton and Deo Publishing for their ongoing support and encouragement of this series throughout its stages of development 1998–2013.

Cover design is an adaptation by Bernard Madden of Rick A. Robbins, "His LifeLine" (42" x 50" acrylic on canvas, 2002). Online: http://home.comcast.net/~rick1216/LifeLine/LifeLine5.htm. Cover design used by permission of Deo Publishing.

Library of Congress Cataloging-in-Publication Data

Jeal, Roy R.
    Exploring Philemon : freedom, brotherhood, and partnership in the new society / by
    Roy R. Jeal.
        p. cm. — (Rhetoric of Religious Antiquity ; Number 2)
    Includes bibliographical references and index.
    ISBN 978-0-88414-091-7 (pbk. : alk. paper) — ISBN 978-0-88414-092-4 (electronic
    book) — ISBN 978-0-88414-093-1 (hardcover : alk. paper)
    1. Bible. Philemon—Criticism, interpretation, etc. I. Title.
    BS2765.52.J43 2015
    227'.8606—dc23   2015025271

Quotations of Seneca reprinted by permission of the publishers and the Trustees of the Loeb Classical Library from SENECA, VOL. IV, Loeb Classical Library Volume 75, translated by Richard M. Gummere. Copyright © 1917 by the President and Fellows of Harvard College. Quotations of Pliny the Younger reprinted by permission of the publishers and the Trustees of the Loeb Classical Library from PLINY THE YOUNGER: LETTERS, VOLS. I and II, Loeb Classical Library Volumes 55 and 59, translated by Betty Radice. Copyright © 1969 by the President and Fellows of Harvard College. Loeb Classical Library® is a registered trademark of the President and Fellows of Harvard College.

Printed on acid-free paper.

To my son, Dr. Nathan Jeal, with love

CONTENTS

Editorial Foreword

The Rhetoric of Religious Antiquity Series

The Rhetoric of Religious Antiquity (RRA) series uses insights from sociolinguistics, semiotics, rhetoric, ethnography, literary studies, social sciences, cognitive science, and ideological studies in programmatic ways that enact sociorhetorical interpretation (SRI) as an interpretive analytic. This means that SRI is a multidimensional approach to texts guided by a multidimensional hermeneutic. Rather than being a specific method for interpreting texts, an interpretive analytic evaluates and reorients its strategies as it engages in multifaceted dialogue with the texts and other phenomena that come within its purview. It invites methods and methodological results into the environment of its activities, but those methods and results are always under scrutiny. Using concepts and strategies of methods as an interactive interpretive analytic, sociorhetorical interpretation juxtaposes and interrelates phenomena from multiple disciplines and modes of interpretation by drawing and redrawing boundaries of analysis and interpretation.

The corpus of works for the Rhetoric of Religious Antiquity series is writings in the environment of the first four centuries of the emergence of Christianity. The primary corpus is the New Testament, but full-length studies and commentaries may be produced on writings with some significant relationship to study of the New Testament, such as Wisdom of Solomon, Sibylline Oracles, Didache, Epistle of Barnabas, Protevangelium of James, or Infancy Gospel of Thomas.

The Approach of SREC Commentaries

Sociorhetorical Exploration Commentaries (SREC) enact the interactive interpretive analytic of SRI by exploring, analyzing, and interpreting multiple textures of texts. Interpreters begin sociorhetorical commentary with a description of the blending of rhetorical belief systems that occurs through the sequence of pictures the discourse evokes, which the authors call rhetography. This beginning point is motivated by insights both from conceptual blending theory and from rhetorical interpretation of early Christian discourse. Underlying this beginning point is a presupposition that spoken or written discourse begins its persuasive work by creating a sequence of pictures in the mind. As the commentators proceed, they interpret the rhetography in wisdom, prophetic, apocalyptic, precreation, miracle, and priestly belief systems in emergent Christian discourse to present an initial interpretation of the blending of belief systems that was occurring during the first Christian century.

After the beginning focus on the picturing of belief and action in texts being interpreted, commentators analyze the texts from the perspective of their inner texture, intertexture, social and cultural textures, ideological texture, and sacred texture. This section is called textural commentary. The strategies of analysis and interpretation are guided by a presupposition that humans create patterns of images and reasonings in the inner texture of their elaborations by recruiting great ranges of "background meaning" and building them into rich systems of belief and action through processes of "pattern completion" that create "emergent structures."

The final step in the commentary is the presentation of the rhetorical force of the text as emerging discourse in the Mediterranean world. An overall goal of the commentary, therefore, is to analyze and interpret how emerging Christian belief systems blended graphic imagery and reasoned argumentation into newly configured Mediterranean discourse. Emerging out of contexts within first century Mediterranean Judaism, early Christians lived in the Roman Empire in the context of Greek philosophy, a wide range of ritual practices, and multiple modes of social, cultural, and ideological perspectives. The sociorhetorical commentary in these volumes explores and exhibits the emergent modes of discourse in the highly diverse environment of religious belief and practice especially during the first-century-CE Mediterranean world.

What Stands in Common among SREC Volumes?

Every author of an SREC volume uses nomenclature present in *The Tapestry of Early Christian Discourse: Rhetoric, Society and Ideology* (1996) and *Exploring the Texture of Texts: A Guide to Socio-rhetorical Interpretation*

(1996).[1] This means that each author includes a section titled "Textural Commentary" and within this section refers to basic textures of a text described in the two 1996 publications (inner texture, intertexture, social-cultural texture, ideological texture, sacred texture) and multiple subtextures within the basic textures, such as opening-middle-closing, repetitive, and progressive texture within inner texture.

In addition, each author works with six emergent Christian rhetorolects of the first century CE and with conceptual blending/integration among these rhetorolects. A rhetorolect is a mode of discourse "identifiable on the basis of a distinctive configuration of themes, topics, reasonings, and argumentations" that develops in cultures.[2] The six basic rhetorolects that have been identified since 1996 are wisdom, prophetic, apocalyptic, precreation, miracle, and priestly.[3] The initial publication that guided the RRA group in interpretation of conceptual blending/integration was *The Way We Think*, by Gilles Fauconnier and Mark Turner.[4] Since then, a series

---

1. Vernon K. Robbins, *The Tapestry of Early Christian Discourse: Rhetoric, Society and Ideology* (London: Routledge, 1996); Robbins, *Exploring the Texture of Texts: A Guide to Socio-rhetorical Interpretation* (Valley Forge, PA: Trinity Press International, 1996), 7–39. See also David B. Gowler, L. Gregory Bloomquist, and Duane F. Watson, eds., *Fabrics of Discourse: Essays in Honor of Vernon K. Robbins* (Harrisburg, PA: Trinity Press International, 2003).

2. Vernon K. Robbins, "Socio-rhetorical Interpretation," in *The Blackwell Companion to the New Testament*, ed. David E. Aune (Oxford: Blackwell, 2010), 197.

3. Vernon K. Robbins, "The Dialectical Nature of Early Christian Discourse," *Scriptura* 59 (1996): 353–62; Robbins, "Argumentative Textures in Socio-rhetorical Interpretation," in *Rhetorical Argumentation in Biblical Texts: Essays from the Lund 2000 Conference*, ed. Anders Eriksson, Thomas H. Olbricht, and Walter Übelacker, ESEC 8 (Harrisburg, PA: Trinity Press International, 2002), 27–65; Robbins, *The Invention of Christian Discourse*, vol. 1, RRA 1 (Dorset, UK: Deo, 2009); Robbins, "Precreation Discourse and the Nicene Creed: Christianity Finds Its Voice in the Roman Empire," *R&T* 18 (2012): 1–17; David A. deSilva, "A Sociorhetorical Interpretation of Revelation 14:6–13: A Call to Act Justly toward the Just and Judging God," *BBR* 9 (1999): 65–117; deSilva, "The Invention and Argumentative Function of Priestly Discourse in the Epistle to the Hebrews," *BBR* 16 (2006): 295–323; Roy R. Jeal, "Starting Before the Beginning: Precreation Discourse in Colossians," *R&T* 18 (2011): 287–310; Duane F. Watson, ed., *Miracle Discourse in the New Testament* (Atlanta: Society of Biblical Literature, 2012); Vernon K. Robbins and Jonathan M. Potter, eds., *Jesus and Mary Reimagined in Early Christianity*, WGRWSup 6 (Atlanta: SBL Press, 2015).

4. Gilles Fauconnier and Mark Turner, *The Way We Think: Conceptual Blending and the Mind's Hidden Complexities* (New York: Basic Books, 2002).

of additional publications by members of the RRA group has played an important role.[5]

Since authors understand SRI as an interpretive analytic rather than as a method, they have the freedom to select and foreground certain aspects of the texts more than, or even rather than, others. But every author has agreed to write an SREC volume within the following format: after an introductory chapter to the volume, which includes an explanation of the particular way the author will apply SRI as an interpretive analytic, each volume presents commentary on the text in a sequence of rhetography, English translation display, textural commentary, and rhetorical force as emergent discourse.[6]

The rhetography section presupposes knowledge of the essay titled "Rhetography: A New Way of Seeing the Familiar Text" and is regularly informed by other essays and books as well.[7] The rhetorical force section presupposes ongoing discussion and debate among New Testament scholars concerning the rhetorical role of a particular writing in emerging Christianity in the Mediterranean world. This means there are two "primary" foci in the rhetorical force section: (1) rhetorical force in emerging Christianity itself and (2) rhetorical force in emergent social, cultural, ide-

---

5. Vernon K. Robbins, "Conceptual Blending and Early Christian Imagination," in *Explaining Christian Origins and Early Judaism: Contributions from Cognitive and Social Science*, ed. Petri Luomanen, Ilkka Pyysiäinen, and Risto Uro, BibInt 89 (Leiden: Brill, 2007), 161–95; Robbins, *Invention of Christian Discourse*; Robert von Thaden Jr., *Sex, Christ, and Embodied Cognition: Paul's Wisdom for Corinth*, ESEC 16 (Dorset, UK: Deo, 2012); Thaden, "Pauline Rhetorical Invention: Seeing 1 Corinthians 6:12–7:7 through Conceptual Integration Theory. A Cognitive Turn," in *Cognitive Linguistic Explorations in Biblical Studies,* ed. Bonnie Howe and Joel B. Green (Berlin: de Gruyter, 2014), 101–21.

6. See Robbins, "Socio-rhetorical Interpretation," 192–219, esp. 203–208; Robbins, "Socio-rhetorical Criticism," in *The Oxford Encyclopedia of Biblical Interpretation*, ed. Steven L. McKenzie (Oxford: Oxford University Press, 2013), 311–18.

7. Vernon K. Robbins, "Rhetography: A New Way of Seeing the Familiar Text," in *Words Well Spoken: George Kennedy's Rhetoric of the New Testament*, ed. C. Clifton Black and Duane F. Watson, SRR 8 (Waco, TX: Baylor University Press, 2008), 81–106; Robbins, *Invention of Christian Discourse*; David A. deSilva, "Seeing Things John's Way: Rhetography and Conceptual Blending in Revelation 14:6–13," *BBR* 18 (2008): 271–98; Roy R. Jeal, "Blending Two Arts: Rhetorical Words, Rhetorical Pictures and Social Formation in the Letter to Philemon," *Sino-Christian Studies* 5 (June 2008): 9–38.

ological, and religious discourse and conceptuality in the broader Mediterranean world at the time of the writing (and perhaps later).

What Are Some of the Variations among SREC Volumes?

Freedom for Each Author

Each author is given a range of freedom within the overall sequential framework of rhetography, English translation display, textural commentary, and rhetorical force as emergent discourse. Some authors think it works well to write textural commentary in the sequence in which the textures were presented in *The Tapestry of Early Christian Discourse* and *Exploring the Texture of Texts*: inner texture, intertexture, social-cultural texture, ideological texture, sacred texture. Other authors think it is too constraining to write textural commentary in a sequence like this. Therefore, authors are allowed to write textural commentary in whatever "order" of textures and subtextures they consider most workable for the text on which they are commenting. To indicate to the reader what texture the author is interpreting, bold letters introduce the major five textures (or combinations thereof), and italics introduce subtextures, like *repetitive texture* within **inner texture**.

This SREC Commentary on Philemon

Within the established sequence for writing SREC commentaries, Roy R. Jeal has chosen to interpret Philemon from the perspective of all the textures and subtextures in *Exploring the Texture of Texts*. Since Philemon is only 335 words long, he decided to divide the sequential commentary on the basis of the opening, middle, and closing of the letter. After the introduction, he presents the rhetography, English translation, and *repetitive texture* of the entire text. Then he presents textural commentary on the **inner textures, intertexture, social and cultural texture, sacred texture**, and rhetorical force as emergent discourse of the opening (vv. 1–7), middle (vv. 8–20), and closing (vv. 21–25). After this, he concludes the volume with a chapter on the **ideological texture** and rhetorical force as emergent discourse of the entire text of Philemon.

Jeal's decision to write this commentary on Paul's short Letter to Philemon using each SRI texture and subtexture makes it appropriate to publish it as the first Sociorhetorical Exploration Commentary in the Rhetoric of Religious Antiquity series. Its comprehensive presentation of multiple textural analyses of Philemon allows the possibility for this commentary to function as a guide or manual for authors of other SREC commentaries as they select the modes they wish to foreground as they interpret units of text. The editors anticipate that subsequent SREC volumes regularly will present a selection of textural interpretive-analytic strategies, rather than always using all of them, because the length of their texts will not allow them the luxury of the comprehensive approach in this volume. Some commentators may desire to give only certain textural analytic-interpretive strategies prominence so they can introduce approaches they consider important for moving SRI into territory not yet in view.

Preface

Yes, I think words were born to play with each other, they don't know how to do anything else, and contrary to what people may say, there are no such things as empty words.[1]

But my people, inspired by what to them might seem an actual, renewed meeting with me—for the African has a capacity for disregarding distances of space and time—on leaving the solicitor's quarters laid their way round by the post office, looked up the Indian professional letter-writer in his stall there and had this learned man set down for them a second message to me. In such way the letter, first translated in the mind of the sender from his native Kikuyu tongue into the lingua franca of Swahili, had later passed through the dark Indian mind of the scribe, before it was finally set down, as I read it, in his unorthodox English. Yet in this shape it bore a truer likeness to its author than the official, conventional note, so that as I contemplated the slanting lines on the thin yellow paper, I for a moment was brought face to face with him.[2]

The letters of the New Testament were meant to be read, heard, and felt by their audiences. Their rhetorical energy was meant to affect people, to move them to believe, to strengthen their belief, and to live life out in ways appropriate to belief in Jesus Christ and the gospel. The letters describe and address life as it was encountered by Christ-believers in real social, cultural, and ecclesial situations. Paul the apostle's Letter to Philemon is made up of full, powerful, interactive words that bring us, even at this long distance and time from their composition, face-to-face with Paul, Philemon, Onesimus, and the situation that confronted them.

---

1. José Saramago, *The Cave*, trans. Margaret Jull Costa (Orlando: Harcourt, 2002), 173.

2. Isak Dinesen [Karen Blixen, pseud.], "Echoes From the Hills," in *Shadows on the Grass* (Chicago: University of Chicago Press, 1960), 119–20.

The words of the Letter to Philemon interact with each other on the field of play in multiple ways. They place images in the mind. They argue. They move ideas along. They have sounds, intonations, rhythms, movements, and indeed beauty about them. They indicate ideologies, and they evoke new ideologies. They introduce sacred ideas about faith in Christ Jesus and the implications of that faith. They call for a new ethic for an emerging society in the ancient Mediterranean world. The sociorhetorical analysis and interpretation in this commentary aims to look at these things, interpret them, and articulate them carefully. Words are our stock in trade as readers and interpreters, and our task is to learn and talk about them clearly, to explain how they are coherent and compelling. We examine the words to understand how they play and interweave together to bring us into contact with people, Christ-believers, who lived long ago, so that we may be better people today.

Because Philemon is short, I have had the luxury of engaging in a full-bodied sociorhetorical interpretation (SRI) that examines every line of the letter multiple times. Since SRI is an analytic rather than a method, each analytical procedure views the same text through a different lens, with the goal of coming, not to repetition, but to a comprehensive view of the features and the effect—the rhetorical force—of the letter as it emerged in its ancient setting. Structurally, therefore, the commentary moves through the analyses or "textures" of SRI as it has developed during recent decades. Following the introduction to Philemon, the commentary considers rhetography, textural commentary, and rhetorical force as emergent discourse. The textural commentary moves sequentially according to the *opening, middle,* and *closing textures* of the letter. The sections can be read individually or in varied sequences. I have aimed for as much depth as possible. I am aware that other commentaries in the SREC series will employ the analytic in other ways.

Philemon is about teaching and learning wisdom. Paul is at work "on the ground," working through an emerging issue that affected him, Philemon, Onesimus, and many others. The letter is about how life should be lived faithfully, honestly, honorably, and productively in the new society, the *ekklēsia* of Christ-believers. There are important and dramatic implications for life in the household, the polis, and the cosmos. While it brings us face to face with a situation and with fascinating characters from the past, it also brings us face to face with ourselves in our own ecclesial, household, and sociocultural experiences. Surely this is a good thing.

This commentary does not do everything. It does not refer to all the secondary literature. It does not take an adversarial approach that tries to move ahead in tension with the work of other interpreters. The bibliography lists only the materials explicitly indicated in the commentary. There is more to do. The interpretation of biblical texts, including sociorhetorical interpretation, never ends. Each generation and each person must be taught by the texts. There is always more to learn.

Sincere thanks are due to many. I thank Vernon K. Robbins and Duane F. Watson, editors of the series, for their confidence in and support of my work. I am highly appreciative of the generous support of the Pierce Program in Religion of Oxford College of Emory University, which made possible the publication of this volume. I am grateful to my friends and colleagues of the Rhetoric of Religious Antiquity research group who, now for a long time, have engaged together in deep, revealing, and delightful sociorhetorical interpretation of fascinating texts. Vernon K. Robbins, the developer of SRI and man of ideas and energy who has brought it forward, has worked tirelessly to lead the RRA group to propose ever new ideas and approaches to interpretation. He has listened carefully to the thoughts of all, has pushed, persuaded, and been persuaded, with firmness but also with sensitivity and care. I am grateful for Vernon's personal friendship, which has involved many early-morning walks; discussions by email, Skype, and in person; much encouragement; and, for this volume on Philemon, support, criticism, editing, and love for these tasks. I thank many friends who have indicated their interest and support with questions, comments, criticism, and encouragement. I am deeply grateful for the support of my family, who ask questions about how things are going, engage in conversation, ask whether I am about to finish something, and encourage me to keep at it. Jackie, my wife, has always supported me in more ways than I can say.

Roy R. Jeal
February 2015

Abbreviations

Ancient Sources

Ann.	Tacitus, *Annales*
Ant.	Josephus, *Jewish Antiquities*
De an.	Aristotle, *De anima*
Digest	a compendium of Roman law drawn together from laws long in force by the (Eastern) emperor Justinian in the sixth century
Ep.	Pliny the Younger, *Epistulae*; Seneca, *Epistlae morales*
Eph.	Ignatius, *To the Ephesians*
Eth. nic.	Aristotle, *Ethica nicomachea*
Inst.	Quintilian, *Institutio oratoria*
Leg.	Plato, *Leges*
Lucil.	Seneca, *Ad Lucilium*
Mart. Pol.	Martyrdom of Polycarp
Opif.	Philo, *De opificio mundi*
Pol.	Aristotle, *Politica*
Prob.	Philo, *Quod omnis probs liber sit*
Rhet.	Aristotle, *Rhetoric*
Rom.	Ignatius, *To the Romans*
T. Sim.	Testament of Simeon
T. Zeb.	Testament of Zebulun

Secondary Resources

AB	Anchor Bible
ABD	*Anchor Bible Dictionary*. Edited by David Noel Freedman. 6 vols. New York: Doubleday, 1992
BBR	*Bulletin for Biblical Research*

BDAG	Walter Bauer, William F. Arndt, F. Wilbur Gingrich, and Frederick W. Danker. *A Greek-English Lexicon of the New Testament and Other Early Christian Literature*. 3rd ed. Chicago: University of Chicago Press, 2000
BDF	F. Blass and A. Debrunner. *A Greek Grammar of the New Testament and Other Early Christian Literature*. Translated and revised by Robert W. Funk. Chicago: University of Chicago Press, 1961
BibInt	Biblical Interpretation Series
BSac	*Bibliotheca Sacra*
ConC	Concordia Commentary
ECC	Eerdmans Critical Commentary
ESEC	Emory Studies in Early Christianity
ICC	International Critical Commentary
JBL	*Journal of Biblical Literature*
JSNT	*Journal for the Study of the New Testament*
KJV	King James Version
LXX	Septuagint
LCL	Loeb Classical Library
LSJ	Henry George Liddell, Robert Scott, and Henry Stuart Jones. *A Greek-English Lexicon*. 9th ed. with revised supplement. Oxford: Clarendon, 1996
MM	J. H. Moulton and G. Milligan. *Vocabulary of the Greek New Testament*. 1914–1929. Reprint, Grand Rapids: Baker, 1995
NA[28]	*Novum Testamentum Graece* (Nestle-Aland 28th rev. ed.). Edited by Barbara and Kurt Aland et al. Stuttgart: Deutsche Bibelgesellschaft, 2012
NIB	*The New Interpreter's Bible*. Edited by Leander E. Keck. 12 vols. Nashville: Abingdon, 1994–2004
NICNT	New International Commentary on the New Testament
NIGTC	New International Greek Testament Commentary
NRSV	New Revised Standard Version
NTG	New Testament Guides
NTS	*New Testament Studies*
PNTC	Pillar New Testament Commentary
RBECS	*Reviews of Biblical and Early Christian Studies*
RRA	Rhetoric of Religious Antiquity
RSV	Revised Standard Version

R&T	Religion and Theology
SBLDS	Society of Biblical Literature Dissertation Series
SBLGNT	*The Greek New Testament SBL Edition.* Edited by Michael W. Holmes. Atlanta: Society of Biblical Literature, 2010
SREC	Sociorhetorical Explorations Commentaries
SRI	Sociorhetorical Interpretation
SRR	Studies in Rhetoric and Religion
TDNT	*Theological Dictionary of the New Testament.* Edited by Gerhard Kittel and Gerhard Friedrich. Translated by Geoffrey W. Bromiley. 10 vols. Grand Rapids: Eerdmans, 1964–1976
UBS[4]	*The Greek New Testament.* 4th rev. ed. Edited by Barbara Aland et al. Stuttgart: Deutsche Bibelgesellschaft/United Bible Societies, 1994
WGRWSup	Writings from the Greco-Roman World Supplement Series
WUNT	Wissenschaftliche Untersuchungen zum Neuen Testament
ZECNT	Zondervan Exegetical Commentary on the New Testament
ZNW	*Zeitschrift für die Neutestamentliche Wissenschaft*

Glossary[1]

Argumentative texture. The reasoning that occurs inside a text. Rhetorical argument may be logical, asserting or prompting syllogistic reasoning, or qualitative, where the sequence of images, descriptions, and values encourages the reader to accept the portrayal as true and real. Argumentation moves people to thought, belief, understanding, and action.

Conceptual blending. The formation of new and emergent cognitive structures when topoi from particular and clear input frames (or mental spaces) are brought together and elicit understandings of new concepts and conditions not previously understood.

Frames. Cultural narrative and conceptual structures that prompt images and environments of thought. Frames provide reference patterns by which new experiences are assessed, choices are made, and values and behaviors are established. Input spaces within frames blend together in the human mind, inducing new, emergent cognitive structures, concepts, and conditions not previously understood.

Ideological texture. How people consciously or unconsciously see and understand the spatial and mental worlds in which they live. It involves beliefs, values, assumptions, philosophies, points of view, expectations, notions of right and wrong, behaviors, justifications of positions whether well-argued or not, doctrines, systems, politics, and power structures that affect people and things in the cultures in which they live. The particular alliances and conflicts nurtured and evoked by the language of a text, the language of interpretations of a text, and the way a text itself and inter-

---

1. See the comprehensive glossary in Vernon K. Robbins, *The Invention of Christian Discourse* (Dorset, UK: Deo, 2009), 1:xxi–xxx.

preters of the text position themselves in relation to other individuals and groups.

Inner texture. The various ways a text employs language to communicate. This includes linguistic patterns, voices, movements, argumentations, and structural elements of a text; the specific ways it persuades its audiences; and the ways its language evokes feelings, emotions, or senses that are located in various parts of the body.

Intertexture. The representation of, reference to, and use of phenomena in the world outside the text being interpreted. This world includes other texts; other cultures; social roles, institutions, codes, and relationships; and historical events or places.

Narrational texture. The texture of the voices (often not identified with a specific character) through which words in texts speak. The narrator may begin and continue simply with an assertion that describes, asserts, or greets. Narration may present argumentation or introduce people who act, which creates storytelling or narrative.

Opening-middle-closing texture. The basic rhetorical structure of the beginning, the body, and the conclusion of a section of discourse. In a text, this texture indicates where the basic functional sections are located and how they operate rhetorically. These subtextures provide a sense of wholeness or completeness to a text.

Progressive texture. Progressions and sequences of grammar and ideas in a text. Progressions indicate how the rhetoric moves ahead linguistically, thematically, spatially, and topically.

Repetitive texture. Repetition of words, phrases, and topoi that help identify social, cultural, and ideological networks of meanings and meaning effects in the rhetoric in a text.

Rhetography. The progressive, sensory-aesthetic, and argumentative textures of a text that prompt graphic images or pictures in the minds of listeners and readers that imply certain truths and realities.

Rhetorical force as emergent discourse. The emerging discourse of a social, cultural, ideological, and/or religious movement like early Christianity as it moved audiences by eliciting belief, behavior, and community formation.

Rhetorolects. An elision of "rhetorical dialect" that refers to the emergent modes of discourse created by early Christ-believers, who shaped and reshaped language so that they could articulate their new faith understandings about Jesus Christ and the implications of that faith for life in their communities (the *ekklēsia*) and in Mediterranean societies. Modes of discourse are identifiable on the basis of distinctive configurations of themes, images, topics, reasonings, and argumentations. Six major rhetorolects are prominent in first Christian discourse: wisdom, prophetic, apocalyptic, precreation, priestly, and miracle discourse.

Sacred texture. The manner in which a text communicates insights into the relationship between humanity, the cosmos, and the divine. It addresses redemption, commitment, worship, devotion, community, ethics, holy living, spirituality, and spiritual formation.

Sensory-aesthetic texture. The features in a text that indicate, reflect, or evoke things discerned through visual, oral, aural, olfactory, tactile, gustatory, textual, prosaic, poetic, intellectual, and other sensory and aesthetic human characteristics.

Social and cultural texture. The social and cultural nature and location of the language used and the social and cultural world evoked and created by a text.

SRI (sociorhetorical interpretation). A range of heuristic analytics that analyzes and interprets texts using features of rhetorical, social, and cognitive reasoning to help commentators learn how the texts under examination function to influence thinking and behavior. The *socio-* refers to the rich resources of modern social, cultural, and cognitive sciences. The *rhetorical* refers to the way language in a text is a means of communication among people. A major goal of SRI is to nurture an environment of fullbodied interpretation that encourages a genuine interest in people who live in contexts with values, norms, and goals different from our own.

Steps. In this commentary the term "step" is employed to indicate specific movement ahead in the progressive texture of the letter. Sociorhetorical analysis shows that sometimes there is variation in the steps both among the textures and between the textures and the rhetography. The steps sometimes do not correspond, because different functions may be in play as the interweaving of the rhetoric advances.

Texture. Emerging from a metaphor of figuration as weaving, the concept of texture in relation to a text derives from Latin *texere* (to weave) that produces an arrangement of threads in the warp and woof of a fabric. SRI extends the metaphor of texture to the metaphor of tapestry, approaching a text as a thick network of meanings and meaning effects that an interpreter can explore by moving through the text from different perspectives.

Topos, topoi (pl.). A place to which one may go mentally to find arguments. The topics by which argumentation is made. Thus topoi are landmarks in the mental geography of thought which themselves evoke networks of meanings in their social, cultural, or ideological use.

Wisdom rhetorolect. Discourse that interprets the visible world by blending human experiences of geophysical, social, cultural, and institutional human experiences with beliefs about God especially through parental and familial nurturing and caring modes of understanding. Wisdom is about doing good in the world and living faithfully, fruitfully, and ethically. Its special rhetorical effect is to conceptualize the function of spaces, places, and people through practices characteristic of households and other teaching-learning environments.

Editors' Note

The English translation of Philemon was made by the author, based on his exegetical insights. Other biblical texts are from the New Revised Standard Version, except where noted. Quotations from Latin and Greek authors follow the texts and translations of the Loeb Classical Library.

Introduction

This wonderful letter portrays Paul as a man of deep emotions who employs moving, subtle, manipulative, and simultaneously clear rhetoric. It presents Philemon as a caring person who has the good of his fellow Christ-believers in mind and works to meet their needs. Onesimus is presented as recently becoming a Christ-believer and like a child to Paul and, as one who has been Philemon's slave, one owned as property by another person. There is an implicit concern that, despite Philemon's love, faith, and good works for Christians (ἅγιοι, "holy ones"), he might not be inclined to treat Onesimus as generously. It is apparent that Paul thinks Philemon needs to be encouraged to treat Onesimus in the same way he, Philemon, "refreshes" others and with the same courtesy he treats Paul himself. While the lines of thought are clear—Paul wants Philemon to receive his slave Onesimus as a "beloved brother," as if Onesimus were Paul himself—the nuancing of ideas and language, the blending of words, the pictures the words convey, and the frames of cognitive understanding make the letter a very complex discourse for analysis.

This is a short letter as Pauline letters go, the shortest in the corpus, at 335 words. It is also the most directly personal letter in the collection. It was meant to affect Philemon intellectually, emotionally, and behaviorally and to do so directly in the context of his faith as a Christ-believer, in the context of the *ekklēsia* (the assembly of holy ones) that met in his house, and in the context of his relationship with Paul. It is hard to imagine that it did not have its desired effect. Strangely, it seems, at least at first glance, Onesimus, the object of Paul's appeal to Philemon, is a slave who has become a Christ-believer through his contact with Paul during a separation from his owner. For Paul there is no doubt about what should happen next, because he thinks in well-developed and clear theological, practical, and Christian ways. The good Philemon does not yet have such a fully developed understanding. Many interpreters become occupied (and preoccupied) with historical questions: Was Onesimus a runaway slave? Was he a messenger from Philemon to Paul? Did he seek Paul out? Was he a thief? Where was Paul located? And with more sociohistorical and ethical questions: Was Paul in favor of or against slavery? Why did Paul not explicitly call for the abolition of slavery? Did Paul mean for Philemon to manumit Onesimus? If so, why did he not say so explicitly? What was the nature of slavery in the Roman world, and how did it relate to the situation indicated in the letter? They become similarly occupied with certain theological questions: Does Philemon have any theological point? Why is it in the New Testament canon? These are all important—though generally not fully answerable—considerations, and they receive notice in this commentary; but the goal here is to identify, analyze, and interpret what the text and the arguments *do* and *how they go about doing it*. This is to ask, identify, and understand what is going on in the letter. So this commentary is less concerned with historical and sociohistorical conclusions and more concerned with the rhetorical force of the letter as a small but dramatically significant piece of the distinctly Christian discourse that was emerging in the Mediterranean world of the first century CE.

What the Letter to Philemon surely does show is that "in Christ"—in the critical space where Paul, Philemon, Onesimus, and the other named persons and all the holy ones are now located—things are different than they are in Mediterranean cultural, political, social, and religious practice. In this new space, a distinctly wisdom space, there is freedom, brotherhood, and partnership for all. There is a new society that is concerned for life as it should be in the community, much more than for how it operates in and is accepted by the larger culture. Philemon is expected to get the idea, specifically as regards himself and Onesimus, and to act accordingly.

Sociorhetorical Interpretation

Sociorhetorical interpretation is a heuristic analytic—or, perhaps better, a range of analytics—that, rather than being a "method" employing a series of scientific steps or formulae that are performed and produce predictable results according to a conceptual framework, is a kind of "multiple accounts evaluation" that analyzes (and reanalyzes) texts using features of rhetorical, social, and cognitive reasoning in order to help interpreters learn how the texts being examined function to influence thinking and behavior. It has been designed with the interpretation of biblical texts (and

other religious texts of the ancient Mediterranean)[1] in mind, focusing on
the New Testament and closely connected documents. Analysis aims to
discover phenomena in the texts as they emerge in their social, anthro-
pological, and rhetorical contexts and as they bring about religious and
theological cognition. It is not an adversarial approach that aims to move
interpretation and understanding ahead by comparison and contrast with
other interpretations. Rather, it employs the analytic for continuing discovery of the rhetoric of topoi, pictures, textures, and emergent structures that the texts set in recipients' minds and by which the audiences are
meant to be socially and religiously formed and reformed. Sociorhetorical
interpretation aims to show *how* texts such as the Letter to Philemon *function* rhetorically and socially.

A leading characteristic of sociorhetorical interpretation is the way
it identifies and examines the multiform and multivalent geometry of
the texts of the New Testament and of Mediterranean antiquity. Texts are
imagined to be analogous to a tapestry,[2] a woven textile that presents pictures, stories, argumentation, sensory, and aesthetic details. This means
that they draw on features (or threads) from other texts, material culture,
social, and cultural agency and many other realms. They employ and
create ideologies, and they relate to the sacred and the spiritual realm. In
doing all this, they present a multidimensional fabric and picture that fills
spaces of various kinds and that both conveys and elicits meaning. The
interweaving of threads forms textures that are not flat, two-dimensional
broadcloth fabrics, but are both coarsely and finely textured images that
have depth and shapes of all possible kinds. This geometry[3] brings the
shapes together yet recognizes that they interweave in multiple ways and
in multiple directions and that they turn and can be turned, and every
turning reveals something not noticed before.

Sociorhetorical interpretation does a very important thing for understanding and for writing about biblical texts: rather than trying to judge
them from, as it were, the outside—whether to show that what they say
is correct, true, historically accurate, inspired, inspiring, authoritative, or

---

1. Hence the general title of the series, the "Rhetoric of Religious Antiquity."
2. See the programmatic work of Vernon K. Robbins, *The Tapestry of Early Christian Discourse: Rhetoric, Society and Ideology* (London: Routledge, 1996).
3. For me the concept of "geometry" is informed by Margaret Visser, *The Geometry of Love: Space, Time, Mystery, and Meaning in an Ordinary Church* (Toronto: HarperPerennial, 2000), and by many life experiences.

the word of God, on the one hand, or wrong, false, historically fabricated, misleading, misguided, simply mistaken, on the other—it lets them stand in judgment over their interpreters. It avoids being bound by the static sources, situations, and structures of discourse, being concerned more with the *interplay* of them in the production and evocation of ideas, thoughts, and behaviors. The point here is that sociorhetorical interpretation attends to what the texts actually say and do, observing the rhetography or images cast on the imagination, the **inner textures** and **intertextures**, the **ideologies**, indeed to the **sacredness** of the texts apart from external methodological or moral constraints. Sociorhetorical interpretation is not aiming to make a point for its own or for some third party's sake. It is aiming to learn, to understand.[4] The text should be heard in its own self-presentation. Because it is a heuristic analytic, it can be performed multiple times. There is no final, definitive analysis or interpretation. Discovery is always a continuing process. It encourages one to do all one can, but allows for and encourages more to be done heuristically by others. Sociorhetorical interpretation aims to show (in visuality, visual exegesis, rhetography), to describe (textural analysis), and to explain the power (rhetorical force) of biblical and religious discourse as it emerged and was employed in the ancient Mediterranean.

While sociorhetorical interpretation takes the classical rhetorical tradition indicated in the famous handbooks seriously, it recognizes that ancient Mediterranean, early Christian, and biblical rhetorics are broader than the handbooks indicate. The three species of classical rhetoric (judicial, deliberative, epideictic), for example, do not adequately address the range of situations and kinds of discourse indicated in the New Testament.[5] Rather than addressing the law courts, political assemblies, or civil ceremonies, early Christian and New Testament discourse addresses situations centered in "households, political kingdoms, imperial armies, imperial households, temples, and individual bodies of people."[6] Early Christians did what groups and communities of all kinds and in all places do:

---

4. On this, see especially Christopher Bryan's "A Digression: 'Great Literature'?" in *Listening to the Bible: The Art of Faithful Biblical Interpretation* (Oxford: Oxford University Press, 2014), 56–65.

5. See the discussion in Roy R. Jeal, *Integrating Theology and Ethics in Ephesians: The Ethos of Communication* (Lewiston, NY: Mellen, 2000), 35–43.

6. See Vernon K. Robbins, *The Invention of Christian Discourse* (Dorset, UK: Deo, 2009), 1:1–3. This point is noted by others in regard to New Testament texts, e.g., Neil

they shaped and reshaped language in ways that expressed their beliefs, their worldview, and what had been revealed to them. This reshaped language was meant to be delivered to Christ-believing audiences who could recognize the discourse in light of their belief. New Testament documents like the Letter to Philemon are, therefore, living things whose features require interpreters to be imaginative, looking for these features of reshaping and the development of ideas, getting as close as we can by explanation of their meanings in our own words while recognizing that analysis and interpretation must be done again by every generation of interpreters.[7] Sociorhetorical interpretation helps overcome a negative hermeneutic of suspicion with a hermeneutic of openness and hope. It aims to examine the letter in a living, vital, breathing world where there are human, ethical, and eternal concerns, not only (or merely) concerns for facts and factual, reconstructed situations.

Rhetorolects: Distinctive Rhetorical Dialects or Modes of Discourse

One of the important developments employed by sociorhetorical interpretation is the recognition that early Christians, in their shaping and reshaping of language, were creating their own emergent discourse so that they could articulate their understanding of faith in Jesus Christ and its implications for life in their community and in societies. This discourse became identifiable by its distinctive rhetorical dialects or modes of speaking and writing.[8] Sociorhetorical interpretation calls these modes of discourse rhetorolects (*rhetórolect*; an elision of "rhetorical dialect"). Each rhetorolect is a mode of discourse "identifiable on the basis of a distinctive configuration of themes, topics, reasonings, and argumentations" that develops in cultures.[9] Early Christians employed at least six major

---

Elliott, *The Arrogance of Nations: Reading Romans in the Shadow of Empire*, (Minneapolis: Fortress, 2010), 20.

7. See Richard B. Hays, "Crucified with Christ: A Synthesis of the Theology of 1 and 2 Thessalonians, Philemon, Philippians, and Galatians" in *Pauline Theology*, ed. Jouette M. Bassler (Philadelphia: Fortress, 1994), 1:227–46, here 228.

8. See especially Vernon Robbins, "The Dialectical Nature of Early Christian Discourse," *Scriptura* 59 (1996): 353–62; Robbins, "Socio-rhetorical Interpretation," in *The Blackwell Companion to the New Testament*, ed. David E. Aune (Oxford: Blackwell, 2010), 192–219. Robbins, *Invention of Christian Discourse*, 1:7–9, and *Invention of Christian Discourse*, vol. 2, forthcoming.

9. Robbins, "Socio-rhetorical Interpretation," 197.

rhetorolects: wisdom, prophetic, apocalyptic, precreation, miracle, and priestly.[10] An analogy that provides a helpful illustration is the ancient Greek concept of modes of music. Thomas Cahill points out,

> In our Western music we still know the modes "major" and "minor." The Greeks had five modes, known to us by their names—Ionian, Aeolian, Lydian, Dorian, and Phrygian—which referred also to ethnic groupings within Greece. Each of these modes, each of which had submodes, was easily recognized by listeners, and each created a characteristic mood, just as we might say, "That sounded like a Scottish ballad. This sounds like a Spanish dance." Each Greek mode was constructed from an invariable sequence of relationships between the notes that no other mode possessed, more distinct than E flat major is from C minor, perhaps at times more akin to Asian music with its larger intervals and quarter tones. The Dorian was martial, the Phrygian engendered contentment, the Mixolydian (one of the submodes) was plaintive, the Ionian softly alluring, apparently making seduction easier. In all, Greek music probably sounded something like the late medieval music of Europe with its emphases on catchy, easily singable melodies, exaggerated rhythms, and humble instrumental accompaniment—Gregorian chant gone wild in the streets.[11]

The rhetorolects in early Christian discourse, similarly, both describe and create particular and often specialized understandings.[12] They correspond to the "spaces" in which actions of God and humans occur.[13] While this commentary points to the use of prophetic, priestly, and apocalyptic rhetorolects and spaces in Philemon, the letter is a rhetorical discourse strongly focused on wisdom because it is concerned with how Christ-believers should behave toward other Christ-believers in *ekklēsia* and household locations and in all sociocultural situations.

---

10. For a full description and discussion see Robbins, *Invention of Christian Discourse*, 1:7–9, 90–120. There may be more rhetorolects that interpreters will identify.

11. Thomas Cahill, *Sailing the Wine-Dark Sea: Why the Greeks Matter* (New York: Doubleday, 2003), 87.

12. What Robbins calls "the invention of Christian discourse."

13. See especially the chart in Robbins, *Invention*, 1:109, for a clear description of rhetorolects and their respective spaces.

Wisdom

Sociorhetorical interpretation understands Philemon as a wisdom text. It employs overall a wisdom rhetorolect, has a wisdom goal, and has a view toward wisdom space. Wisdom in the context of New Testament discourse has to do with the lives early Christians were called to live in their ancient Mediterranean social, cultural, and religious world. Christ-believers lived in locations, in social spaces, where they interacted with people and behaviors of diverse kinds. They lived in and under the authority of the Roman Empire and of the emperor. They faced pressures to conform to social, political, religious, and legal ideologies, norms, and expectations. Major questions for them in their Mediterranean setting would naturally have been "How should we live our new lives of faith?" and "What should we do?" These questions arise because believers like Paul recognized that things are different "in Christ" (ἐν Χριστῷ, Phlm 8, 20, 23) because Jesus is recognized as Lord (vv. 3, 5, 25) and eternity is in view (v. 15). These ideological perspectives call for clear thought and understanding in the Mediterranean context. Much of the New Testament was produced to address these issues. Wisdom discourse was the natural response to the situation.

> Wisdom rhetorolect interprets the visible world.... [It] blends human experiences of the household, one's intersubjective body, and the geophysical world (firstspace) with the cultural space of God's cosmos (secondspace). In the lived space of blending (thirdspace), people establish identities in relation to God who functions as heavenly father over God's children in the world. People perceive their bodies as able to produce goodness and righteousness in the world through the medium of God's goodness, which is understood as God's light in the world. In this context, wisdom belief emphasizes "fruitfulness" (productivity and reproductivity) in the realm of God's created world.[14]

Wisdom is, therefore, about doing good in the world and about living faithfully, fruitfully, and ethically. The discourse developed out of a variety of language and rhetorical modes and ideologies, particularly the Old Testament and other Jewish discourses, and also drew on moral and behavioral notions from the broader Mediterranean realm of thought.[15]

---

14. Ibid., 1:xxix–xxx; see also 1:121–74.
15. Ibid., 1:121–74.

Its motivation, however, relies on the conviction that God is the Father of all, that Jesus is Lord and Christ, that he is alive in the present time even though he had been dead, and that humans are responsible to Christ's authority and that they can in fact do good things. The normal location of wisdom is in physical bodies in the household, the space where people live out much of their lives.

Philemon was invented, spoken, written, and delivered with such wisdom in mind. While the man Philemon was a notably loving and faithful person who had other Christ-believers in mind (Phlm 5), there is more wisdom for him as someone who is a believer living in Mediterranean culture. Philemon is physically located in a household, which, adding to the complexity of households, is the location of the church, the *ekklēsia* (καὶ τῇ κατ' οἶκόν σου ἐκκλησίᾳ, v. 2). He has membership in and commitment to the *ekklēsia*. He has a commitment to the new relational situation among believers. He is also a slave owner. The rhetoric of the letter is aimed directly at the social formation of Philemon as he stands in this household situation. It is specifically designed and presented to persuade him to receive his slave Onesimus, over whom he has power, as a "beloved brother" (οὐκέτι ὡς δοῦλον ἀλλὰ ὑπὲρ δοῦλον, ἀδελφὸν ἀγαπητόν, 16). It aims to craft a wisdom space where Philemon receives Onesimus, who himself has become a Christ-believer (vv. 10–13).

This wisdom discourse moves to the development of an *ecclesial* space. The letter must be seen as a pastoral and deeply theological text. It envisions a kind of "ecclesiastical discipline"[16] where all believers, even if they are or have been slaves in the ancient Roman Mediterranean, are, in their physical bodies, family members and participants in the assembly of believers, the ecclesial space. Philemon's social formation in this way is Paul's goal and is effectively the same thing as Philemon's sacred or spiritual formation.[17]

Rhetography

Sociorhetorical Explorations Commentaries privilege "rhetography" as the starting point for analysis and commentary.[18] This is because what is

---

16. Marianne Meye Thompson, *Colossians and Philemon*, Two Horizons Commentary (Grand Rapids: Eerdmans, 2005), 201.

17. See the sections on **sacred texture**.

18. For this reason rhetography is placed first in the commentary, followed by a translation of the text of Philemon.

"seen" or otherwise sensed is first and fundamental to understanding. The word *rhetography* is an elision of "rhetoric" and "graphic,"[19] indicating the interrelationship and function of the visual and the persuasive features of texts. Visible, written texts are composed of recognizable letters of alphabets that are shaped into words and grammaticalized into phrases, clauses, sentences, and paragraphs. The sounds that correspond to these constructions are understood by people when they are read silently, read aloud, and heard. What we see in texts with our eyes or hear with our ears draws most (if not all) of us quite naturally into the visuality or visual art of the words. We "see" scenes and visualize persons, places, and things; we "hear" sounds and notice colors and other sensory phenomena; we visualize and hear and feel the emotions that the rhetoric of the words conveys. The written art (words) and the visual art (pictures evoked by the words) intersect or blend in the mind in the visual imagination and contribute dramatically to interpretation and understanding. Texts are themselves visual things[20] that, when they are most effective, evoke or cause the mind to recall the visual. The rhetography is a way of telling the story that texts aim to get across to people. Interpretation of the imagery is visual exegesis.[21]

Aristotle, in the *Rhetoric* (*Ars Rhetorica*), speaks of employing metaphors that "set things before the eyes" (*Rhet.* 3.11.1 [Freese, LCL]), in order to create a sense of reality in the minds of audience members. He had in mind the notion that rhetoricized combinations of words have a visual aspect and a visual function that elicit mental images that human minds

---

19. See Vernon K. Robbins, "Rhetography: A New Way of Seeing the Familiar Text," in *Words Well Spoken: George Kennedy's Rhetoric of the New Testament*, ed. C. Clifton Black and Duane F. Watson (Waco, TX: Baylor University Press, 2008), 81–106.

20. Particularly for modern people who generally read texts individually and silently. The first recipients (or most of them) of New Testament texts heard them read aloud.

21. For a full theoretical account including modern theories of rhetography/visuality, see my article, "Visual Interpretation: Blending Rhetorical Arts in Colossians 2:6–3:4" in *Biblical Rhetography through Visual Exegesis of Text and Image*, ed. Vernon K. Robbins, Walter S. Melion, and Roy R. Jeal, ESEC (Atlanta: SBL Press, forthcoming). See also Jeal, "Blending Two Arts: Rhetorical Words, Rhetorical Pictures and Social Formation in the Letter to Philemon," *Sino-Christian Studies* 5 (2008): 9–38; Jeal, "Clothes Make the (Wo)Man," *Scriptura* 90 (2005): 685–99; and Jeal, "Melody, Imagery, and Memory in the Moral Persuasion of Paul," in *Rhetoric, Ethic and Moral Persuasion in Biblical Discourse*, ed. Thomas H. Olbricht and Anders Eriksson (London: T&T Clark, 2005), 160–78.

employ for understanding: "I mean that things are set before the eyes by words that signify *actuality*" (ἐνέργεια, *Rhet.* 3.11.2 [Freese, LCL]).

Words can convey both actuality and metaphor according to Aristotle (*Rhet.* 3.11.2). The idea is that words are able to portray the inanimate in an animated way (*Rhet.* 3.11.3) that "gives movement and life to all, and *actuality is movement*" (κινούμενα γὰρ καὶ ζῶντα ποιεῖ πάντα, ἡ δ᾿ ἐνέργεια κίνησις, *Rhet.* 3.11.4 [Freese, LCL]). This means that things are *seen* in the imagination to be energized, working, functioning, active.[22] When he begins his discussion of style (λέξις), Aristotle states that it is necessary to give attention to it in order to make things clear and visible by presenting φαντασία, that is, a show, an impression, an appearance in the imagination (*Rhet.* 3.1.6). This is to say that, in Aristotle's view, rhetoric, words, and literature elicit visual images in the mind that are linked, indeed necessary, to understanding (belief) and action (behavior). Quintilian addressed how eloquent speech functions and the importance of awakening the emotions of the audience so that it is drawn into symbolic worlds where ideas are understood (Quintilian, *Inst.* 6.2.24–36).

> The prime essential for stirring the emotions of others is, in my opinion, first to feel those emotions oneself. (*Inst.* 6.2.26 [Butler, LCL])

> Consequently, if we wish to give our words the appearance of sincerity, we must assimilate ourselves to the emotions of those who are genuinely so affected, and our eloquence must spring from the same feeling that we desire to produce in the mind of the judge. (*Inst.* 6.2.27 [Butler, LCL])

How can these emotions be produced in the speaker and grasped by listeners?

> There are certain experiences which the Greeks call φαντασία, and the Romans visions [*visiones*], whereby things absent are presented to our imagination with such extreme vividness that they seem actually to be before our very eyes. (*Inst.* 6.2.29 [Butler, LCL]).

> From such impressions arises that ἐνέργεια which Cicero calls illumination and actuality, which makes us seem not so much to narrate as to exhibit the actual scene, while our emotions will be no less actively

---

22. Ἐνέργεια appears as "actuality" in the LCL version translated by J. H. Freese quoted here. The word means "energy," "working," "function," "action."

stirred than if we were present at the actual occurrence. (*Inst.* 6.2.32 [Butler, LCL])

Ned O'Gorman demonstrates, by reading Aristotle's *Rhetoric* together with *De anima* (*On the Soul*), that there is a visual aspect to Aristotle's rhetorical theory.[23] According to *De anima*, sight is the most developed sense (3.3). *Phantasia* (φαντασία), brought on (primarily)[24] by visual perception, conveys understanding to the mind and, indeed, to the soul (ψυχή).[25] *Phantasia* brings what is not seen in visual reality to the human mind in the visual imagination.[26] By it things are interpreted to be meaningful, to be right or wrong, and it is critical to perception, deliberation, and understanding (*De an.* 3.3.5–3.7.8).[27]

According to Aristotle, style (λέξις) evokes *phantasia* for the purpose of clarity of idea and understanding ("but all this [i.e., style] is appearance/imagery for the listener/audience"; ἀλλ᾽ ἅπαντα φαντασία ταῦτ᾽ ἐστι καὶ πρὸς τὸν ἀκροατήν, *Rhet.* 3.1.6).[28] Style is what brings things before the eyes. The mind visualizes and blends scenes, persons, actions, and material things that appear to be, but are not, material realia. Such mental imagery and blending has a rhetorical function. It has emotional, pathos effects that lead to the development of opinion. It is an integral part of persuasion and the development of correct judgments and correct behaviors. The texts communicate things beyond themselves *in what they picture*. The language is not only the language of words but also the language of the visual imagination.

---

23. Ned O'Gorman, "Aristotle's *Phantasia* in the *Rhetoric*: Lexis, Appearance, and the Epideictic Function of Discourse," *Philosophy and Rhetoric* 38 (2005): 16–40.

24. But also by the senses of sound, smell, taste, touch. The sensibilities affected are visual, oral, aural, olfactory, tactile, gustatory, textual, prosaic, poetic, and intellectual. See ibid., 19. Sound is particularly important for ancient Mediterranean documents since they were first spoken, then transcribed, then read aloud to their audiences. Sound evokes the visual.

25. Ibid., 17.

26. Ibid., 20.

27. Ibid., 20–21.

28. See ibid., 22–27. The LCL translation by J. H. Freese mistakenly renders the line as "But all these things are mere outward show for pleasing the hearer."

Textures

Following consideration of the rhetography of a text and an English translation, Sociorhetorical Exploration Commentaries provide an analysis of "textures."[29] This analytical rather than methodological approach[30] examines various textures first to discover what they are and then to interpret how their function has rhetorical power, that is, to *explore* how they *do* things to people. The approach is exploratory, not final, aiming to see ever more broadly and deeply into the artistry and power of the rhetoric. As with the rhetoric of any tapestry, any artistic work, and any verbal or written discourse, there are many textures that may be considered. In the commentary, I have looked at the series of textures according to the taxonomy set out by Vernon Robbins in *The Tapestry of Early Christian Discourse* and *Exploring the Texture of Texts*. Descriptions of the textures are provided in the sections of the commentary as they go along. Here, however, are brief statements about what each texture considers.

Inner textures are concerned with the language, the medium of communication, of the texts under consideration. Analysis involves identifying and examining words, patterning, voices, movement, argumentation, and the structural and sensory artistry of the language.

Opening-middle-closing texture is the basic rhetorical structure of the letter. All texts (and generally coherent units of texts) have these parts or variations of them. The terms correspond to "beginning" (or "introduction"), "body," and "ending" (or "conclusion"). *Opening-middle-closing texture* provides a sense of wholeness or completeness to a text.

Repetitive texture refers to repetitions of words, grammaticalizations, and topoi, which produce patterns that help identify major themes in the rhetoric and social relations in a text.

Progressive textures are the sequences of grammar and ideas in a text. They indicate where the rhetoric moves ahead linguistically, thematically, spatially, and/or topically.

Narrational texture is observed in the storytelling or narrative presented by the (implied) narrator or speaker. It listens to the voice(s) that

---

29. Here see especially Robbins, *Tapestry*; and Robbins, *Exploring the Texture of Texts: A Guide to Socio-rhetorical Interpretation* (Valley Forge, PA: Trinity Press International, 1996).

30. See above on sociorhetorical interpretation.

conveys the ideas of the discourse. The narration is the story as it is being told in a text.

Argumentative texturing is about the reasoning that occurs inside a text. The rhetorical argument may be logical or qualitative. This texturing is meant to move people to thought, understanding, belief, and action.

Sensory-aesthetic texture is revealed in the features that indicate, reflect, or evoke things discerned through visual, oral, aural, olfactory, tactile, gustatory, textual, prosaic, poetic, and intellectual sensibilities. This texturing produces a recognizable "feel" in a text.

Intertextures are the connections and interactions between a text being studied and phenomena outside it. This involves "intertextuality," connections with other texts, but also relationships with any observable external phenomena.

Social and cultural texture refers to the "social and cultural nature and location" of the language used and the "social and cultural world" evoked and created by a text.[31] It employs social topoi and categories that denote social and cultural situations addressed and created in the rhetorical discourse.

Ideological texture has to do with how people see and understand the spatial and mental worlds in which they live. It involves the beliefs, values, assumptions, philosophies, points of view, expectations, notions of right and wrong, behaviors, justifications of positions whether well-argued or not, doctrines, systems, politics, and power structures that affect people and things in the cultures in which they live.

Sacred texture is the texture of the relationships among humans, the created order, and God, between and among humanity, the cosmos, and the divine. This is the texturing that addresses redemption, commitment, worship, devotion, community, ethics, holy living, spirituality, and spiritual formation.

Rhetorical Force as Emergent Discourse

Sociorhetorical Exploration Commentaries conclude with analysis of the rhetorical force of the text as emergent discourse in the ancient Mediterranean world. This analysis recognizes that Philemon, like all New Testament and early Christian discourse, is "emergent," because it presents the

---

31. Robbins, *Exploring*, 71–94.

developing thinking, theology, and faith of some early Christ-believers set
down in writing, transmitted, and preserved as they came to it and went
along in their lives. Paul and other New Testament authors did not arrive
fully formed, speaking and writing with fully developed beliefs and doctrines. They understood and interpreted Jesus Christ, the new faith and
the new society, and their implications as they came to understand more
about them and as they encountered circumstances—such as those of Philemon and Onesimus—that called for thoughtful interpretation and the
application of interpretation to the actual conditions of the new reality.
This *emerging* discourse was shaped with powerful and dramatic *rhetorical
force* in order to move audiences—real people in real locations and circumstances—employing the dynamics of the visual and the textural, that
is, the sociorhetorical, to elicit belief, behavior, and formation among the
people individually and collectively as the *ekklēsia*. This rhetorical force
evoked, encouraged, and strengthened faith and indicated, reminded of,
and sometimes corrected behavior appropriate to the faith. In other words,
the rhetorical force of the emergent discourse was meant to shape the lives
of people. In this process new modes of discourse were created that, while
drawing on other existing modes, are new and strategic communications
that affect audiences. The rhetorical force of the Letter to Philemon powerfully influenced, I presume, Philemon, Onesimus, the *ekklēsia*, and other
early Christ-believers. It influences us as readers and listeners to it now.

Reading a Sociorhetorical Exploration Commentary

The layout of the commentary makes clear that it is not structured in a
verse-by-verse or even paragraph-by-paragraph fashion as is frequently
done. It does work through Philemon in a careful, structured way as it
employs the analytic indicated above, but it flows differently than is usual
in Bible commentaries. It can be read usefully in several ways. Some readers might like to read the entire book from beginning to end, but many
will find it most helpful to work through the first section on rhetography,
perhaps followed by the English translation of Philemon, and then go
immediately to the final section on rhetorical force as emergent discourse.
This approach in itself provides a complete sociorhetorical interpretation
of Philemon and creates the possibility for readers to select sections of the
textural commentary they wish to read according to interest. The sections
of the textural commentary offer a complete analysis of the entire letter.
The analyses of **inner textures** are the most complex, as they interpret

features of the letter in multiple ways. Reading the textural analyses will flesh out and enhance understanding.

Contextualizing reading, of course, will be very important. The commentary does not lend itself easily to looking up a particular verse, phrase, or word in order to get an interpretation regarding a particular issue or concern, although that can be done with a little work. Every line of Philemon is covered multiple times as the commentary goes along. Rather than reading specific sections of the commentary to try to find an answer to a particular question or to a concern about a word, phrase, or idea, it is important to read larger portions in order to come to a fuller understanding of what may be at stake for the author, the audiences, and for readers then and now.

The Text

The Greek text of Philemon is a clean, strongly attested document of 335 words in the NA[28], UBS[4], and SBLGNT editions of the Greek New Testament (334 words without the disputed [καί] in verse 11).[32] The letter occurs in many manuscripts and had early—though not universal—reception. The relatively small number of variants indicated in the apparatuses date from about the fifth century CE and later. There are no troubling alternate readings. Variants occur with respect to the addition of a few words, alternate ordering of words, and some differences in pronouns. None demand dramatic alterations to meaning or rhetorical force. It seems likely that the variants are to be attributed to efforts at correcting the letter's language in order to clarify or to make wording look and sound like Paul's usage elsewhere. Examples include the following:

- Some manuscripts add the word ἀγαπητῇ ("beloved") to καὶ Ἀπφίᾳ τῇ ἀδελφῇ in verse 1, probably to agree with the sentiment regarding Philemon.
- Some manuscripts have the reading "faith and love" rather than "love and faith" in verse 5, apparently to agree with Paul's more usual word order.

---

32. For a more detailed discussion, see Markus Barth and Helmut Blanke, *The Letter to Philemon*, ECC (Grand Rapids: Eerdmans, 2000), 104–8.

- Some manuscripts add the imperative form προσλαβοῦ ("receive") to verse 12 to read ὃν ἀναπεμψά σοι, αὐτόν τοῦτ᾽ ἔστιν τὰ ἐμὰ σπλάγχνα προσλαβοῦ ("whom I send back to you, receive him, this one [who] is my own viscera"). This variant is likely intended to agree with the usage in verse 17.

A number of commentators have preferred to interpret πρεσβύτης ("old man") in verse 9 as if it were its homonym πρεσβεύτης ("ambassador"; see Eph 6:20). There is no textual evidence for this reading, though the RSV uses "ambassador."[33] In the end it is clear that the preferences of the editors of the Greek editions are to be respected and followed.

The Author

Paul is the undoubted author of the letter.[34] It is important to be aware, however, of what it means to have been the author of a document during the Greco-Roman era and how Hellenistic and New Testament letters were produced. Our modern notion of an individual person sitting at a desk or table preparing and sending a letter must not be projected back directly and imposed on how letters in the first-century CE Mediterranean were prepared.[35] Several people would normally be involved in the writing process. Already from the beginning it is clear that Timothy is named as cosender of the letter (Παῦλος δέσμιος Χριστοῦ Ἰησοῦ καὶ Τιμόθεος ὁ ἀδελφός, v. 1). At the end of the letter Epaphras, Mark, Aristarchus, Demas, and Luke are named as coworkers with Paul who send greetings to Philemon (Ἀσπάζεταί σε Ἐπαφρᾶς ὁ συναιχμάλωτός μου ἐν Χριστῷ Ἰησοῦ, Μᾶρκος, Ἀρίσταρχος, Δημᾶς, Λουκᾶς, οἱ συνεργοί μου, vv. 23-24). While the narrational voice of the letter is certainly Paul's, Timothy must be nearby and is imagined as a participant in the message. It seems likely that the others are not far away, and since they send greetings they can be imagined to be listening in. Paul

---

33. See Barth and Blanke, *Letter to Philemon*, 107, 321-22; and Allen Dwight Callahan, *Embassy of Onesimus: The Letter of Paul to Philemon* (Valley Forge, PA: Trinity Press International, 1997), 31-32, who discuss both meanings for πρεσβύτης.

34. The few disputes about authenticity have never been convincing; see Joseph A. Fitzmyer, *The Letter to Philemon: A New Translation with Introduction and Commentary*, AB 34C (New York: Doubleday, 2000), 8-9.

35. On this see Margaret Ellen Lee and Bernard Brandon Scott, *Sound Mapping the New Testament* (Salem OR: Polebridge, 2009), 11-57.

speaks the letter aloud, dictating it to a scribe, perhaps, but not necessarily, dictating to Timothy.

We cannot know the precise conditions of the composition of Philemon, but we can gain insights from what is known generally about how written materials were produced. Writing was a collaborative process where one person spoke aloud and another wrote down what was spoken.[36] Usually other persons would be involved in gathering, manufacturing, or preparing the required writing materials such as stylus, ink, wax tablets, and papyrus.[37] Paul spoke his letters aloud, the exceptions being where he explicitly stated he was writing in his own hand, as is observed in Phlm 19 (ἐγὼ Παῦλος ἔγραψα τῇ ἐμῇ χειρί, ἐγὼ ἀποτίσω; cf. Gal 6:11; 2 Thess 3:17). It was common for the scribe to set down the spoken words first on wax tablets (*cerae*) and, subsequently, to transcribe them on to papyrus.[38] It is possible, perhaps likely, that this method was used by Paul and his coworkers to prepare the Letter to Philemon. Writing on wax tablets could be easily corrected or revised as dictation went along or at some later time. A text could be corrected, altered, or amended when it was transcribed in final form to papyrus. Papyrus was expensive, so writing on it directly from dictation would be avoided. Papyrus also required some amount of preparation by smoothing the writing surface with an ivory or shell tool or pumice. The scribe typically sat on the floor or ground, using a propped leg to support a wax tablet or some papyrus. The actual physical writer or scribe usually became forgotten, though Tertius raises his own voice as a writer of the Letter to the Romans (Rom 16:22). Apart from the physical acts of writing and transcribing, the process depended on sound spoken and sound heard. The letter would have been dictated by Paul in one session, but revised in the transcription to papyrus when Paul could have entered his own handwritten words. The scribe wrote what was heard spoken aloud, giving best effort to record the grammar, sound, and wording correctly, perhaps even to make corrections. Writers spoke aloud with

36. See ibid., 29–30, with Greco-Roman examples.

37. See the video descriptions by Daniel B. Wallace, *Scribal Methods and Materials*, The Center for the Study of New Testament Manuscripts, iTunesU, https://itunes.apple.com/us/itunes-u/scribal-methods-materials/id446658178.

38. Lee and Scott, *Sound Mapping the New Testament*, 16–18, with examples. See "Ancient Writing Materials: Wax Tablets," University of Michigan Library website, http://www.lib.umich.edu/papyrus-collection/ancient-writing-materials-wax-tablets. See more images in an Internet search of "wax tablets."

a view to the text being read aloud to its recipient(s). Consequently, the entire authorial process was oriented to sound and was decidedly rhetorical.[39] Texts were intentionally composed to be spoken.[40] The Greek words for reading, verb ἀναγινώσκω and noun ἀνάγνωσις, refer not to silent reading but to public vocal reading, hence to the hearing of a message read aloud to an audience.[41] Few people read individually or silently. What was spoken and heard was rhetorical and dependent on the minds of author and recipients much more than on the written text. Authors arranged topoi, imagery, and argumentation in their minds, and recipients similarly interpreted and understood topoi, imagery, and argumentation in their minds. An author's message was conveyed by spoken and heard sounds.

Who Delivered the Letter?

The intermediate step of letter production was physical transport of the letter and delivery of its rhetorical presentation aloud. Based on the narration and names of greeters in Col 4:7–17, particularly the appearance of the name Onesimus (Col 4:9), many have taken the view that the Letter to Philemon was transported and delivered by Tychicus, accompanied by Onesimus, who was "sent back" to Philemon by Paul (Phlm 12).

> Tychicus will tell you all the news about me; he is a beloved brother, a faithful minister, and a fellow servant in the Lord. I have sent him to you for this very purpose, so that you may know how we are and that he may encourage your hearts; he is coming with Onesimus, the faithful and beloved brother, who is one of you. They will tell you about everything here.
>   Aristarchus my fellow prisoner greets you, as does Mark the cousin of Barnabas, concerning whom you have received instructions—if he

---

39. Lee and Scott, *Sound Mapping the New Testament*, 24–28. They are texts prepared for utterance. See the helpful comments of Bryan, *Listening to the Bible*, chapter 10, "The Drama of the Word," 114–26.

40. Lee and Scott, *Sound Mapping the New Testament*, 69. They were not, however, composed or delivered by "performance." On this see Larry W. Hurtado, "Oral Fixation and New Testament Studies? 'Orality,' 'Performance' and Reading Texts in Early Christianity," *NTS* 60 (2014): 321–40.

41. See Rudolf Bultmann, "Ἀναγινώσκω, ἀνάγνωσις," *TDNT* 1:343–44; Jeal, *Integrating Theology and Ethics in Ephesians*, 28n71; see also Lee and Scott, *Sound Mapping the New Testament*, 24.

comes to you, welcome him. And Jesus who is called Justus greets you. These are the only ones of the circumcision among my co-workers for the kingdom of God, and they have been a comfort to me. Epaphras, who is one of you, a servant of Christ Jesus, greets you. He is always wrestling in his prayers on your behalf, so that you may stand mature and fully assured in everything that God wills. For I testify for him that he has worked hard for you and for those in Laodicea and in Hierapolis. Luke, the beloved physician, and Demas greet you. Give my greetings to the brothers and sisters in Laodicea, and to Nympha and the church in her house. And when this letter has been read among you, have it read also in the church of the Laodiceans; and see that you read also the letter from Laodicea. And say to Archippus, "See that you complete the task that you have received in the Lord." (Col 4:7–17)

Greeters mentioned in the closing of Philemon are noted in Colossians, with more information given about some of them. Onesimus, here called "faithful and beloved brother,"[42] which sounds like Paul's description and request for him in Phlm 16, is "one of you," which many have taken to mean that he is a resident of Colossae and a member of the *ekklēsia* there. This implies that Philemon, too, was resident in Colossae. Letter carriers were commonly present when the document was prepared and when it was read aloud to its recipients.[43] This connection depends, of course, on the view that Philemon and Colossians were written at or about the same time and that the Onesimus of Col 4 is the same Onesimus of Philemon. Both of these notions are questionable, because the overall content and themes of the two letters are vastly different and, more particularly, because the view and role of Onesimus seem to be very different in Colossians compared to Philemon.[44] Onesimus was a common name for male slaves, and there is nothing in either Colossians or Philemon specifying the same person as referent. Still, while the evidence is not certain, it is possible to imagine that the Onesimus who met the prisoner Paul was himself

---

42. As is, interestingly, Tychicus (Τυχικὸς ὁ ἀγαπητὸς ἀδελφός).

43. See the report of an essay presentation by Peter M. Head, "Onesimus and the Letter to Philemon: New Light on the Role of the Letter Carrier," *RBECS*, 31 May 2012, http://rbecs.org/2012/05/31/peter-m-head-letter-carrier.

44. The disputed authorship of Colossians is actually not itself an objection to the Tychicus theory. Authorship, as we have seen, had a measure of fluidity to it because of its oral nature and the input of scribes. The real issue is whether Colossians and Philemon were written at about the same time, i.e., when Paul was imprisoned and met Onesimus. See below, n. 69.

the letter carrier and deliverer of the message to Philemon. Paul is explicit about sending Onesimus to Philemon. Could Onesimus have made his own personal, vocal appeal to Philemon, along with the letter? We cannot know, but the possibility is intriguing. It is plausible that Onesimus knew Paul was preparing a letter to Philemon and knew he was going to be sent back to Philemon. Against this is the question of why Paul would direct Onesimus to undertake a long and arduous journey back to a slave owner who had power over his life and future. But Paul did have confidence in the now Christ-believing Onesimus and confidence that Philemon would do the right thing despite significant social pressure.

The Audience

The intended end stage of letter-writing is delivery to the audience, the recipients of the communication. The audience members are not, in the ancient Mediterranean context, readers of letters, or few of them are; they are listeners. Letters and other documents were read aloud to their recipients as audible, aural communications from the sender. As we noted above in the discussion of the author, texts were first spoken aloud with the expectation that they would be spoken aloud again by a reader and heard, interpreted, and understood by audiences as meaningful *sounds*. This means that oral delivery and aural reception of the letter were as rhetorical as its composition. As with the precise circumstances of composition, we cannot know exactly how the letter was heard, what intonations and nuances were conveyed, nor how they were received and interpreted. But we can surmise that, even if Paul's words had been amended during the scribal and delivery process, Philemon understood Paul's argumentation.

The clearly intended recipient of the letter is Philemon. Despite some amount of historical speculation that it was directed toward Archippus,[45] a natural reading that notes the repetitive uses of second person singular pronouns demonstrates that Philemon is the single person meant to get the message. It is equally clear that other people were members of a larger audience who, though not direct recipients of the argumentation, were present with Philemon or were near enough to listen, that they heard the letter and its message, and that they were at least tangentially interested

---

45. See John Knox, *Philemon among the Letters of Paul* (1935; repr., New York: Abingdon, 1959); and Sara C. Winter, "Paul's Letter to Philemon," *NTS* 33 (1987): 1–15.

parties. People were "looking over his shoulder," observing Philemon's reactions and behaviors. These persons are Apphia, Archippus, and the *ekklēsia* that met in Philemon's home (καὶ Ἀπφίᾳ τῇ ἀδελφῇ καὶ Ἀρχίππῳ τῷ συστρατιώτῃ ἡμῶν καὶ τῇ κατ᾽ οἶκόν σου ἐκκλησίᾳ, v. 2). While it is a nice, romantic notion, there is no evidence to support the common view that Apphia was Philemon's wife and Archippus his son. We cannot know who this woman and man were, other than being persons known to Paul and Philemon. Other people were present with Paul who were members of the audience—certainly Onesimus—and incidentally, but perhaps not unimportantly, Timothy, Epaphras, Mark, Aristarchus, Demas, and Luke (vv. 1, 23–24). Philemon's knowledge of persons in multiple spaces being privy to his letter from Paul, including God and Christ Jesus, places implicit pressure on him to do the right thing regarding Onesimus. All of these audience members are real beings, human and divine, understood to be alive and conscious of the persons and situation under consideration.

Philemon and the others with him are Christ-believing gentiles who are members of the assembly, the *ekklēsia*. They are ἅγιοι, holy ones (vv. 5, 7), for whom Philemon has provided significant and memorable care. They are imagined as faithful people who are acquainted with Paul. Paul imagines them as coworkers in the gospel. There is a difference, however, between the kind of recipient Philemon is and the kind of recipients the others are. Philemon is the person being called on to act, to receive Onesimus as his beloved brother. As the recipient who is expected to do something, to respond intellectually and behaviorally, he is a judge, a κριτής. The other third-party listeners are spectators, θεωροί,[46] people who watch and contemplate, who learn as observers. Spectators are influential, however, and will themselves be moved to take points of view that coincide with those of an author or speaker. The physical space of Philemon and those with him is the household. Philemon is the owner of the home, the paterfamilias who possesses authority. He is sufficiently affluent to have a home large enough to accommodate the *ekklēsia*, which could have been composed of thirty or more persons. It appears that his home was spacious enough for him to be able to accommodate Paul in hospitality space (ἅμα δὲ καὶ ἑτοίμαζέ μοι ξενίαν, v. 22). Clearly he had at least one slave, perhaps more, and it is reasonable to imagine family members also living in the

---

46. See Aristotle, *Rhet.* 1.3.1–3; LSJ 797; Wilhelm Michaelis, "θεωρέω," *TDNT* 5:318; G. W. H. Lampe, *A Patristic Greek Lexicon* (Oxford: Clarendon, 1961), 649.

house. Some interpreters wonder, if Philemon had been a Christ-believer for some time, why Onesimus the slave was not a believer before he met Paul. It would be common for an entire household to follow the religious and other social, cultural, and behavioral views and practices of the senior householder. There is no evidence leading to determining a reason for why Onesimus was not a believer before his separation from Philemon.

Canonicity

To some readers Philemon has seemed to be an odd or questionable letter for inclusion in the New Testament canon. It is very short relative to the other letters in the Pauline corpus (though not so short relative to ancient Hellenistic letters more generally), and its argument is personally focused on Philemon and his reception of Onesimus. Its apparently highly manipulative rhetorical ethos can seem to be unfairly pressuring Phile-mon. Many have considered its direct personal concern to be peripheral to the issues addressed in the New Testament. Many have claimed the letter has no theological or doctrinal content.[47] Even though it is in the canon, its brevity and personal argument have often pushed it to the neglected edge of scholarly study. Why would an apparently private matter, even if Apphia, Archippus, and the *ekklēsia* are listening in and applying pressure to Philemon, be preserved and become part of wider canonical concern? It is not enough simply to say that it was included in the New Testament canon, because it was written by Paul the apostle and its authority relies on his name.[48] It is clear that Paul wrote other letters that were not included in the canon and are lost (see 1 Cor 5:9; 2 Cor 2:4; Col 4:16), and it may be imagined that some of them were short and personal.

We cannot say, of course, just why this letter was included. But it is not peripheral at all to early Christian thought, and it has no lack of theology.

---

47. As Norman R. Petersen, *Rediscovering Paul: Philemon and the Sociology of Paul's Narrative World* (Philadelphia: Fortress, 1985), 201. See also Robert McL. Wilson, *A Critical and Exegetical Commentary on Colossians and Philemon*, ICC (London: Bloomsbury, 2014), 317. Fitzmyer, *Letter to Philemon*, 34, notes that St. Jerome (ca. 347–420 CE) reported that people said the letter "has nothing that can edify us."

48. Some interpreters have suggested that Philemon was preserved by Onesimus, presumed to be the bishop mentioned in Ignatius, *Eph.* 1.3; 2.1; 6.2. See Barth and Blanke, *Letter to Philemon*, 201–2; Thompson, *Colossians and Philemon*, 201.

Indeed, interpretation of it demands theological thinking.[49] Sociorhetorical analysis reveals aspects of what Paul believed had been brought into the world in Christ Jesus and how those things may be lived out in a wisdom space and context. In the wisdom, household location, love and faith, refreshment, family inclusion (brotherhood), and freedom are provided for *all* persons, including slaves who, in the social and cultural setting of the Roman Empire, were persons with no inherent or legal status in family affairs.[50] They were there to do as they were directed for the wishes and comforts of their masters. In Paul's understanding, all Christ-believers, including slaves and other disenfranchised persons, are members of the *ekklēsia* and are to be received and treated as family members (Onesimus is a *brother*). This means that slaves are not to be treated as slaves, even if they have formerly been considered to be "useless" (v. 11). Those who have been slaves are now, in Christ, no different from those who are not or have never been slaves. This is how Paul in Christ sees the world; it is the ideology he presents.[51] Because of Christ the world is a changed space. It is apparent that early Christians who were interested in preserving authoritative documents saw such values in Philemon.

Occasion/Circumstances

The occasion and circumstances of the letter are straightforward enough, even if they allude to larger social, cultural, historical, and sacred contexts. Philemon, slave owner, and Onesimus, slave (δοῦλος, v. 16), are separated from each other, or, to use the grammar of the text, Onesimus "has been separated" from Philemon (τάχα γὰρ διὰ τοῦτο ἐχωρίσθη πρὸς ὥραν, v. 15). *This is the foundational circumstance of the letter.* Because the language is given in the passive voice, the impression is given of a "divine passive" where God is the implicit subject of the separation and Onesimus the object.[52] No other reason is given for the separation. During the separation, Onesimus and Paul have met and Onesimus has become a Christ-believer. Paul, who is imprisoned when the letter is composed, imagines

---

49. See Fitzmyer, *Letter to Philemon*, 34–40.

50. See the commentary on **intertexture** and **social and cultural texture**.

51. On this see the **ideological texture** and rhetorical force as emergent discourse sections in the commentary.

52. Of course Onesimus *is* the subject of the verb, but the passive voice means that the action is being done *to* him, presumably by God.

Onesimus now as someone who serves with him, or at least can serve if Philemon will permit it (χωρὶς δὲ τῆς σῆς γνώμης οὐδὲν ἠθέλησα ποιῆσαι, v. 14), in the service of the gospel (μοι διακονῇ ἐν τοῖς δεσμοῖς τοῦ εὐαγγελίου, v. 13). Paul has become so close to Onesimus that he views him as his own child, figuratively or spiritually "begotten" by Paul during his imprisonment (παρακαλῶ σε περὶ τοῦ ἐμοῦ τέκνου, ὃν ἐγέννησα ἐν τοῖς δεσμοῖς Ὀνήσιμον, v. 10), as his own viscera (τοῦτ᾽ ἔστιν τὰ ἐμὰ σπλάγχνα, v. 12). Formerly perceived to be "useless" to Philemon, now he is "useful" (τόν ποτέ σοι ἄχρηστον νυνὶ δὲ σοὶ καὶ ἐμοὶ εὔχρηστον, v. 11). Paul, for his part, does not see the separation as being permanent. He is sending Onesimus back to Philemon (ὃν ἀνέπεμψά σοι αὐτόν, v. 12) with the request that Philemon receive the Christ-believing Onesimus as a "beloved brother" (οὐκέτι ὡς δοῦλον ἀλλὰ ὑπὲρ δοῦλον, ἀδελφὸν ἀγαπητόν, v. 16), as if Onesimus were Paul himself (προσλαβοῦ αὐτὸν ὡς ἐμέ, v. 17). Paul suggests that if Philemon is materially aggrieved due to the separation, he himself, Paul, will cover any amount owing (εἰ δέ τι ἠδίκησέν σε ἢ ὀφείλει, τοῦτο ἐμοὶ ἐλλόγα· ἐγὼ Παῦλος ἔγραψα τῇ ἐμῇ χειρί, ἐγὼ ἀποτίσω, vv. 18–19). Paul is confident that Philemon will do the right thing (πεποιθὼς τῇ ὑπακοῇ σου ἔγραψά σοι, εἰδὼς ὅτι καὶ ὑπὲρ ἃ λέγω ποιήσεις, v. 21). The simple fact is that we do not know more about the occasion and circumstances of the letter than this.

Still, the pressure to reconstruct the historical situation of Philemon has moved interpreters to spend much time and take up much space hypothesizing about the situational context of the letter, without, it should be admitted, any hard evidence. Most commentaries also include discussions of slavery in the ancient Mediterranean basin, some of them very extensive.[53] Why were Philemon and Onesimus separated? It is known that slaves could be separated from owners for many reasons: conducting business for the owner, delivering letters, assisting other persons, working where required and directed by the owner. Or they might be runaways, or they might seek asylum from an owner or from a difficult situation. There are a number of theories about why Onesimus and Philemon were separated.[54]

---

53. For example, Barth and Blanke, *Letter to Philemon*, 3–102.

54. For a very helpful survey see Larry J. Kreitzer, *Philemon*, Readings: A New Biblical Commentary (Sheffield: Sheffield Phoenix, 2008), 38–69. See also J. Albert Harrill, *Slaves in the New Testament: Literary, Social and Moral Dimensions* (Minneapolis: Fortress, 2006), 6–16, 165–92. See also the essays in Matthew V. Johnson, James

1. Most common is the construct that claims Onesimus was a run-away slave, a *fugitivus* according to Roman law.[55] This theory is usually taken to mean that Onesimus had committed the offense of leaving Philemon without permission, thereby becoming a fugitive. It is equally plausible, however, to imagine that Philemon (although already a Christ-believer) had abused Onesimus, causing him to depart.[56] Onesimus, in this scenario, is frequently described as a thief who had stolen from Philemon (based on the wording of verse 18) and made a run for it.

2. A second hypothesis is that Onesimus had been sent to Paul, either by his owner, Philemon,[57] or by the church in Colossae,[58] perhaps with messages or with some kind of assistance for Paul. This would mean, obviously, that Onesimus was not a *fugitivus*, but a servant of Philemon or the *ekklēsia*, who was on a mission to Paul. It would also mean that Onesimus was well trusted by Philemon and/or the *ekklēsia*. Paul writes to request that Onesimus be released in order to engage in gospel work with him.

3. Another hypothesis is that Onesimus was a slave who was seeking sanctuary in a religious site such as the temple of Asclepius in Pergamon.[59] This would mean that Onesimus was indeed a runaway, but that he knew *fugitivi* could, in some circumstances, legally seek asylum in religious structures. A variation on this view is that Onesimus sought out Paul (apparently knowing where to look) in the hope that Paul would be an *amicus domini* (friend of the master) who would intervene on his behalf with Philemon.[60]

A. Noel, and Demetrius K. Williams eds., *Onesimus Our Brother: Reading Religion, Race, and Culture in Philemon* (Minneapolis: Fortress, 2012).

55. See, among many examples, John G. Nordling, "*Onesimus Fugitivus*: A Defense of the Runaway Slave Hypothesis in Philemon," *JSNT* 41 (1991): 97–119; Nordling, *Philemon*, ConC (Saint Louis: Concordia, 2004), 3–4; John M. G. Barclay, *Colossians and Philemon*, NTG (Sheffield: Sheffield Academic, 1997), 98–102.

56. Cain Hope Felder, "The Letter to Philemon," *NIB* 11:885–86; Barth and Blanke, *Letter to Philemon*, 73.

57. Knox, *Philemon*, 1959.

58. Winter, "Philemon," 1–15, who extends Knox's ideas. Winter claims that Onesimus was the slave of Archippus, not Philemon, and that the *ekklēsia* met in the home of Archippus.

59. See below on **social and cultural texture**.

60. This view is favored by, among others, James D. G. Dunn, *The Epistles to the*

If Paul was incarcerated when they met, then, practically speaking, Paul's location in prison would be a kind of (unlikely) sanctuary for Onesimus.

4.   Yet another hypothesis, proposed by Allen Dwight Callahan,[61]
      is that Onesimus was not a slave, hence not a *fugitivus*, but was
      the actual genetic "in the flesh" brother of Philemon and also a
      brother "in the Lord" (οὐκέτι ὡς δοῦλον ἀλλὰ ὑπὲρ δοῦλον, ἀδελφὸν
      ἀγαπητόν, μάλιστα ἐμοί, πόσῳ δὲ μᾶλλον σοὶ καὶ ἐν σαρκὶ καὶ ἐν
      κυρίῳ, v. 16). Callahan suggests that the concern of the letter is
      about encouraging Philemon to receive Onesimus as a *beloved*
      brother, not simply as a brother. Callahan claims that the con-
      junction ὡς, "as," in Phlm 16 indicates that Paul's argumentation
      calls for Onesimus not to be received *as if* he is a slave but *as if* he
      is a beloved brother. The slavery, on this view, is a "virtual," not
      real, condition.[62] This construction has not been widely accept-
      ed.[63] One major purpose of the construction is to offer an alterna-
      tive to and argument against the common starting point for study
      of the letter, namely that Onesimus was a runaway, that is, that
      Onesimus was "a criminal and a fugitive."[64] While it seems clear
      that Onesimus was indeed a slave, it is in fact true that it is not
      necessary and not particularly helpful to think of him as criminal
      and fugitive.

How did Paul and Onesimus meet? Again, historical reconstructions
have proliferated, though they follow lines similar to the theories of separation listed above.

1.   The fugitive and thief Onesimus traveled to the known (to him)
      location (Rome? Caesarea? Ephesus?) of the imprisoned Paul,

---

Colossians and to Philemon, NIGTC (Grand Rapids: Eerdmans, 1996), 304–7; S. Scott
Bartchy, "The Epistle to Philemon," *ABD* 5:307–8; Brian Rapske, "The Prisoner Paul in
the Eyes of Onesimus," *NTS* 37 (1991): 187–203; and Peter Lampe, "Kleine 'Sklavenflucht' des Onesimus," *ZNW* 76 (1985):135–37.

    61. Allen Dwight Callahan, *Embassy of Onesimus: The Letter of Paul to Philemon*
(Valley Forge, PA: Trinity Press International, 1997).

    62. Ibid., 10.

    63. See Fitzmyer, *Letter to Philemon*, 18–20; Kreitzer, *Philemon*, 65–67.

    64. Callahan, *Embassy of Onesimus*, 4.

was received by Paul, and became a Christ-believer. On this hypothesis, Paul is harboring a criminal. Alternatively, Onesimus by chance (or providentially?) came into contact with Paul or, perhaps, was arrested and imprisoned by chance (or by providence?) in the same jail in which Paul was located.

2. Onesimus, having a grievance with Philemon, fled to seek sanctuary at a religious site and, somehow in the process (chance? arrest? providence?), came into contact with Paul, who was imprisoned nearby, and became a Christ-believer. This theory reduces the pressure on Paul, who would not be harboring a criminal fugitive, but only supporting a refugee or assisting a fellow prisoner.

3. Onesimus was sent by Philemon and/or the *ekklēsia* to the known location of Paul's imprisonment.

4. Onesimus fled to seek out Paul as an *amicus domini* who would appeal to Philemon on his behalf. Somehow he located and came into contact with Paul.

The general assumptions in these scenarios are that Onesimus fled Philemon from Colossae and that he came into contact with the imprisoned Paul. Neither assumption is certain and the evidence ranges from nonexistent to meager. It is possible, for example, that Onesimus and Paul met *prior* to Paul's imprisonment.

A slave would most likely be incarcerated in a prison for slaves, not in a place where Paul would have been held.[65] It is very difficult to envisage how a slave, working independently, could have come into contact with a prisoner, even if the slave did know the location of the imprisonment. Apart from being a Christ-believing slave who had become closely associated with Paul, Onesimus's status and location at the time of the writing of the letter are unknown. We do not know whether he was a *fugitivus*, a thief, a messenger, a truant seeking asylum, or something else (such as the estranged brother of Philemon). We know that Philemon and Onesimus, owner and slave, were separated (v. 15), but we do not know the reason(s) for or circumstance(s) of the separation. We do not know the circumstances of how Paul and Onesimus met. We do know that Onesimus has become a Christ-believer. No amount of reconstruction or analysis of the metanarrative is determinative or even helpful for reconstructing anything else about

---

65. Fitzmyer, *Letter to Philemon*, 13.

the historical situation. Examination of Col 4:7–17 offers only incidental and possibly disputable information that tells us nothing about the situations indicated in Philemon. The limitless hypotheses[66] are so unlikely that they can scarcely be considered. They are fascinating, of course, and interesting for their own sake, but they do *not* add to our understanding of the letter; indeed, they have the potential to detract from or skew understanding, because they lead to interpretations oriented toward contrived situations. The possibilities remain just that, possibilities, but they are very far from being probabilities. The complete situational history remains unknown. In this commentary, we will leave it there.[67]

Locations and Date

Consideration of locations and dating—as with studies of the chronology of Paul's life and writings—necessarily involves speculation and dispute without full resolution. In the speculative process, though, it is important to think of "locations" in the plural, because there are both senders and receivers of letters and, in the case of Philemon and other Pauline letters, multiple parties directly involved with the content of the letter. There are, of course, Paul and Timothy, the declared authors (v. 1), and Onesimus, who is present with Paul when the letter is composed (vv. 10–13). It is likely that other named persons, Epaphras, Mark, Aristarchus, Demas, and Luke, are also present with Paul or near enough to be in contact with him (vv. 23–24). If Col 4:7–17 is connected with Philemon, then there seem to be even more people in view at the composition location (Tychicus, Jesus Justus). Epaphras is called "my fellow prisoner in Christ Jesus" (Ἐπαφρᾶς ὁ συναιχμάλωτός μου ἐν Χριστῷ Ἰησοῦ, v. 23), which might or might not indicate that Epaphras is incarcerated with Paul or in another location.[68]

---

66. See, for numerous examples, Barth and Blanke, *Letter to Philemon*, 145–50. Houlden is a rare commentator who notes that we do not know the situation and cannot know it from the letter or from any available information (J. Leslie Houlden, *Paul's Letters from Prison: Philippians, Colossians, Philemon, Ephesians* [London: Penguin, 1970], 226).

67. For a thoroughgoing analysis see Peter Arzt-Grabner, "How to Deal with Onesimus? Paul's Solution within the Frame of Ancient Legal and Documentary Sources," in *Philemon in Perspective: Interpreting a Pauline Letter*, ed. D. François Tolmie (Berlin: de Gruyter, 2010), 113–42.

68. There is a range of possible meanings: Epaphras could be incarcerated with Paul; he could be incarcerated in another location; he could be understood as a

On the receiving side are Philemon, Apphia, Archippus, and the *ekklēsia* gathered in Philemon's home.

Paul calls himself "prisoner of Christ Jesus" (δέσμιος Χριστοῦ Ἰησοῦ, v. 1), and it is hard not to take him literally and not to imagine him being physically incarcerated when the letter was composed. But where? Directly linked to this question is the location of Philemon and the people closely connected with him. Where were they? The straightforward fact is that we do not know with much certainty where any of them were located. The letter does not provide any information regarding the geographical locations of the imprisoned Paul with Onesimus, Timothy, and others or of Philemon, Apphia, Archippus, and the *ekklēsia* that met in Philemon's home. This fact causes much perplexity regarding aspects of the circumstances and the dating of the letter. The only clear information given is that the leading characters in the visual scene are separated by a significant distance, making the letter itself necessary for communication.

Onesimus is being "sent back" to Philemon (v. 12). Paul expects to travel to Philemon's location and stay in Philemon's house (v. 22). Many interpreters have assumed that the situation described in Col 4:7–17, where Tychicus and Onesimus are described as traveling shortly to Colossae, indicates that Philemon was a resident of that town, not far from Laodicea and Hierapolis (see Col 4:13) in the Lycus Valley in Phrygia. This assumption has resulted in Colossians and Philemon frequently being closely connected in people's minds and in commentaries on the two letters being bound together in single volumes. It presumes that both letters were prepared and sent at about the same time. It is possible that Colossians and Philemon are this closely related, but it is not historically certain.[69] Colossians seems to indicate that Paul had not himself ever been to Colossae or the Lycus towns (Col 2:1) and that Epaphras,[70] mentioned

---

metaphorical or spiritual prisoner of Christ Jesus along with Paul. See below on *repetitive texture*.

69. The question of the authorship of Colossians becomes significant to many at this point (see above, n. 44). The majority of scholars think that Colossians is deutero-Pauline, written after Paul's death, but before 100 CE. On this see Raymond E. Brown, *An Introduction to the New Testament* (New York: Doubleday, 1997), 615–17. I suggest, given what we have learned about how Hellenistic letters were composed, that the important question is not about the authorship of Colossians, but whether it was composed and sent while Paul was still alive. See my forthcoming commentary on Colossians.

70. Who is unlikely to be the same person as Epaphroditus, mentioned in Phil 2:25; 4:18.

only in Philemon (v. 23) and Colossians (1:7; 4:12), had proclaimed the gospel there.[71] Colossians could have been composed later than Philemon, using names and circumstances recalled from earlier times during Paul's ministry. Conjecture rules the day due to lack of information. However, the sharing of names makes a reasonable, indeed the only, starting point, a possibility with strong plausibility, namely, the presumed residence of Philemon in Colossae or at least in the relatively small Lycus Valley region in Phrygia.[72] We can build possible scenarios on this basis.

At the time of the letter's composition, Paul could have been imprisoned in Caesarea Maritima (Acts 23:23–26:32) or Rome (Acts 28:14–31). Onesimus and Paul had met and were apparently together. Rome seems much too far away from Colossae (direct distance approximately 1,500 kilometers) and much too expensive to reach for Onesimus to have traveled there, whether entirely on his own or with assistance. Caesarea Maritima was much closer to Colossae (approximately 800 kilometers), hence a somewhat more plausible location, but still a long distance, whether overland or by sea. The third possibility is that Paul was imprisoned in Ephesus, much closer (approximately 200 kilometers) and more readily reachable for Onesimus. The major problem with this third hypothesis is that there is no record of Paul being imprisoned there. Some interpreters suggest that several of Paul's statements about difficulties he experienced in Ephesus support an incarceration there (Rom 16:7; 1 Cor 15:32; 16:9; 2 Cor 1:8–9; 6:5; 11:23–24).[73] Of the three possible locations, Ephesus is more strongly plausible, on the view that Philemon was resident in the Lycus Valley.[74] On this hypothesis, Philemon was written sometime during the span of years from 54 to 58 CE. A fourth, less plausible hypothesis, taking seriously the language of 2 Cor 11:23 about imprisonments in the plural, is of an unreported imprisonment for some short period of time in some

---

71. Epaphras is a bit of an anomaly when Philemon and Colossians are compared. In Col 4:12 he is referred to as "one of you," but in Phlm 23 as Paul's fellow prisoner who sends greetings to Philemon.

72. For a general history of the Lycus Valley as regards the New Testament, see F. F. Bruce, "Colossian Problems Part One: Jews and Christians in the Lycus Valley," *BSac* 141 (1984): 3–15.

73. See Fitzmyer, *Letter to Philemon*, 10.

74. There are other hypothetical scenarios if it is considered that Paul was released from prison in Rome and was able to travel and work up until about 65–67 CE. See Barth and Blanke, 126, n. 48; Jerome Murphy-O'Connor, *Paul: A Critical Life* (Oxford: Oxford University Press, 1998).

unknown location, presumably in Asia Minor. The wording of the letter that offers information useful for dating is where Paul calls himself "an old man" (τοιοῦτος ὢν ὡς Παῦλος πρεσβύτης, v. 9), which indicates that he was more than fifty years old when the letter was composed.[75] This makes dating in the mid- to late 50s or later plausible.

The fact remains that we do not know the precise geographical and physical locations relevant to the letter. We are left with something less than probabilities and likelihoods, only with possibilities. I have here engaged in a level of historical reconstruction where Colossae is the location of Philemon and people close to him and Ephesus is the location of Paul and those near him, but nothing leads to final decisions. What we do know is that Philemon and Onesimus are separated; we take as a given that Paul is in prison at some distance from Philemon, that Paul and Onesimus have met, and that Onesimus is being sent back to Philemon. As is suggested in the section on **social and cultural texture** in the commentary, it is actually best, for interpretive purposes, to avoid hard conclusions. We are studying an intensely personal letter that leaves out things already understood by the correspondents. What we do have is the rhetoric of the letter.

Purpose and Goals

The purpose of the Letter to Philemon comes across clearly from reading verses 16 and 17: Paul wishes to move Philemon, carefully yet without allowing Philemon any other righteous option, to receive Onesimus, not as a slave but as a beloved brother and as if he were Paul himself. We presume that Onesimus was agreeable to this.[76] How Paul gets to this point and how he employs language to move Philemon to do what he wants is taken up in the commentary. The rhetoric and argumentation are focused on Philemon, not on Onesimus or slavery, even though these are critical features of the texturing of the letter. The result is anticipated, not enacted. Paul aims to influence Philemon's understanding, behavior, and

---

75. Paul is usually estimated to have been born ca. 5 to 10 CE. See Brown, *Introduction*, 423. See below on **intertexture**.

76. Did Onesimus want to return to Philemon? We cannot know his views but can only presume he accepted Paul's leadership in these matters. Was Paul being excessively patriarchal regarding his "child" Onesimus? See the introduction and essays in Johnson, Noel, and Williams, *Onesimus Our Brother*, and Harrill, *Slaves in the New Testament*, 16. See below on **social and cultural texture**.

faithfulness in Christ. Onesimus has become a Christ-believer and is to be treated as all other Christ-believers in kinship, community, and partnership relationships. Philemon viewed Paul as a "partner" (κοινωνός). He would not, therefore, receive Paul into his home and into the *ekklēsia* that met in his home as a slave. Onesimus should be treated in the same way, as partner, as an equal, not as slave. As partner and brother, Paul in fact (as a feature of his argumentation) mentions that he planned to come to receive hospitality—including physical space in a room—from Philemon (ἅμα δὲ καὶ ἑτοίμαζέ μοι ξενίαν, v. 22). Given this, Philemon could scarcely imagine that Paul wanted anything less provided for Onesimus. The clear meaning is that Onesimus will in fact "no longer" (οὐκέτι)[77] be a slave. Although Paul does not call explicitly for manumission, it would be, for Philemon, easily surmised and a logical and understood goal.[78] Paul builds a powerful yet concise, nearly irresistible, rhetorical case. The goal and anticipated result of the letter is major social formation for Philemon, Onesimus, and for the new society of "holy ones," the *ekklēsia*. Onesimus is a partner, like Paul, not a slave. This in fact is the explanation of the letter: it was written because Paul wanted Philemon to go against the expectations of his geographical, social, and cultural locations and receive his (former) slave as a brother and as if he were Paul himself.

There are a number of subsidiary goals. Paul aims to place much moral and Christ-believing, ideological pressure on Philemon while subtly expressing himself in loving, brotherly terms. He does this in a highly rhetoricized manner (vv. 8–9). Throughout the letter, Paul aims to support both the idea and the reality of the new society of believers, the "holy ones," the *ekklēsia*, that meets in Philemon's home. Certainly he has the same concern for the *ekklēsia* everywhere. Knowing the value of the good

---

77. Rather than μηκέτι, which would be expected and would suggest *possibility* rather than the *indicative reality* of οὐκέτι. It is too relativizing to interpret the comparative conjunction ὡς in verse 16 (οὐκέτι ὡς δοῦλον) to indicate the idea "in spite of," that is, that Onesimus should be treated as a brother "in spite of" (presumably *despite* is actually meant?) still being a slave (as David W. Pao, *Colossians and Philemon* ZECNT [Grand Rapids: Zondervan, 2012], 347, 395–96), with the implication that Paul was not (and Philemon need not be) concerned for Onesimus's legal and physical status as a slave. See the commentary on *argumentative texture*, **intertexture**, and **social and cultural texture**. See also much discussion in the commentaries, e.g., Barth and Blanke, *Letter to Philemon*, 414–20.

78. Whether he did formally emancipate Onesimus is, of course, not known, despite the legendary stories of Onesimus eventually becoming a bishop.

things Philemon has done for the holy ones as a man of love and faith, Paul has in mind to promote his continuing work of refreshment of the viscera of believers (vv. 5–7). Paul clearly shapes his rhetoric in order to place Philemon in a position where it would be very difficult to refuse his requests. He draws in Apphia, Archippus, and the entire *ekklēsia* that meets in Philemon's home as observers, informing them of his requests to Philemon, in order to intensify the pressure. Paul very strongly and stylishly aims to impress Philemon with the notion that Onesimus is indeed a "useful" person, even if he was formerly seen to be "useless" (v. 11). Paul emphasizes this by stating that he would like "to keep" the now productive Onesimus himself for gospel service (v. 13).[79] Paul also aims to show that God is at work in people's lives. He suggests that the separation of Philemon and Onesimus was a divine act with a divine purpose in mind. This divine purpose has an apocalyptic goal beyond the immediate situation in which Paul, Onesimus, and Philemon are participants. In Paul's mind it has a view toward eternity (ἵνα αἰώνιον αὐτὸν ἀπέχῃς, v. 15). The letter also has the goal of giving Onesimus hope for avoidance of penalty and punishment and for peaceful Christian living with Philemon. Paul presents a case against slavery in subtle, indirect ways. One of the results the letter anticipates is a kind of social equalizing where there is a lowering of the relatively wealthy homeowner and slave owner and a raising of the relatively poor, propertyless slave. In the process, Paul the prisoner and the "holy ones" of the *ekklēsia* are also imagined in a rising condition due to the anticipated actions of Philemon.

Despite the occasionally stated view that Philemon has "no theology" and the reality that the letter has often been overlooked by scholars, these purposes and goals demonstrate the letter's major concerns for Christian social formation and theology.[80] It tells us much about Paul's gospel logic and ideology as "a carefully crafted witness to an emerging

---

79. Harrill, *Slaves in the New Testament*, 14–16, hypothesizes that the purpose of the letter was to request that Onesimus "be apprenticed to Paul for service in the gospel." Harrill claims that Philemon is a "letter of recommendation" with similarities to apprenticeship contracts. The language of Phlm 16–17, however, makes the central purpose clear enough.

80. On the importance of Philemon for understanding Paul and his theology see now N. T. Wright, "Return of the Runaway?" in *Paul and the Faithfulness of God* (Minneapolis: Fortress, 2013), 3–74.

Christian ethos."[81] No one may be considered a slave in Christ (vv. 8, 20, 23), the property of another human, even if one has been a slave until now in Roman or legal terms. This because there is, certainly in Paul's understanding, full and complete freedom because of what Christ has done.[82] It turns out that Philemon is one of the keys to understanding Paul and to grasping his underlying thinking, his approach to faith and behavior, and his Christ-believing theology. In Christ people are free and are brothers and sisters. There is a new society where love and freedom are gifts and are to be used in the practice of wisdom. This coheres fully with the Christ-believing theology Paul presents elsewhere in his corpus of letters. Humans are by the grace and action of God in Christ free, in family relationship, partners in the gospel and in the assembly of believers, the *ekklēsia*. Onesimus, now a Christ-believer, is therefore free, and Philemon may not treat him in the way slaves were treated according to the social and cultural expectations and traditions (and indeed laws) of Mediterranean and Roman societies. This is what N. T. Wright calls "the profound, and profoundly revolutionary, theology" leading to "the social and cultural earthquake which Paul is attempting to precipitate— or, rather, which he believes has already been precipitated by God's action in the Messiah."[83] The sociorhetorical analysis of this commentary shows how the letter presents this theology. Philemon is a key text because it gets at nothing less than the nature of the new life, the new society, the communal life, the ecclesial life, the new existence, of Christianity. Paul also turns out to be deeply theologically oriented. He functions as a committed Christ-believer, having faith and theological aims in mind. He has the continuation of living in Christ Jesus, that is, wisdom living, in mind. He uses wisdom rhetorolect, overall, to support this and to get what he wants.

It is worth noting that Philemon has been employed at various times to take a strong stand against slavery and, at others, to stand strongly in support of it.[84] These interpretive claims have more to do with the interpreters and their own sociocultural locations than with Paul, Philemon,

---

81. Luke Timothy Johnson, *The Writings of the New Testament: An Interpretation*, rev. ed. (Minneapolis: Fortress, 1999), 387.

82. See especially the discussions in the sections on **intertexture** and **social and cultural texture** and **ideological texture** in the commentary.

83. Wright, "Return of the Runaway," 9.

84. For a very helpful survey of the history of the interpretation of Philemon see Kreitzer, *Philemon*, 39–173.

Onesimus, and the document itself. There is, of course, a natural tendency to see oneself and one's own time and culture when looking at something from the distant past. Interpreters are people of their own times. Ancient texts can seem to be symbols of modern understandings, and people inevitably see themselves at least in some ways in the stories told by ancient texts, particularly at points that seem flattering to their ideologies.[85] Biblical scholars know this and frequently mention it. Understanding does become bound up with the interpreters themselves, and it can be difficult to separate them from each other. The sociorhetorical analytic aims to assist careful thinking about the purposes and goals of the text by investigating and explaining how the document brings about theological thinking and aims.

Epistolary and Rhetorical Structure

New Testament letters are typically analyzed, at least in major part, according to the standard epistolary structure of ancient Hellenistic letters. A look at the range of commentaries and scholarly articles demonstrates this. For many interpreters this is the "proper" way to engage in the exegetical task.[86] This is structural analysis that is a kind of form criticism.[87] It is aimed at the task of developing an understanding of a letter in its historical circumstances. Certainly Philemon and other New Testament letters have epistolary structure,[88] even if it varies fairly significantly across the corpus, and Sociorhetorical Exploration Commentaries take it into account. Epistolary analysis, however, does not reveal everything. It identifies and helps explain the epistolary framework (though interpreters frequently disagree about where one structural feature ends and another begins), but it does not in itself provide a full understanding of letter's function, particularly

---

85. This is why it is impossible for people today to be Christians in exactly the same way first-century CE believers were Christians, even though the Bible is taken to be authoritative Scripture and a sure guide for faith and practice.

86. "The proper interpretation of any Pauline letter must involve an analysis of the letter's structure and its epistolary conventions" according to Jeffrey A. D. Weima, "Paul's Persuasive Prose: An Epistolary Analysis of the Letter to Philemon," in Tolmie, *Philemon in Perspective*, 29–60, here 29.

87. See ibid., 29. See Jeal, *Integrating Theology and Ethics in Ephesians*, 26–27.

88. Four typical parts: prescript (or introductory greeting), thanksgiving, body, postscript (closing greeting). Not all of the New Testament letters employ this pattern exactly.

with regard to argumentation and the force of argumentation.[89] Consequently, many interpreters employ additional approaches in their work.

Many scholars analyze New Testament letters according to the forms
and styles of classical rhetoric. While this approach has been very fruit-
ful, the problem with it is that the letters actually are *not* speeches or ora-
tory, even if they were composed by being spoken aloud, transcribed, and
spoken and heard aloud when they were received.[90] New Testament letters
frequently display oratorical features, but they are still letters. Philemon
is *like* a deliberative speech in some respects (i.e., it is a kind of wisdom
discourse, as described above), and it might be delivered *like* a speech, but
it is *not* a speech prepared for and delivered in the public square or for
politics. It is a letter that has profound rhetorical force intended to move
Philemon ideologically and behaviorally. It relies on sound spoken and
sound heard, the voice of Paul, and the voice of the reader. Many aspects
of classical rhetoric are helpful, particularly for stylistic analysis. But in its
social, rhetorical, and ecclesial context it remains a letter, not a speech.[91]
The New Testament has its own rhetorical features and categories that do
not correspond neatly to Greco-Roman rhetorical methods.

While interpreters differ about where the body ends and the closing
begins, an analysis of the epistolary structure of Philemon has this typical pattern:

> Prescript (introductory greeting) (vv. 1–3)
> Thanksgiving and prayer (vv. 4–7)
> Body (vv. 8–22; or vv. 8–18 or vv. 8–20, with closing vv. 19–22 or vv.
>   21–22)
> Postscript (closing greeting) (vv. 23–25)

Rhetorical structure according to the formation of speeches presented by
the classical rhetoricians, while also divergently presented by interpreters, could have this fairly typical pattern (with the epistolary prescript and
postscript removed):

---

89. See the commentary on *opening texture*. See also Jeal, *Integrating Theology and
Ethics in Ephesians*, 26–27.

90. As indicated in the description above.

91. The classical handbooks of rhetoric and the *progymnasmata*, it is worth
noting, address the formation, not the analysis, of speeches.

Exordium (vv. 4–7)
Narratio (vv. 8–16)
Argumentatio (*probatio*) (vv. 17–21)
Peroratio (v. 22)

In this Sociorhetorical Explorations Commentary, however, the sociorhetorical analytic is guided by the inner stages of *opening-middle-closing texture* and *progressive texture* and by what seems to be the natural forward movement of what is seen or imagined visually (rhetography), heard narrationally (*narrational texture*), presented argumentatively (*argumentative texture*), and perceived sensorily (*sensory-aesthetic texture*). *Opening-middle-closing texture* sets the foundational pattern:

Opening (vv. 1–7)
Middle (vv. 8–20)
Closing (vv. 21–25)

Within this structure, various steps and topoi move the rhetoric, meaning, theology, and thinking of Philemon along. The term "step" is employed to indicate specific movement ahead in the progressive texture of the letter. While readers may anticipate neat and consistent structural arrangements of texts in a commentary, the multidimensional approach of sociorhetorical analysis reveals that structural arrangements of "steps" do not always correspond across the textures. Readers should not be surprised to see variations among the steps as they read through the sections of the commentary. It is a function of sociorhetorical interpretation to reveal these differences. As an interpreter analyzes and reanalyzes the text from the various vantage points of sociorhetorical interpretation, it becomes clear that sometimes the interweavings of images and ideas overlap, sometimes they are elaborated or abbreviated, and sometimes they are reshaped, recolored, and reoriented. Different textural functions often produce differing movements in the discourse that in turn produce variation of the steps. These steps and topoi are fully described in the commentary.

Rhetography[1]

Opening Rhetoric (Verses 1–7)

Step One (Verses 1–7)

The Letter to Philemon begins by casting images of persons and situations on the visual imagination. First Paul appears in the rhetograph as a male human. He is visualized as a prisoner (δέσμιος) of the second person to appear, Christ Jesus. Paul is thus seen in the situation of imprisonment[2] under the authority of Christ Jesus, another male, who stands in the visualization as the power figure. Seen with Paul, presumably also under the authority of Christ Jesus, is Timothy, another male figure, who is pictured in the kinship role of "brother" (ὁ ἀδελφός). Listeners and readers will begin already to imagine a situation where Paul, who speaks with a prophetic voice from prophetic space yet as a prophet confined under the authority of Christ, addresses them with what will likely be important words and ideas. Paul speaks powerfully, but his power is clearly not his own; it belongs to Christ, for whom he speaks prophetically. Paul is visualized to be speaking to Philemon, who stands in another space, a productive, *wisdom*, household space, and who functions as a coworker (fellow worker, συνεργῷ ἡμῶν) of Paul and Timothy and as one loved by them (τῷ ἀγαπητῷ … ἡμῶν). With Philemon in the wisdom space is Apphia, the sister (τῇ ἀδελφῇ); Archippus, the fellow soldier (τῷ συστρατιώτῃ ἡμῶν) with Paul and Timothy; and the church (ἐκκλησία) that meets in Philemon's house.[3] Apphia, Archippus, and the church are in literary terms

---

1. For a description of rhetography, see the introduction.
2. See the more frequent image of Paul as slave or bond servant (δοῦλος) of Christ. Paul does not here call himself "apostle" as in other letters (e.g., Col 1:1).
3. While the grammar is slightly ambiguous, it is most likely that Philemon's house is the one in view.

"flat" or "static" characters, that is, persons who perform a function necessary to the visual and rhetorical flow, but whose nature and characteriza-
tion are not developed or altered as the scenes progress. Philemon's house
is pictured in the imagination as the location of the church assembled,[4]
perhaps in a room containing various furnishings. Paul is speaking to Philemon, Apphia, Archippus, and the entire *ekklēsia*, although in the picture
he is addressing Philemon most directly. The opening scene thus visualizes
a group of people—as many as might reasonably fit in someone's house—
who stand relationally to each other as *ekklēsia* and who know each other.[5]
Philemon, Apphia, and Aristarchus may be leaders of this church.[6] As Paul
speaks, standing at some distance from the household scene as a prisoner
to and alongside Christ Jesus (along with brother Timothy), Philemon and
the people in his house church hear him. Paul speaks in his prophetic and
authoritative voice, but now also from a priestly space,[7] proclaiming grace
and peace (χάρις ὑμῖν καὶ εἰρήνη) as a greeting to Philemon and the church.

While Paul stands in prophetic space, speaking under Christ's authority
as his prisoner, he is seen simultaneously in the priestly space, employing
priestly rhetorolect to address Philemon directly as an individual.[8] Paul is
seen stating that he gives thanks to God for Philemon, always remembering[9] him in his prayers. Observing Paul make this statement immediately
places the interwoven image of Paul actually remembering, thanking God
and praying for Philemon in the audience's mind. This is a very significant
rhetorical move, because it focuses the rhetograph on the message Paul is
addressing to Philemon, who stands now with Paul in the foreground, and
moves Apphia, Archippus, and the church out to the edges of the picture.
Paul engages in his priestly actions, because he is hearing (ἀκούων) good
things about Philemon.

---

4. Since the word *ekklēsia* means "assembly."

5. As "church" they can be visualized as people who engage in worship and community practices together.

6. Some have speculated that Apphia was Philemon's wife and Archippus his
son, all together in the same house. The rhetograph does not give any reason to take
this view.

7. Here in what SRI calls priestly rhetorolect.

8. The shift to the singular pronoun σου in verse 3 indicates that Philemon is now
addressed individually.

9. Or "making mention" or "making a memory."

Vision is focused on Philemon for the remainder of the first step,[10] and on his wisdom-space actions, which Paul, still visualized as the speaker, describes and anticipates, using wisdom rhetorolect. According to Paul's description, Philemon is seen as a person with love and faith for the Lord Jesus and for all the holy ones. Philemon cares deeply for Christ Jesus, who is still visualized as holding Paul, the speaker, as prisoner and for the holy ones, among whom are the people of Philemon's house church, those people with whom he interacts regularly, who will be immediately observed again at the edges of the rhetograph. Paul's priestly prayer activity has particular aims (ὅπως, "so that"). The prayers are offered with a view to Philemon's observable faith (and presumably his love) for Jesus and the holy ones, becoming active in every good thing, which Paul (and Timothy and others, τοῦ ἐν ἡμῖν[11]) are already observably doing for Christ. This wisdom rhetorolect envisions good activity that Philemon is not yet visibly practicing, but in which Paul is currently engaged. The activity itself is not named and so is not seen clearly, but it is good activity and Paul is doing it. Paul is, then, not only visualized to be speaking but also engaged in unnamed good actions. The picturing here is actually very striking. Philemon is a faithful, loving man who offers his own house as an assembly place for the *ekklēsia*. Yet it is already apparent that there is a specific and now visible gap in his faithful activity. Paul prays that the gap will be closed. Paul envisages Philemon engaging in the good activity as do Philemon himself and other listeners to/readers of this rhetoric—including Apphia, Archippus, and the house church. This visualization has a distinct rhetorical force, because it suggests, indeed it very nearly demands, that the already faithful Philemon start practicing the behavior that Paul and others are seen to be practicing. Listeners and readers viewing the rhetograph want to see Philemon doing the good thing.

Paul is now observed, coming toward the end of this first step in the rhetoric of the letter, to be making an argument.[12] He is visualized and heard saying that he has had much joy and comfort from Philemon's love

---

10. Clearly indicated by the vocative singular ἀδελφέ at the end of verse 7.

11. The variant reading ὑμῖν ("you") is not as strongly attested as the reading ἡμῖν ("we"). See Joseph A. Fitzmyer, *The Letter to Philemon: A New Translation with Introduction and Commentary*, AB 34C (New York: Doubleday, 2000), 98. For a view in favor of "you," see Markus Barth and Helmut Blanke, *The Letter to Philemon*, ECC (Grand Rapids: Eerdmans, 2000), 288–89.

12. Argument is indicated by the conjunction γάρ.

(and presumably Philemon's faith), because the felt needs, the deepest
affections of the saints—for whom Philemon is still seen to care deeply—
have been refreshed by Philemon. Philemon is clearly visualized as a con-
genial and helpful person who has the concerns of others in mind. His
work of refreshing the affections of the saints presents a graphic image to
the mind, because the word σπλάγχνα literally means "entrails," "viscera,"
and even "bowels."[13] It thus portrays things that are hidden and intimate
for humans, reflecting their deepest feelings and emotions.[14] But the word
"for" (γάρ) portrays Paul making an argumentative point: Philemon has
indeed refreshed many and is presently observed doing so, and Paul is
seen to be quite joyful about it, but the word "for" brings out the visual
and argumentative connection with Paul's prayers for him: Philemon does
good things, but the gap in his behavior needs to be closed. The argument
portrayed has the following features:

> Case: Paul prays for Philemon's faithful behavior so that it will
> match his own in some specific way.
> Rationale: Philemon is already lovingly and faithfully caring for
> the saints and has refreshed the affections of many. This implies/
> anticipates that he will fill in the missing part of the picture.
> Anticipated result: Philemon engages in the unnamed behavior.

The rhetograph of Philemon caring for people rhetorically casts the image
of Philemon practicing the as yet unnamed behavior on the imagination.
An expectation of future activity comes clearly to mind.

The final discursive picture that Paul presents to Philemon is the word
"brother" (ἀδελφέ). Philemon is now visualized in the same relationship
to Paul as is Timothy (v. 1). He is the prisoner's brother. The vocative form
indicates that Paul is speaking from his prophetic and imprisoned space
directly to Philemon, who is in wisdom, behavioral space. The imagery
has an almost palpable effect. Although Philemon is deficient in some specific behavior, Paul addresses him as "brother," as one with whom he has a
relationship, but also, and more significantly, as the one he is calling, in a
brotherly way and with a brotherly tone, to see an important point and to
act accordingly. The familial image, rather than the imagery indicated by

---

13. See Ceslas Spicq, *Theological Lexicon of the New Testament* (Peabody, MA:
Hendrickson, 1994) 3:273–75. See the repetition of this word in Phlm 12, 20.

14. Thus the metaphorical notion of what people refer to as the "heart."

some other honorific, presents a happy and loving scene where Philemon could hardly reject the appeal to the behavior to which he is being called. There is a visual pressure on Philemon to do what Paul wants.

This first step functions as a visual, rhetographical setup. Paul the prisoner of Christ Jesus begins by describing a pleasing social situation involving Philemon, the church that meets in his house, and the loving care Philemon has provided for people. Listeners and readers, including Philemon himself in particular, observe a happy scene that obviously should continue. Paul wants the happy scene to be extended by an additional action by Philemon, who will be drawn into the picture and will stand in a morally persuasive situation that will be very difficult to deny. The picturing of the good that Philemon has already done for "the holy ones" itself makes an argument for his continuation in another area. This is blended prophetic rhetorolect, where Paul's prophetic discourse blends with priestly and wisdom discourse material to produce another, anticipated space where Philemon is observed to be practicing the behavior for which Paul wishes. The picture is leading, as will be seen soon enough, to a particular social formation.

Middle Rhetoric (Verses 8–20)

Step Two (Verses 8–9)

Having set the visual stage, Paul, in this step, adds to the rhetograph by employing two colorings, one bright and bold and the other slightly self-deprecating, and then brings into the picture the person who is at the focus of his concern. Paul is observed speaking once again in prophetic mode, tying his progression in thought[15] carefully to his introductory rhetoric (διό, "therefore"), this time presenting himself in a bold and authoritative manner, situated strongly enough to command Philemon to do the right thing. Paul claims this boldness from his visible spatial location "in Christ," where he is still imagined to be Christ's prisoner. He speaks boldly, but his power to do so is derived from being located in Christ. Apart from Christ he has no prophetic command. Yet to soften this empowered and sharp rhetoric, Paul shifts his language to show that he prefers to speak out of love (ἀγάπη). He pictures himself to Philemon (and to the holy ones in

---

15. See below on **progressive texture**.

Philemon's house who are observing nearby), then, as an imposing, commanding presence, on the one hand, while simultaneously as a loving, encouraging (παρακαλῶ) presence, on the other. Making himself appear more loving and encouraging still by shifting to priestly rhetorolect, Paul presents his appearance self-deprecatingly as an "old man" and (again) as "a prisoner of Christ Jesus."[16] This is Paul now working in the space of a priest, as someone who sacrifices, in this case himself, to serve the lord Jesus Christ (see v. 3) and as one who has grown old in the process of serving and sacrificing. The picturing itself is, quite obviously, making a very persuasive point, an argument in fact, that is drawing Philemon along to act in the way Paul has in mind. The compelling image of old prisoner Paul, the one who loves and encourages, who does not shout out commands (though he could), is difficult to shut out of the mind and difficult to refuse.

Step Three (Verse 10)

By repeating the verb παρακαλῶ,[17] Paul shifts the visualization, bringing into focus the unnamed behavior that now emerges with a clear image of a named person, Onesimus. Paul addresses Philemon directly, using the same encouraging and beseeching yet authoritative and sacrificing tones and presence regarding Onesimus. Onesimus now appears in the rhetograph as another male human, someone recognizable to Philemon (and the *ekklēsia* in his house, the people lurking at the edge of the picture). Onesimus is known and visualized in a complex way also by Paul, who envisions Onesimus in social and kinship terms as his own family member and as his child (τοῦ ἐμοῦ τέκνου).[18] This already graphic image, however, is embellished by picturing Paul, the old man-prisoner, in near female, birth-giving terms as the one who has begotten, generated, or given birth to the child Onesimus (ὃν ἐγέννησα). Paul now is seen in multiple visual roles. He is prophetic speaker, priestly self-sacrificer, prisoner located in Christ, old man, advocate, and in some sense parent to Onesimus. The

---

16. On the view that this should read "ambassador" rather than "old man," see the introduction. Paul speaks and is to be visualized as an "old man," that is, in the ancient Mediterranean, one more than fifty years of age.

17. A *repetitive texture*. This repetition forms an interlocking of rhetorical ideas in these steps.

18. Onesimus was, of course, not literally a child.

overall portrayal is surprising. Without saying it explicitly, it is seen very clearly that Philemon's anticipated good behavior has somehow to do with Onesimus.

This step in the rhetography provides a visual argument with both explicit and implicit features. Paul employs an "I could, but will not" rhetorical form of argumentation, where he is seen in an empowered position from which he could command Philemon to act in a specific way, but, portraying himself as an elderly prisoner and claiming to speak to Philemon in a loving way, he is moving Philemon along toward the practice of the still unnamed action that involves a now pictured person, Onesimus, who appears as Paul's "child." Paul is playing Philemon in a highly rhetoricized and manipulative fashion. Philemon is being drawn along in the images that are presented to him and in the presence of his *ekklēsia* friends as observers and witnesses toward a position that he will find difficult to refuse. The blending follows a prophetic-priestly-wisdom sequence that is aimed at producing a wisdom space inhabited by Philemon.

Step Four (Verse 11)

Now the picturing shifts to look directly at Onesimus, who has just come into sight in the preceding step. Onesimus is brought into sharp focus for Paul, Philemon, and the church meeting in Philemon's house in multiple ways. All of these persons already know—unlike other readers of the letter at other times and places—that Philemon has some important history with Onesimus. The characters appearing in the rhetograph know that Onesimus is a slave[19] owned by Philemon and visualize him that way. As a slave, though, Onesimus is seen in two views: how he appeared at some past time ("then," ποτέ) and how he is seen in the present ("now," νυνί). This double visualization of Onesimus shows him in two moral modes of behavior: useless (ἄχρηστον) and useful (εὔχρηστον). Philemon, who continues to be the singular recipient of the message of the letter (σοί), is persuaded by Paul to visualize Onesimus harshly and frankly as he is remembered, as a "useless" slave who, for some unstated and unvisualized reason, is separated from Philemon.[20] Onesimus, in this view, is situated in the midground in a very dim and unfavorable light in the memory of

---

19. Something not explicit (δοῦλος) until verse 16.
20. As verse 15, ἐχωρίσθη, "he has been separated."

the characters in the scene, who are observed to be pondering the past. Thoughts are immediately transferred to the present (νυνὶ δέ), where Onesimus appears, in stark contrast, as a "useful" person to Philemon and, perhaps surprisingly, to Paul, too. This view places Onesimus in a new, favorable, and bright light in the visualization. Rhetorically, the visual (and oral and aural) wordplay seen (and spoken and heard) in the contrapuntal words ἄχρηστον and εὔχρηστον[21] comes across in the visualized before/after, then/now scenes that they place in the mind.[22] This double imagery has a third picture added to it by the very name Onesimus, which Philemon would surely know means "useful" or "useful one."[23] Philemon could hardly miss the complex of images.

This step employs wisdom rhetorolect that observes the attitude and behavior of Onesimus within a ποτέ/νῦν, then/now structure. Paul portrays Onesimus as having undergone some observable change. The portrayal is a visual rhetoric that draws Philemon along more deeply into a place from which there will be no honest, faithful, or social escape. Philemon is called, by means of the picturing, to remember and to identify[24] with images he knows from the past and to make the visual contrast with how Paul describes the present. Philemon is being called to see things in a new way. The rhetograph itself continues to make the argument. The pictorial artistry argues and draws people along to places they never before imagined they would go. The useless slave is useful.

Step Five (Verses 12–14)

With the now useful Onesimus clearly in focus and with Philemon seen to be under significant rhetorical pressure, the already imprisoned and sacrificing Paul is observed in this step to be speaking again in priestly rhetorolect, blending it with prophetic and speaking of the responses he

---

21. *Homoioptoton* (when a series of words has the same case or inflection) and *homoioteleuton* (when words or clauses have endings with the same sound).

22. Here the actual *visual* phonemes themselves, that is the alphabetic letters (and corresponding vocalizations and sounds), function in the rhetorical argument in their paronomasic similarity.

23. See BDAG, 570, s.v. Ὀνήσιμος. This was a common name for slaves.

24. On identification as a rhetorical feature see Roy R. Jeal, "Rhetorical Argumentation in Ephesians," in *Rhetorical Argumentation in Biblical Texts*, ed. Anders Eriksson, Thomas H. Olbricht, and Walter Übelacker, ESEC 8 (Harrisburg, PA: Trinity Press International, 2002), 310–24, here 316–17.

wants from Philemon in wisdom rhetorolect. Paul is seen now to be sending Onesimus back to Philemon (ὃν ἀνέπεμψά σοι). This already appears to be a generous action, because Paul has just mentioned how "useful" Onesimus is now to him (v. 11). The generous and sacrificial act is made even more rhetorically effective with Paul's pictorial description of his own deepest felt needs or affections, that which is felt in his viscera, or entrails (σπλάγχνα),[25] being personified in Onesimus. The repetition of the image of σπλάγχνα, the same visual aspect of human feeling that "brother" Philemon has "refreshed" for many others (v. 7), dramatically and rather manipulatively reminds Philemon of his previously observed and precedent-setting activity that Paul wishes him to repeat. That is, Philemon is called to action not only on behalf of Onesimus but also for Paul's benefit. Paul and Onesimus are pictured together, still as prisoner-parent and child (v. 10), but also as emotionally close. This imagery is meant to *do* something to Philemon, to move him emotionally.

Paul speaks from a power space in the next clause, where he is seen to be wanting to have Onesimus stay with him, even as he sends him back to Philemon. He speaks emphatically, emphasizing the imagery of his own wish by using the first person pronoun (ἐγώ). But this image is ameliorated by Paul's claims in the following three clauses of this step. In a purpose (ἵνα) clause, Paul presents the picture of Onesimus serving on Philemon's behalf if Paul kept him back. This imagines Philemon in a serving role, similar to the view of him indicated earlier (v. 7), and it visualizes Philemon's service being beneficial for Paul's gospel work. Paul reminds Philemon once again that he is seen as a prisoner (see vv. 1, 9, 10) and so is sacrificing a great deal by sending Onesimus back.[26] In a contrasting clause, Paul portrays himself now in an unwilling pose,[27] that is, as being unwilling to keep Onesimus back, without the anticipated visualization of Philemon's consent. This, of course, places considerable pressure on Philemon to give consent; indeed it envisions his consent in advance, along with the service that consent will provide to Paul. In another purpose clause, Philemon is pictured freely consenting to Paul's wish to have Onesimus work with him. While Paul envisions that the consent is not forced (μὴ ὡς κατὰ ἀνάγκην), the visually apparent pressure on Philemon is enormous. It is easy to imag-

---

25. See above on verse 7.

26. For Paul the terms "prisoner of Christ" and "prisoner of the gospel" are closely related notions.

27. Switching from βούλομᾳ in v. 13 to θέλω now in v. 14.

ine Philemon listening to Paul in the rhetograph, sweating, looking over his shoulder toward the people who are members of his house church, conscious of the good thing he should do (τὸ ἀγαθόν σου) and so visually identifying with the desired behavior. The picture cast in the imagination makes it more difficult for Philemon to refuse—to appear in a power role over Onesimus and Paul, and unlike how he appeared previously, as one who refreshes the holy ones—than for him to consent. Philemon is not directly commanded, but the rhetograph does not allow him any honor were he to refuse. To refuse would to be to inhabit and be seen in a space of social and religious shame.[28] Paul appears to be behaving very sacrificially in this step. Philemon is being pressured to behave in a similar way.

Step Six (Verses 15–16)

The pressure on Philemon shifts in this step, but it does not ease. Paul stands again in his authoritative foreground space, but he appears to be slightly cautious, coloring the scene with the suggestion of a question by employing the word "perhaps" (τάχα). Both Philemon and Onesimus are in the rhetograph with Paul, but they stand far apart from each other. Philemon is invited to look back at the scene when Onesimus was separated from him. As he looks back, Paul addresses him, wondering if Onesimus might have been separated from Philemon temporarily and, as shall be seen, for a purpose. The language evokes a complex imagery. Employment of an aorist passive verb (ἐχωρίσθη) shows that Onesimus is not seen leaving Philemon by his own power, but is seen being moved away from Philemon by another power. Philemon is left to imagine God (or perhaps Christ Jesus, who is still envisioned to hold Paul as prisoner) as the person who took Onesimus away. This separation is visualized as temporary (for an hour; for a while, πρὸς ὥραν). Viewed this way, the separation is not cast with a dark, negative coloring, but is bright and hopeful of something better. This imagery calls Philemon to look at the separation in a much

---

28. Notions of honor versus shame were very important in ancient Mediterranean culture. In her book *Beyond Fate*, 2002 Massey Lectures [Toronto: House of Anansi, 2003], 41), Margaret Visser points out that "the civilizations of the West have striven hard and consciously for two thousand years and more to liberate themselves from the thrall of honour and shame—those two, for honour and shame go together; they are two sides of the same coin." "Our Christian heritage has replaced—ideally replaced—the notion that a person is what he or she is in the eyes of other people."

different way. It may be that some purpose will now become visible. The scene has now become colored with expectancy. Philemon cannot now turn his eyes away from the scene.

Purpose, as Paul sees it, in the separation of Onesimus from Philemon and, it also begins to become clear, purpose for Paul's call on Philemon's behavior is now revealed in apocalyptic rhetorolect. Perhaps it has all occurred "so that" Philemon "might have him [Onesimus] back[29] forever, no longer as a slave but more than a slave, a beloved brother." For Paul, something life-changing has happened to Onesimus and to himself: Onesimus has become Paul's "child," his personified viscera (vv. 10–12).[30] They are viewed in close, bonded, parent-child relationship. For Paul and now, he envisions, for Philemon, too, an apocalyptic change has occurred relative to Onesimus. The old master-slave relationship of the former time (then) has been transcended by an apocalyptic, "forever" (αἰώνιον) and socially transcended present (now). Philemon has this new social situation placed visibly in his mind *by* Paul's language. The language conveys a vision of new apocalyptic space, and the vision makes a dramatic rhetographic point. Philemon's former view of his relationship with Onesimus is subverted and overthrown. Philemon now visualizes Onesimus in precisely the same way that he sees the holy ones whose affections, viscera, he has refreshed. He now visualizes Onesimus in the same way Paul sees him, as brother (see v. 7). Onesimus the slave is now seen above, beyond the social status and physical role of slave (ὑπὲρ δοῦλον). This vision, with which Philemon is being encouraged to identify himself, is socially formative. It lays out an apocalyptic situation far beyond normal Mediterranean expectations for the owner-slave relationship. The sociocultural opposites are not now viewed as slave and owner, but, with "forever" in sight, the opposites now are slave and "beloved brother." An owner is seen and heard to call his slave "brother" forever. Implicit in the apocalyptic visioning is the *ekklēsia*, the believing community, that meets in Philemon's house, to which Onesimus is seen to be traveling and of which he will shortly be a member. The house church is envisioned having a social formation that includes a slave as a brother. The house church is not separated into internal social groups, but *is* a social group. The social

---

29. Aorist subjunctive ἀπέχῃς, agreeing syntactically with the τάχα.

30. This means, implicitly, that Onesimus is seen as one who has become a believer in Christ Jesus, a "brother," "fellow soldier," perhaps a "prisoner" of Christ.

convention of slavery is rejected in this community. These images are unexpected by Philemon, but are nevertheless now visible to him.

Paul, shifting back into his prophetic space, strengthens the vision with the final clause of this step. Paul especially visualizes Onesimus as his brother[31]—just as he visualizes Philemon as his brother (v. 7). Much more, then, does Philemon now, in an apocalyptically altered present, visualize Onesimus as *his* brother, both in the flesh and in the Lord. To see Onesimus as brother in the flesh and in the Lord is to visualize the physical, bodily man and to see him located, in the rhetograph, in Christ Jesus, who holds Paul as prisoner. Philemon is not able to avoid this rhetoric and the visualization of "brother" cast on his mind.

Step Seven (Verses 17–20)

Now Paul is observed to alter the tone of the picture by speaking to Philemon with a directive: accept Onesimus as if he were Paul himself. Philemon, along with everyone viewing the scene, will visualize himself doing what Paul requires (προσλαβοῦ, imperative). The rhetorical embellishment "if therefore you have me as partner" places, indeed manipulates, Philemon once again into a corner (see vv. 7–16) from which there is no righteous escape. Paul has already portrayed Philemon as a coworker (v. 1), a person of love and faith (v. 6), and one who has refreshed many (v. 7), but he casts a rhetorical and visual double image where Philemon is seen to be Paul's partner while simultaneously suggesting that the same fellowship is conditional (εἰ, if he is partner[32]). Both Paul and Philemon know that their partnership is strong, but the suggestion of questioning—as if either party is uncertain about it—places pressure on Philemon from yet another angle. The image of Philemon refusing to accept Onesimus as a brother, refusing to accept him as if he were Paul himself, shows him in a starkly negative, mean-spirited role. All viewers, including Paul and Philemon, know that such an image does not belong in and cannot remain in the rhetograph. Philemon knows that the picturing can continue only when he is seen to be receiving Onesimus as a brother.

Paul is seen to intensify the imagery by allowing a similar kind of conditional picture to appear again. Here Onesimus is portrayed as one who

---

31. A shift for Paul, who until now has been viewing Onesimus as his child.
32. Grammatically a first-class conditional.

might have done Philemon wrong (εἰ, "if "). Since this imagery is presented conditionally, some significant time after its possible occurrence, the wrong action itself is not part of the current scene. Onesimus might have wronged Philemon, but the wrong action is not visible. Paul is envisioned to be inviting Philemon to charge the debt to him. This image is doubly emphasized by the picture of Paul taking the stylus in his own hand, writing his own words down in the letter (ἐγὼ Παῦλος ἔγραψα τῇ ἐμῇ χειρί),[33] and employing the first person pronoun to stress both that he writes down what he is saying and that he will pay (ἐγὼ ἀποτίσω). Paul is presenting Philemon with his personal assurance as one who is still seen as Philemon's "partner." Paul is seen here in both prophetic and priestly spaces, as one who makes a proclamation and who sacrifices his own property for another person.

The rhetorical and rhetographic pressure is not yet over for Philemon. Paul is seen pressing him with a manipulative flourish by now saying, "not that I say that you owe yourself to me!" The image is morally powerful for Paul and socially awkward for Philemon. Paul clearly has the upper hand as he is envisioned paying Philemon while Philemon owes much more, his own life, to Paul.[34] Philemon is being formed socially in the picture. The social and ideological force of Paul's rhetoric affects how he is likely to respond. This step in the rhetoric ends with Paul observed calling to Philemon in a more conciliatory way once again as "brother" (see v. 7) and speaking in an altered role where he calls for a benefit not for Onesimus, but for himself. Paul calls to his brother now in a pleading, hesitant, perhaps pensive tone[35] for the benefit, visually located in the Lord Christ Jesus for whose sake both of them work, of Philemon's acceptance of Onesimus as a brother. Then Paul's voice is seen to call Philemon back to gaze at an earlier scene, the scene where Philemon refreshes the affections, the viscera, the hearts of the holy ones (v. 7). Paul draws on the goodness of Philemon seen earlier in his relations to other people and beckons him to do the same thing for him.[36] Paul is visualized calling Philemon for

---

33. Perhaps intensely significant since Paul typically spoke or dictated his letters to an amanuensis. Here he is seen writing directly himself.

34. Whatever images there may be from the past in the minds of Paul and Philemon are not made explicit. It can be presumed that Paul's proclamation of Christ and Philemon's belief in Christ are in their memories.

35. Indicated in the optative mood of the form ὀναίμην, meaning something like "might I possibly have."

36. Note the *repetitive texturing* of "refresh" and "viscera."

refreshment, located again visually in Christ. The refreshment consists of the by now socially shaped Philemon, who can visualize Onesimus as "brother" just as Paul appears as his "brother." The argument works on the rationale of the precedent of Philemon's previous actions: he refreshed others; now he should refresh Paul, too.

This step employs a blend of wisdom and prophetic/priestly rhetorolects, which Paul uses to portray Philemon and himself doing the right things. Philemon, in wisdom space, is visualized receiving Onesimus—who might have done him wrong—and giving up something of himself for the sake of Paul's refreshment. Paul, in prophetic and priestly space, declares and visibly writes with authority, while simultaneously offering (sacrificially) to pay for Onesimus's wrongs. Philemon is manipulated, is pushed around—the rhetoric is that strong—with the wisdom visualization that he actually owes Paul everything, his life. It is hard to visualize Philemon doing anything other than giving in to what Paul wants. The next steps show that Paul sees it that way too.

Closing Rhetoric (Verses 21–25)

Step Eight (Verse 21)

In this step, the portrayal depicts Paul still writing to Philemon, but his gaze shifts to the past, where Philemon's behavior is observed. The perfect participle[37] πεποιθώς ("being confident") indicates that Paul (and all those viewing the scene with him) have been affected by observation of Philemon's acts of "obedience," probably his work with Paul ("coworker," v. 1) and, particularly, his loving and faithful "refreshing of the saints" visualized in verse 7. This observation assures Paul that Philemon will obey, that is, do the right thing, now. The vision of the past has set a precedent for the present. Paul's look into his memory of the past has so convinced him about Philemon that he is visualized as "knowing" or "having knowledge," indicated in the perfect participle εἰδώς, that Philemon will do more than he says. Paul is visualized in a mood of certainty, and Philemon, all this implies, will soon be seen receiving his "brother" Onesimus.

Paul is seen here to be speaking from prophetic space as a spokesman for doing what is right. His prophetic rhetorolect is blended with wisdom

---

37. Completed action with ongoing effect.

rhetorolect, Philemon's space, where Philemon acts out the prophetic message, indeed more than the message requires.

Step Nine (Verse 22)

In this step Paul is visualized making a rather bold and imposing demand on Philemon: "But at the same time, prepare hospitality space for me, for I hope that because of your prayers I shall be restored to you." This indicates a shift away from conciliatory action that pleads with Philemon and persuades him to do the right thing. Paul calls Philemon—who, he has already stated, will do more than he says—while Philemon is accepting Onesimus (ἅμα, "at the same time") to prepare hospitality space (reception, food, lodging) in, presumably, the house in which Philemon lives and in which the *ekklēsia* meets. The image of Philemon engaging in this task is placed in everyone's mind. These images are immediately followed by the depiction of Paul in hopeful expectation (ἐλπίζω γάρ) of a visualized future time, when he will be present with Philemon. Philemon is visualized in prayer that this face-to-face picture will be realized. Paul, who is visualized still as a prisoner of Christ Jesus, conveys the image of himself returned, being handed over to Philemon to reside in his lodging by the passive verb χαρισθήσομαι. Paul the prisoner does not act on his own power in this view. The image envisioned is of the prisoner being given to Philemon. This stands as a very graphic counter-portrayal to the former ("then") owner-slave relationship of Philemon and Onesimus. Onesimus the slave is now the brother of Philemon. Paul the brother is now the prisoner-slave of Philemon. There is a social reversal and, therefore, a social re-formation of expected situations by unexpected situations. Paul, to be sure, is visualized paying for Onesimus's debt to Philemon (see vv. 18–19).

This step shows Paul speaking in blended wisdom and priestly rhetorolects, directing Philemon to take specific action while showing that he gives of himself, indeed is given by Christ, for Philemon's benefit in memory of their friendship as brothers who serve each other.

Step Ten (Verses 23–25)

The final rhetorical step shows Paul in his prophetic space, offering greetings and a concluding blessing. Yet even this closing visual scene is rhetographically powerful. The picture has from first glance (vv. 1–2) indicated that not only Paul and Philemon are privy to the depictions, because other people are seen at the periphery, watching and listening. This fact is pressed home in this closing picture, where Epaphras, Mark, Aristarchus, Demas, and Luke are seen sending their greeting to Philemon, perhaps waving, from where they are located, just past Paul. Epaphras appears as a prisoner with Paul, while the others appear as Paul's coworkers, as of course does Philemon himself (v. 1). All are visualized as coworkers together, sharing a greeting. It will be obvious to Philemon that there are other people who know the situation between Onesimus and himself. They are watching. It is like saying, "They know about you, Philemon. Keep that in mind." They have their own expectations of Philemon, their coworker, which align with Paul's expectations. What Philemon sees now, at the end of the letter, exerts a visual peer pressure. He is pressured by his honor before his friends to receive Onesimus as his brother. The need to avoid social shame presses on him.

The final verbless greeting images the Lord Jesus Christ blessing, gracing Philemon. The picture of the grace of Jesus coming to Philemon suggests the similar image of Philemon's grace being extended to Onesimus.

Translation

The translation aims to be as direct as possible while presenting the dynamic nature of the rhetoric of the letter's discourse and tone and rendering it in clear English.

Opening (Verses 1–7)

[1] Paul, a prisoner of Christ Jesus, and brother Timothy, to our much loved fellow worker Philemon, [2] and to our sister Apphia and our fellow soldier Archippus, and to the assembly at your house: [3] Grace and peace to you from God our Father and our Lord Jesus Christ.

[4] I thank my God, always making remembrance of you in my prayers, [5] hearing of the love and faith which you have for the Lord Jesus and for all the holy ones, [6] so that the partnership of your faith might become energized in the knowledge of every good thing among us, for Christ. [7] For I have much joy and comfort from your love, because the viscera of the holy ones have been refreshed by you, brother.

Middle (Verses 8–20)

[8] Therefore, having much boldness in Christ to command your obedience, [9] I appeal, rather, through love—I do this as Paul, an old man, but now also a prisoner of Christ— [10] I appeal to you for my child—whom I have birthed in chains—*Onesimus*, [11] who formerly was *useless* to you, but now is *useful*—to you and to me— [12] whom I send back to you, this one who is my own viscera— [13] whom I strongly wish to keep to myself, so that he might serve me on your behalf in the chains of the gospel.

[14] But apart from your consent I wish to do nothing, so that you do not do the good thing out of necessity, but voluntarily. [15] For perhaps this is why he was separated from you for a while, so that you might have him back forever, [16] no longer as a slave, but more than a slave, a beloved

brother—certainly to me, but much more to you, as in the flesh also in the Lord.

[17] If therefore you have me as partner, receive him as me. [18] But if he has wronged you or owes you anything, charge it to me. [19] I Paul, I write this in my own hand: I will repay it—not that I say that you owe yourself to me!

[20] Yes, brother, might I possibly have this benefit from you in the Lord? Refresh my viscera in Christ!

Closing (Verses 21–25)

[21] Confident of your obedience, I write to you knowing that you will do even more than I say. [22] But at the same time, prepare hospitality space for me, for I hope that because of your prayers I shall be restored to you.

[23] Epaphras my fellow prisoner in Christ Jesus greets you, [24] as do Mark, Aristarchus, Demas, Luke, my coworkers.

[25] The grace of the Lord Jesus Christ be with your spirit.

Textural Commentary

Repetitive Texture

Repetitions of words, grammar, and topoi point out major ideas and themes in the rhetoric and social situations in and related to a text. They are major clues regarding the nature and concerns and argumentation of a text. While there are many repetitions, the most obvious and striking *repetitive texturing* in Philemon is in the abundance of first- and second-person-singular verbs (including participles) and pronouns.[1] This feature makes the rhetoric direct and personal between Paul and Philemon despite the presence of other persons who are visualized in the rhetograph. The verb forms naturally carry their own pronominal meanings and thus are not lexical or semantic repetitions, but first- and second-person-singular repetitions. Plural pronouns ("us," "our," "you," "your"; ἡμῖν, ἡμῶν, ὑμῖν, and ὑμῶν) appear in the opening and closing, but in by far most of the letter first- and second-person-singular verbs and pronouns (and related nouns and adjectives) carry the rhetorical narrative and argumentation. There are no plural verbs in the letter. Statistically the usage falls into this pattern:[2]

- twenty-one first-person-singular verb forms, all with Paul as subject; most have Philemon as direct or indirect object;
- nine second-person-singular verbs, all with Philemon as subject;
- six third-person-singular verbs, three with Onesimus as subject, two with qualities as subject, and one with Epaphras as subject (with additional greeters, v. 24);
- "of you," "of your," "your" (σου), ten occurrences, all refer directly to Philemon;

---

1. For some general comments on vocabulary and language see Markus Barth and Helmut Blanke, *The Letter to Philemon*, ECC (Grand Rapids: Eerdmans, 2000), 108–19.

2. There are also several relative pronouns with Onesimus as referent.

- "you," "to you" (σοι), seven occurrences, all refer directly to Philemon;
- "you" (σε), three occurrences, all refer directly to Philemon;
- "your" (σῆς), one occurrence, referring directly to Philemon;
- "my" (μου/ἐμοῦ), six occurrences, all refer directly to Paul;
- "to me" (μοι/ἐμοί), six occurrences, all refer directly to Paul;
- "me," "my," "to me" (με, ἐμε, ἐμα, ἐμῆ), one occurrence each, all refer to Paul;[3]
- "I" (ἐγώ), four occurrences, all refer directly to Paul.

These repetitions make it clear that Paul has Philemon directly in mind throughout the letter, even though there are other persons listening in. The rhetorical discourse and its force are focused closely on Philemon and the singular response Paul wants from him. Paul sets the rhetorical stage by praising Philemon using singular pronouns (vv. 4, 5, 6, 7) and anticipates Philemon's positive response similarly (vv. 20, 21). In the central argument, Paul employs singular verbs and pronouns to make his case to Philemon (vv. 10, 11, 12, 13, 14, 16, 19). The request is from one person, and only one person is expected to grapple with the ethical, social, and gospel notions of the request and with Onesimus's future. This analysis also makes it clear that the *repetitive texturing* of first- and second-person words form the foundation for the *argumentative texturing* of the letter.[4] The argument employs a repetitive pattern of I-me-you-with-regard-to-him.

The repetition of the description of Paul as a "prisoner of Christ Jesus" (δέσμιος Χριστοῦ Ἰησοῦ, vv. 1, 9) coupled with the repetition of the image of Paul and Onesimus being "in chains" (ἐν τοῖς δεσμοῖς, vv. 10, 13[5]) emphasizes, quite strikingly, the identity of Paul not as apostle, that term he uses to identify himself in other letters, but as one bound morally and faithfully to Christ and, it seems most likely, as a metaphor for his actual condition as a prisoner of the state. The repetition of "prisoner of Christ Jesus" in verse 9 is more emphatic than the occurrence in verse 1, because it is tied directly to Paul's transition toward direct appeal and to Paul's emotive self-description as "an old man" (πρεσβύτης). The repetitions show that Paul is not only a prisoner in chains but also one who

---

3. The emphatic forms, ἐμου (v. 10), ἐμοί (vv. 11, 16, 18), ἐμε (v. 17), ἐμα (v. 12), ἐμῆ (v. 19), draw particular attention to Paul himself.

4. On which see below.

5. The word δεσμοῖς is cognate with δέσμιος.

works at his imprisoned, apostolic, gospel task—having borne or begotten Onesimus in this situation and anticipating continuing gospel service (v. 13)—and that he is not disturbed by either the imprisoned situation or by the work. The imprisonment motif is emphasized even more by the *closing* reference to Epaphras as "my fellow prisoner in Christ Jesus" (ὁ συναιχμάλωτός μου ἐν Χριστῷ Ἰησοῦ, v. 23). The Greek word for "fellow prisoner" (συναιχμάλωτός) is obviously not cognate with the word for "prisoner" (δέσμιος), but suggests that Epaphras is a kind of "prisoner of war"[6] with Paul, one fully and unavoidably engaged in the gospel task.

Repetitions of a number of nouns intensify the rhetorical force of the letter. Repetitions of forms of Christ (Χριστός), Jesus (Ιησοῦς), and Lord (κύριος, vv. 1, 3, 4, 6, 8, 9, 20, 23, 25) set the foundational notions of the object and locus of love, faith, and gospel work (imprisonment for Christ and gospel) in the Lord Jesus Christ. Faith in Christ undergirds everything in the Letter to Philemon. It is central to the rhetorical force of the letter. The threefold occurrence of viscera (σπλάγχνα, vv. 7, 12, 20) is a strong example of *ekphrasis*, descriptive speech that brings things emotively before the eyes, emphasizing to Philemon that he has had and that Paul anticipates that he will have in the near future a powerful effect on people of faith. Philemon has the capacity to touch people inwardly, emotionally, refreshingly. The repetition indicates that Paul knows this capacity. Paul himself (v. 12), at least as regards Onesimus, is also an emotional, visceral person who thinks the human "feel it in my guts" quality is important enough to use it argumentatively. Nouns based on love (ἀγάπη) recur five times (vv. 1, 5, 7, 9, 16). Philemon is a loving guy (vv. 5, 7) who should view Onesimus as a loved brother (v. 16). Paul appeals to Philemon through love, not command (v. 9). These repetitions reveal love as central to the argumentation. The repetitions of forms of "brother" (ἀδελφός, five occurrences), particularly in the vocative, demonstrate how notions of kinship help define Paul's relationship with fellow believers and function in the rhetorical argument to place a kind of familial pressure on Philemon. The use of words based on the κοινων- root (κοινωνία, "partnership, fellowship," v. 6; κοινωνός, "partner," v. 17) support and emphasize the relationship between Paul and Philemon, hence they intensify the rhetorical force placed on Philemon. The relational connections are also demonstrated emphatically by the repetitive use of συν- compound words

---

6. See Gerhard Kittel, "Αἰχμάλωτός," *TDNT* 1:195–97.

(συνεργός, "fellow worker," vv. 1, 24; συστρατιώτης, "fellow soldier," v. 2; συναιχμάλωτός, "fellow prisoner," v. 24). Repetition of the quite personal "I write" (ἔγραψα, from γράφω, vv. 19, 21) points to Paul's sincere, unequivocal intention regarding his request of Philemon as well as to his strong rhetorical intention.

The Opening, Philemon 1–7

Opening Texture

The analysis of the epistolary structure of New Testament letters as ancient Hellenistic letters, which is a kind of form criticism, is important for understanding their standard features—introductory greeting (prescript); thanksgiving; body (often including a paraenesis); closing greeting (postscript).[1] Many analyses of Philemon follow the anticipated and hence readily discovered epistolary form to provide the outline for analysis—what may be imagined as a natural progressive texture.

Prescript (vv. 1–3)
Thanksgiving (vv. 4–7)
Body (vv. 8–22)
Postscript (vv. 23–25)

But formal epistolary characteristic do not tell us everything about meaning and structure, particularly about rhetorical structure, meaning, and force. The boundaries between sections can be less rigid than epistolary

---

1. See, for example, William G. Doty, *Letters in Primitive Christianity* (Philadelphia: Fortress, 1973); Abraham J. Malherbe, *Ancient Epistolary Theorists* (Atlanta: Scholars Press, 1988), E. R. Richards, *The Secretary in the Letters of Paul* (Tübingen: Mohr Siebeck, 1991); Stanley Stowers, *Letter Writing in Greco-Roman Antiquity* (Philadelphia: Westminster, 1986); John L. White, "Ancient Greek Letters," in *Greco-Roman Literature and the New Testament*, ed. David E. Aune (Atlanta: Scholars Press, 1988): 85–105; White, *Light from Ancient Letters* (Philadelphia: Fortress, 1986). For comments see Roy R. Jeal, *Integrating Theology and Ethics in Ephesians: The Ethos of Communication* (Lewiston, NY: Mellen, 2000), 16–22. See also Jeffrey A. D. Weima, "Paul's Persuasive Prose: An Epistolary Analysis of the Letter to Philemon," in *Philemon in Perspective: Interpreting a Pauline Letter*, ed. D. François Tolmie (Berlin: de Gruyter, 2010), 29–60.

theory suggests. Thanksgiving and supplicatory elements, for example, can and do occur at various places in ancient and New Testament letters, not only immediately following opening formulae. These features have social and rhetorical effects rather than thematic functions.[2] Paraenetic language can and does occur in various places in letters, not always, indeed rarely, in discrete sections within the letter body. In a similar way, openings (opening ideas and thoughts) can extend beyond the epistolary form of the prescript and thanksgiving sections. Closings (closing ideas and thoughts) can begin before clear postscripts. Thanksgiving sections frequently signal topoi and arguments to be presented in body sections. Transitional sections sometimes do not fit neatly in either thanksgiving or body sections. Still, New Testament letters, like all texts, have *opening-middle-closing textures* that can be reasonably identified. Transitional sections are sometimes employed to convey the rhetoric internally. *Opening-middle-closing texture* can be observed in narrational terms rather than more tightly defined epistolary terms.

Opening-middle-closing texture identifies the patterns and shifts that indicate where these broad functional sections of a text are located and how they operate rhetorically. While it seems obvious from a common-sense perspective, it is worth mentioning that openings start a rhetorical unit, capture attention, gain the participation of audience members and their minds and emotions, and present preliminary ideas.[3] Middle textures focus in on the topoi, themes, and issues at hand and present the central narration and argumentation.[4] Closings do more than simply terminate; they draw ideas and arguments together, and aim at persuading thought toward resolution, conclusion, and perhaps to action.

Opening-middle-closing texture in Philemon occurs in this pattern:

Opening: verses 1–7
Middle: verses 8–20
Closing: verses 21–25

---

2. See Roy R. Jeal, *Integrating*, 18–19; Terrence Y. Mullins, "Formulas in New Testament Epistles," *JBL* 91 (1972): 380–90.

3. As do *exordia* according to classical rhetoric, though opening ideas can extend beyond the limits of a formal *exordium*.

4. See below on *narrational* and *argumentative textures*.

The opening introduces the characters—apart from Onesimus, the object of concern[5]—who have positions and roles in the narration. These persons, including Paul (with Timothy) as narrator, stand in warm relationship to each other. The praiseworthy Philemon has done much good for the benefit (the viscera) of the holy ones (τὰ σπλάγχνα τῶν ἁγίων), that is, for faithful people like himself.

Progressive Texture

Progressive texture is the existence and role of the sequences or progressions of words, phrases, and clauses observed in texts.[6] Analysis involves identifying where the progressions are located and interpreting how they function. *Progressive texture* helps make sociorhetorical function clear by indicating the sequencing of ideas that are blended together to make the argument and point of the rhetoric and to move thought ahead. Awareness of the progression of the rhetorical sequencing keeps us from getting ahead of ourselves due to previous knowledge or presuppositions about the text.

There are seven opening progressions here that move the discourse ahead.

1.   Verse 1
     [1] Παῦλος δέσμιος Χριστοῦ Ἰησοῦ καὶ Τιμόθεος ὁ ἀδελφός

     [1] Paul, a prisoner of Christ Jesus, and brother Timothy

This sequence initiates the entire discourse by naming and describing the author(s).[7] While naming authors is a standard epistolary feature, descriptors like "prisoner of Christ Jesus" (δέσμιος Χριστοῦ Ἰησοῦ) and "brother" (ὁ ἀδελφός) draw attention to them in particularized ways relevant to the

---

5. Though in fact Philemon is himself Paul's direct object of concern in the letter. Paul wishes Philemon to be concerned, in turn, about Onesimus.

6. Vernon K. Robbins, *Exploring the Texture of Texts: A Guide to Socio-rhetorical Interpretation* (Valley Forge, PA: Trinity Press International, 1996), 9–10.

7. As noted under *repetitive texture*, the first-person verbs and pronouns make it clear that Paul is the author. Still, as noted in the commentary introduction, Mediterranean writing conventions allowed for the participation of multiple persons in letter preparation. It is possible that Timothy was the amanuensis or fulfilled some other role in the production of the letter.

audience and the rhetorical force the letter aims to produce. The sequence is focused on persons recognizable to the audience.

2. Verses 1–2

Φιλήμονι τῷ ἀγαπητῷ καὶ συνεργῷ ἡμῶν
  ² καὶ Ἀπφίᾳ τῇ ἀδελφῇ
  καὶ Ἀρχίππῳ τῷ συστρατιώτῃ ἡμῶν
  καὶ τῇ κατ’ οἶκόν σου ἐκκλησίᾳ

to our much loved coworker Philemon,
  ² and to our sister Apphia
  and our fellow soldier Archippus,
  and to the assembly at your house

This progression moves thought forward by means of dative nouns indicating the identities of the addressees. As with the author(s), particularized descriptors of the addressees point out their respective importance with regard to Paul and Timothy.

3. Verse 3

³ χάρις ὑμῖν καὶ εἰρήνη ἀπὸ θεοῦ πατρὸς ἡμῶν καὶ κυρίου Ἰησοῦ Χριστοῦ

³ Grace and peace to you from God our Father and our Lord Jesus Christ

This progression employs the nominative-case "grace and peace" plus genitive of source to complete the introductory greeting. It is notable that no verbs are employed in the greeting. Grammatical shifts are adequate to make the point without verbs. The focus remains on the entire group of addressees, although God and Jesus Christ are understood as the sources of grace and peace.

4. Verse 4

⁴ Εὐχαριστῶ τῷ θεῷ μου πάντοτε μνείαν σου ποιούμενος ἐπὶ τῶν προσευχῶν μου

⁴ I thank my God, always making remembrance of you in my prayers

The appearance of the first verb shifts thought directly to Paul and Philemon. Paul offers thanks to God for Philemon and prays on his behalf. It is clear that God is considered worthy of the thanks given for Philemon.

5. Verse 5

^{5} ἀκούων σου τὴν ἀγάπην καὶ τὴν πίστιν ἣν ἔχεις πρὸς τὸν κύριον Ἰησοῦν καὶ εἰς πάντας τοὺς ἁγίους

^{5} hearing of the love and faith which you have for the Lord Jesus and for all the holy ones

Here thought moves forward by means of a participle ("having heard") that corresponds to and moves out from Paul's thanksgiving and prayers to what he knows of Philemon's reputation. Philemon is a man of love and faith. His love and faith is centered on the Lord Jesus and all the holy ones. This implies already that Philemon is known to have genuine concern for the benefit of other believers.

6. Verse 6

^{6} ὅπως ἡ κοινωνία τῆς πίστεώς σου ἐνεργὴς γένηται ἐν ἐπιγνώσει παντὸς ἀγαθοῦ τοῦ ἐν ἡμῖν εἰς Χριστόν

^{6} so that the partnership of your faith might become energized in the knowledge of every good thing among us, for Christ

This progression describes the intended and anticipated outcome of Paul's thanksgiving and prayers for Philemon. It picks up on the nuancing of the previous sequence regarding Philemon as a man of love and faith. Paul has here a view to the future (and to persuading Philemon to conform to that particular future) where Philemon's faith will be a shared thing with others and will be energized for good in Christ. This good in Christ presumably has in sight the good of many persons.

7. Verse 7

^{7}χαρὰν γὰρ πολλὴν ἔσχον καὶ παράκλησιν ἐπὶ τῇ ἀγάπῃ σου
    ὅτι τὰ σπλάγχνα τῶν ἁγίων ἀναπέπαυται
    διὰ σοῦ, ἀδελφέ

^{7} For I have much joy and comfort from your love,
    because the viscera of the holy ones have been refreshed
    by you, brother

Moved ahead by the coordinate conjunction "for" (γάρ), Paul supports his hope for the future good Philemon will practice by recalling Philemon's past good work of refreshing the viscera of the holy ones. Thought is also advanced by Paul's reference to Philemon as "brother," a step beyond calling him "beloved" and "coworker."

Narrational Texture

Narrational texture is observed in the storytelling or narrative as it is presented by the (implied) narrator or speaker.[8] It "resides in voices" as they convey ideas through their narrative discourse. The narration is the story as it is being told in a text. Letters actually do have a narrative quality to them[9] because they tell readers and listeners about thoughts, beliefs, actions, or events, or they anticipate thoughts, beliefs, actions, or events in the lives of some people, whether they are authors, recipients, or other persons. The Letter to Philemon provides narration about aspects of the lives of the characters named in it, most particularly and fully the lives of Paul, Philemon, and Onesimus. The sequences and/or patterns in this narration provide an amount of history about some things that have occurred in the past, information about current situations, and requests and expectations for the future. The Letter to Philemon presupposes an implied narrator whom readers and listeners are likely immediately to believe is Paul himself along with the tendency to imagine his voice, but the narrator(s) of the actual words, depending on the situation of their reception, may have been Timothy or another person, or perhaps Philemon or another member of the church that met in his house (v. 2). Nevertheless, the first-person verbs and pronouns throughout the letter make it clear that Paul is the implied narrator. Paul, as a prisoner, speaks about Philemon, the *ekklēsia*, refreshment, Onesimus, separation, return, reception of Onesimus as a brother, and an anticipated visit.

The narrator's voice in step one (vv. 1–3)[10] presents Paul as "a prisoner of Christ" and, it is assumed, a physically incarcerated prisoner in an unnamed location, perhaps Ephesus.[11] Thus not only is Paul the nar-

---

8. See ibid., 15–19.

9. See the section on rhetography, above.

10. The narrational steps do not correspond exactly to the rhetographical or progressive steps.

11. See the commentary introduction. Physical incarceration does not necessarily imply a penal or correctional institution imagined to be a prison or jail. On this see the section "Prisoner" in **intertexture**.

rator telling the story, but he is also a leading character in it. Timothy is "the brother" who is apparently close alongside Paul, possibly functioning as his amanuensis. Philemon is presented both as one beloved by and a coworker of Paul and probably of Timothy and other coworkers named later in the narration, who send their greetings to him (vv. 23–24). Apphia, the sister, and Archippus, brightly described as "the fellow soldier" (τῷ συστρατιώτῃ), and the believers' assembly that meets in Philemon's house are presented as addressees, though, as we have seen, the singular pronoun "your" (σου) indicates that Philemon himself is the direct addressee and object of the letter's message. The narrator offers a greeting of "grace and peace" not explicitly from himself but from "God our Father and the Lord Jesus Christ," setting thereby—as listeners to the narration would expect—a particularized Christian/messianic context to the story.

Step two (vv. 4–7) begins to focus the narration on Philemon. While Paul engages in the priestly activity of thanksgiving and prayer, the story derived from his action and words is that Philemon is a very faithful person. He loves "the Lord Jesus" and takes his faith seriously, extending his love and faith "to all the holy ones," that is, to all believers in Jesus. This has become known to Paul the narrator, who states that he intentionally engages in thanksgiving and prayer on Philemon's behalf, with the intention that (ὅπως) the fellowship of his own faith would become energized with regard to the knowledge of the good he has done for those holy ones. Philemon has "refreshed the viscera of the holy ones," and the narrative states that Paul the narrator's prayers are offered, the implication being that such refreshment will continue. The narration in this way signals the request shortly to be made of Philemon, and anticipates his ongoing "refreshing" behavior. What emerges is that Philemon is a very fine man, a leader, one who cares deeply for others and for whom Paul has deep respect. Paul the narrator is thankful for Philemon. The thought of Philemon elicits thanks and remembrance in Paul's prayers, and joy and encouragement in his inner being (τὰ σπλάγχνα). This narrational sequence clearly centers on the good Philemon. For readers and listeners, this step evokes the expectation of more to come regarding Philemon, and of course it does come in the following steps.

Argumentative Texture

Argumentative texture is the analytic that "investigates multiple kinds of inner reasoning in the discourse"[12] and explains how it functions rhetorically. Reasoning or argumentation may be logical or qualitative. It might be direct or subtle. It might lead to perceptible action or only to anticipated action. Therefore discourse that may not seem to be obviously or directly argumentative frequently makes argumentation as it aims to evoke reactions from audiences. In all cases argumentative textures are persuasive, hence rhetorical. Argumentation is meant to move people to thought, understanding, belief, and action.

In the Letter to Philemon the *argumentative textures* have an overall anticipated result: that Philemon will receive and treat Onesimus as a "beloved brother" (ἀδελφὸν ἀγαπητόν, v. 16). The letter of course precedes the actual response of Philemon, and there is no record of his response.[13] While this anticipated result is explicit, there are multiple and complex arguments along the way. This anticipated result, however, indicates that the argumentative texturing is about social formation. Paul wants Philemon to be persuaded by the nuancing of argumentative topoi to take on a particular social form that stands against what he might have expected. Paul shapes his language to do this, to move Philemon more deeply into the good society of the *ekklēsia*.

Two major steps of the opening make arguments that set the stage for the central argument accomplished in the middle, hinting that there is a major argument to be made, but saying nothing yet about it. The argument of step one (vv. 1–3) is, like many arguments, incomplete and not fully articulated, in that it does not formulate either an explicit rationale or a result, but relies on the imagination to convey the rhetorical idea.

Case: Paul the prisoner and Timothy the brother present themselves with a polite, friendly, and distinctly Christian greeting to Philemon, Apphia, Archippus, and the *ekklēsia* that meets in Phi-

---

12. Robbins, *Exploring*, 21.

13. Though a person named Onesimus is mentioned in Col 4:9 as a "faithful and beloved brother," apparently from Colossae and traveler there with Tychicus. Some scholars point to Bishop Onesimus of Ephesus, or to Bishop Onesimus of Byzantium in the Orthodox tradition, who died apparently as a martyr. There is no certain evidence for the connection of either of these to the Onesimus of the Letter to Philemon.

THE OPENING, PHILEMON 1–7 71

lemon's house. Paul and Timothy are situated in a prophetic space and, despite the social specter of imprisonment, speak initially with a prophetic voice (rhetorolect).

Rational appeal: the verbless but easily understood greeting "Grace and peace to you from God our Father and our Lord Jesus Christ" functions as priestly rhetorolect that provides a fairly clear and rational appeal to the minds and emotions of the addressees even as it intercedes on their behalf. Grace and peace from God and the Lord Jesus are imagined to be coming on the addressees.

Expected but unstated result: the addressees are expected to recognize the case and the appeal implicitly and give their attention to the discourse. Their susceptibility to continuation of the discourse is anticipated.

Here the argumentation already features two topoi that are central to the continuing *argumentative texture* and to the ethos of the discourse: Christ (given as both Christ Jesus and Jesus Christ, vv. 1, 3) and *ekklēsia*. Christ is explicitly "Lord" (κυρίου, v. 3) and implicitly the raised and living savior and Son of God in whom Paul and the addressees believe. The *ekklēsia* is the community of these believers, in this case one that meets in Philemon's house. What emerges is an ecclesial space where Jesus Christ is central to the belief and formation of all concerned. This space and these topoi (with others) will become central to the argumentative texture of the entire letter.

The argumentative texturing of step two (vv. 4–7) is pointedly focused on Philemon as a loving and faithful person. While Paul expresses his own first-person-singular actions of thanksgiving and regular prayers for Philemon, the second-person-singular verbs and pronouns point out that he does these things because he hears (ἀκούων) that Philemon is a man of faith and love for the Lord Jesus and for all the holy ones (i.e., the *ekklēsia*) and wants his own thanksgivings and prayers and Philemon's continuing activity to be beneficial for all believers. The anticipated result of all this is expressed in the difficult ὅπως clause, "so that the partnership of your faith might become energized in the knowledge of every good thing among us for Christ" (v. 6). This suggests that Paul argues for his hope that Philemon's faithfulness will be shared by others for the sake of good. This is a wisdom goal that anticipates productive living in wisdom space. It may be set out as follows:

Case: Paul offers thanksgiving and prayers to God for Philemon.

Unstated rationale: Philemon's loving and faithful behavior and Paul's prayers will benefit persons who are "in Christ."

Anticipated result: other believers benefit from Philemon's good behavior.

In a second argument, signaled by the subordinate conjunction γάρ, Paul continues the texturing of this step by noting that he himself had "much joy and comfort" from Philemon's intentional and thoughtful love (ἐπὶ τῇ ἀγάπῃ σου) and that this was because the viscera—the inner felt needs—of others had been already refreshed by Philemon's good activities (διὰ σοῦ, ἀδελφέ). This anticipates that Philemon will continue his refreshing activity in the future, though Paul does not yet specify the exact nature of the action nor its beneficiary.

Case: Paul, who gives thanks and prays for Philemon, has received much joy and comfort from Philemon's loving behavior.

Rationale: Because Philemon has refreshed the viscera of many holy ones.

Anticipated and unstated result: Philemon will continue the refreshing behaviors in as yet unspecified ways.

The arguments of this step function as *benevolentia* or *captatio benevolentia* that praise Philemon in order to seek his goodwill, as a way of getting him "on side" so that he can be subsequently persuaded in a particular direction.[14] Paul is setting things up with a view toward his more specific and explicit argumentation. There is an expectancy of more persuasive discourse and activity in the ecclesial space.

---

14. See Quintilian, *Inst.* 4.1.16–17.

Sensory-Aesthetic Texture

Sensory-aesthetic texture is concerned with "the range of senses the text evokes or embodies (thought, emotion, sight, sound, touch, smell) and the manner in which the text evokes or embodies them (reason, intuition, imagination, humor, etc.)."[15] *Sensory-aesthetic texturing* has to do with features that indicate or reflect things that are discerned through visual, oral, aural, olfactory, tactile, gustatory, textual, prosaic, poetic, and intellectual sensibilities.[16] These features have powerful rhetorical force. There are patterns and sounds in balanced cola that produce a "feel" and a visual appearance that is recognizable and draws the mind of listeners and readers along. There is appeal to mouth, ear, and sound,[17] to qualities of being, personality, intellect, and affections,[18] and to specified action.[19] In other words, there is a flow of sensations and beauties described in bodily metaphors that appeal to the mind and to certain emotions with the intention of serving the conveyance of meaning and the evocation of behaviors.

Although the Letter to Philemon broaches the ugly (certainly from our modern vantage) social topos of slavery in the Roman world, it is a beautiful, well-formed letter. It is deeply and dramatically sensory by nature with its smooth, stylish, attractive, and frankly creative phrasing.[20] The aesthetics of the letter are, of course, offset by some sensory features of its rhetoric. It is, recalling a word employed three times in the letter, visceral (vv. 7, 12, 20); this *sensory-aesthetic texture* touches the emotions. Viscera can be "refreshed" (ἀναπαύω, vv. 7, 20) and can describe how one feels about another person as Paul feels about Onesimus (v. 12). The viscera are where people are meant to be empathetic to what are otherwise more intellectual notions. Viscera is pathos. This is entirely intentional, as Paul's rhetoric

---

15. Robbins, *Exploring*, 29–30.

16. Some features will be "sensory" and "aesthetic" to some and less so to others. A person's perceptions relate to "taste" and sense of physicality, color, beauty, culturation, and education. But there are some sensory-aesthetic universals that are perceived by most people.

17. Which, according to the taxonomy described by Bruce J. Malina, belongs, in biblical literature, to the "zone of self-expressive speech" (Malina, *The New Testament World: Insights From Cultural Anthropology*, 3rd ed. [Louisville: Westminster John Knox, 2001], 58–76, 69). See Robbins, *Exploring*, 30–31.

18. The zone of "emotion-fused thought" (Malina, *New Testament World*, 69).

19. The zone of "purposeful action" (ibid., 69).

20. As the section on rhetography above already suggests.

is aimed directly at the formation of Philemon's viscera, his entrails, his understanding and practice and emotion as a believer in Christ and as a "brother" (vv. 7, 20), so much so that Philemon will be unable to refuse Paul's requests without appearing to be a very hard person.

There are several beginning and ending, opening and closing, *inclusio* features in Philemon, some of which we will observe as we go along (e.g., vv. 1–3 corresponds to vv. 23–25). There is also a major and overall chiastic *sensory-aesthetic texture* and effect (*commutatio*) that has corresponding end and middle points that have considerable rhetorical force.[21] This texturing is seen in words with the same stem in the opening "I thank" (εὐχαριστῶ v. 4) and the closing "I shall be restored" χαρισθήσομαι (v. 22), and in the central and antithetical same stem words "useless," ἄχρηστον, and "useful," εὔχρηστον (v. 11). Paul begins by declaring his thanksgiving and prayer to God for Philemon (give grace toward; originally "to do a good turn to"[22]) and ends with the notion that he will, through their prayers, be restored to them. The χαρισ- stems make the antithetical point. There is a soft, sensory beginning indicating Paul's prayer wishes for Philemon's good, and a soft, sensory ending indicating that the prayer wishes of Philemon and those associated with him will result in the good of Paul coming to them. Paul *gives* thanks for Philemon in prayers and anticipates, conversely, that he will be restored (χαρισθήσομαι, future passive) to Philemon and others because of prayers. The chiasmus or *commutatio* turns at the virtual midpoint[23] of the letter with the antithetical and strongly euphonic "who formerly was *useless* to you, but now is *useful*—to you and to me"

---

21. I am not often persuaded by analyses of *chiasmus* or criss-cross structure since they often seem to be uneven, unconvincing and, frankly, contrived by interpreters. Interestingly, the term *chiasmus*, though frequently employed by interpreters, was not used by the ancient rhetors as it is by moderns (Heinrich Lausberg, *Handbook of Literary Rhetoric: A Foundation for Literary Study* ed. David E. Orton and R. Dean Anderson [Leiden: Brill, 1998] §723; also p. 855), though they did describe the "antithetic force" of cross arrangements of words and cola. This is ἀντιμεταβολή (Greek) or *commutatio* (Latin). *Commutatio* occurs in "...the opposition of an idea and its converse by means of the repetition of the two word stems, with reciprocal exchange of the syntactic function of both stems in the repetition" (Lausberg §800; see *Rhetorica ad Herennium* 4.21).

22. Moulton and Milligan §1796.

23. There are 154 words preceding εὔχρηστον and 153 following, excluding the final greeting, which is a separate *narrative texture*. Now that Onesimus is useful, things are different. Why has Onesimus become useful? It is not exactly clear except that Paul says so. But it still seems to be a turning point.

(τόν ποτέ σοι ἄχρηστον νυνὶ δὲ σοὶ καὶ ἐμοὶ εὔχρηστον, v. 11). This wordplay, or paronomasia, is enhanced by knowing that the name Onesimus, which immediately precedes it, means "useful." Both the "formerly"/"now" and "useless"/"useful" oppositions make a major sensory point in the argument of the letter: change has taken place; Onesimus has become useful, so things are different now. Things are sensorily and aesthetically different than they were. This knowledge, of course, relies on Paul's word on the matter, but there are visible and felt changes, and the changes will continue with Paul's anticipated release and restoration. There is much more to the *argumentative texture* of the letter, but this is the sensory turning point. This seems to be a quite natural, poetic, not a contrived, rhetoric.

The *sensory-aesthetic texturing* of the opening can be set out and analyzed in the two steps of the following patterning:

Step one (vv. 1–3)
  ¹ Παῦλος δέσμιος Χριστοῦ Ἰησοῦ
    καὶ Τιμόθεος ὁ ἀδελφὸς
  Φιλήμονι τῷ ἀγαπητῷ καὶ συνεργῷ ἡμῶν
    ² καὶ Ἀπφίᾳ τῇ ἀδελφῇ
    καὶ Ἀρχίππῳ τῷ συστρατιώτῃ ἡμῶν
    καὶ τῇ κατ᾽ οἶκόν σου ἐκκλησίᾳ·
  ³ χάρις ὑμῖν καὶ εἰρήνη
    ἀπὸ θεοῦ πατρὸς ἡμῶν
    καὶ κυρίου Ἰησοῦ Χριστοῦ

  ¹ Paul, a prisoner of Christ Jesus,
    and brother Timothy,
  to our much loved fellow worker Philemon,
    ² and to our sister Apphia
    and our fellow soldier Archippus,
    and to the assembly at your house:
  ³ Grace and peace to you
    from God our Father
    and our Lord Jesus Christ

Step two (vv. 4–7)
  ⁴ Εὐχαριστῶ τῷ θεῷ μου πάντοτε μνείαν σου ποιούμενος ἐπὶ τῶν προσευχῶν μου,
    ⁵ ἀκούων σου τὴν ἀγάπην καὶ τὴν πίστιν
    ἣν ἔχεις πρὸς τὸν κύριον Ἰησοῦν
    καὶ εἰς πάντας τοὺς ἁγίους,

⁶ ὅπως ἡ κοινωνία τῆς πίστεώς σου ἐνεργὴς γένηται
    ἐν ἐπιγνώσει παντὸς ἀγαθοῦ τοῦ ἐν ἡμῖν εἰς Χριστόν·
⁷ χαρὰν γὰρ πολλὴν ἔσχον καὶ παράκλησιν ἐπὶ τῇ ἀγάπῃ σου,
    ὅτι τὰ σπλάγχνα τῶν ἁγίων ἀναπέπαυται διὰ σοῦ, ἀδελφέ.

⁴ I thank my God, always making remembrance of you in my prayers,
  ⁵ hearing of the love and faith
  which you have for the Lord Jesus
  and for all the holy ones,
⁶ so that the partnership of your faith might become energized
  in the knowledge of every good thing among us, for Christ.
⁷ For I have much joy and comfort from your love,
  because the viscera of the holy ones have been refreshed by you,
  brother.

The aesthetic plays on the emotions, the heart or, better and more literally, the viscera. Paul does not here appeal to the senses as "apostle," as is common in the openings of his letters (e.g., Rom 1:1; 1 Cor 1:1; 2 Cor 1:1; Gal 1:1), or as a "slave" (Rom 1:1; Phil 1:1; Tit 1:1). He greets Philemon and those with him and around him as a prisoner, a prisoner of Christ Jesus (δέσμιος Χριστοῦ Ἰησοῦ), using precisely the same wording and sound at the beginning of verse 1 and the end of verse 9. In the social and emotional/sensory contexts this sets Paul below Philemon, yet paradoxically also above him as one doing what he does for Christ. Paul, of course, knows why he is writing the letter and wishes to make his own situation correspond in a sensory-aesthetic way to the situation of the person, Onesimus, for whom he is about to make an argument. From the outset of the rhetoric, Paul is not an apostle who issues orders (which he shortly makes explicit, v. 8). Philemon and his house-church community will have Paul's rhetorical situation pretty clearly in mind. It will affect their own situation.

Step one internally employs the chiastic[24] aesthetic of "Christ Jesus ... Jesus Christ" (Χριστοῦ Ἰησοῦ ... Ἰησοῦ Χριστοῦ, vv. 1, 3), which sets out the boundaries of the introductory greeting and, with corresponding genitive endings and sounds, emphasizes the identity of Christ Jesus/Jesus Christ in the rhetoric and social formation Paul has in mind. Paul is a prisoner of Christ, who is the Lord of all with whom the letter is connected. The for-

---

24. See Margaret Ellen Lee and Bernard Brandon Scott, *Sound Mapping the New Testament* (Salem OR: Polebridge, 2009), 227.

mation κυρίου Χριστοῦ Ἰησοῦ is not used elsewhere in the New Testament;[25] the usage regularly occurs with the name Jesus placed first.[26] The chiasmus has a sensory effect: the "Lord Jesus Christ" of verse 3 stands in contrast to the "prisoner of Christ Jesus" of verse 1, closing the greeting, but not closing the opening rhetoric of the letter. It has an internal function indicating that the one to whom Paul is prisoner is the same one who, in reverse order, is the beneficent, personalized Lord Jesus, a person whose own Father is God. The genitive morphology "Lord Jesus Christ" (κυρίου Ἰησοῦ Χριστοῦ) agrees, obviously, with the preceding genitive "our" (ἡμῶν) to indicate that the wish for grace and peace from God is also from the lord Jesus.

This step presents a wonderful melopoeic,[27] balanced sound structure. The first lines,

Παῦλος δέσμιος Χριστοῦ Ἰησοῦ
καὶ Τιμόθεος ὁ ἀδελφός

Paul, a prisoner of Christ Jesus,
    and brother Timothy

are balanced evenly (in Greek) with nine syllables each. The lines addressing the group of recipients are neatly balanced, verbless, dative statements with the first and third lines ending euphonically with the plural pronoun "our" (ἡμῶν; homoioteleuton[28] or parechesis[29]), and the second and fourth ending with dative nouns (*homoioptoton*).[30]

---

25. Though see 1 Tim 1:2; 2 Tim 1:2; Phil 3:8 for the formulation Χριστοῦ Ἰησοῦ τοῦ κυρίου ἡμῶν/μου.

26. It occurs again verse 25.

27. According to the rhetorical categories of Ezra Pound, melopoeia is musical or sound orchestration that directs the flow of meaning by the appeal of sound. See Ezra Pound, *How to Read* (New York: Haskell House, 1971), 25–26. See also Roy R. Jeal, "Melody, Imagery, and Memory in the Moral Persuasion of Paul," in *Rhetoric, Ethic and Moral Persuasion in Biblical Discourse*, ed. Thomas H. Olbricht and Anders Eriksson, ESEC 11 (London: T&T Clark, 2005), 160–78, here 162–65.

28. *Homoioteleuton* occurs when words or clauses have endings with the same sound; Quintilian, *Inst.* 9.3.77–80.

29. *Parechesis* is the repetition of the same sound in words in close succession: Richard A. Lanham, *A Handlist of Rhetorical Terms* (Berkeley: University of California Press, 1968), 71–72; BDF §488, 2.

30. A series of words in the same case or inflection; see Quintilian, *Inst.* 9.3.78; *Rhetorica ad Herennium* 4.20.28.

Φιλήμονι τῷ ἀγαπητῷ καὶ συνεργῷ ἡμῶν
  ² καὶ Ἀπφίᾳ τῇ ἀδελφῇ
  καὶ Ἀρχίππῳ τῷ συστρατιώτῃ ἡμῶν
  καὶ τῇ κατ' οἶκόν σου ἐκκλησίᾳ

to our much loved fellow worker Philemon,
  ² and to our sister Apphia
  and our fellow-soldier Archippus,
  and to the assembly at your house

Both Philemon and Archippus are described by "fellow" (συν-) compound words in the dative case, hence by paromoiosis.³¹ The address to the principal recipient, Philemon, followed by three euphonic and eurhythmic καί phrases identifies and emphasizes the larger audience of the letter. Each "and" raises the senses and expectations toward envisioning more people and the situations in which they stand—sister (kinship) for Apphia; fellow soldier (worker) for Archippus; household (community) for the *ekklēsia*. It is clear that these oral/aural sound features focus on the senses of mouth and ear, of touch, speech, hearing, and visual textures.³²

Step two, the thanksgiving statement, presents the sensory-aesthetic of thanksgiving and prayer.

⁴ Εὐχαριστῶ τῷ θεῷ μου πάντοτε μνείαν σου ποιούμενος ἐπὶ τῶν προσευχῶν μου,
  ⁵ ἀκούων σου τὴν ἀγάπην καὶ τὴν πίστιν
      ἣν ἔχεις πρὸς τὸν κύριον Ἰησοῦν
      καὶ εἰς πάντας τοὺς ἁγίους,
  ⁶ ὅπως ἡ κοινωνία τῆς πίστεώς σου ἐνεργὴς γένηται
      ἐν ἐπιγνώσει παντὸς ἀγαθοῦ τοῦ ἐν ἡμῖν εἰς Χριστόν·
  ⁷ χαρὰν γὰρ πολλὴν ἔσχον καὶ παράκλησιν ἐπὶ τῇ ἀγάπῃ σου,
      ὅτι τὰ σπλάγχνα τῶν ἁγίων ἀναπέπαυται διὰ σοῦ, ἀδελφέ.

⁴ I thank my God, always making remembrance of you in my prayers,
  ⁵ hearing of the love and faith
      which you have for the Lord Jesus
      and for all the holy ones,
  ⁶so that the partnership of your faith might become energized

---

31. Paromoiosis is the parallelism of sound in words and clauses. Paromoiosis can include both homoioptoton and homoioteleuton. See *Rhetorica ad Alexandrum* 1436a.5–13; Aristotle, *Rhet.* 3.9.9.

32. See Robbins, *Exploring*, 30–31.

in the knowledge of every good thing among us, for Christ.
7 For I have much joy and comfort from your love,
 because the viscera of the holy ones have been refreshed by you,
 brother.

Thanksgiving and prayer immediately interweave the mouth, speech, the voice (or at least the mind, where thanksgiving and prayer exist in thoughts), the tongue, and, from the side of the recipient and listeners to the prayers, the ears, hearing, and again the mind.[33] This texturing reveals much about Paul and his practice and character (note the first-person-singular verb forms and the repeated pronoun μου). His own sense of hearing is indicated by his claim that his prayers are informed by his hearing (ἀκούων) about Philemon's love and faith for Christ and for fellow believers. The aesthetic of Philemon's love and faith become visualized and accepted as a reality. Significantly, "faith" typically precedes "love" wording in the Pauline corpus (e.g., 2 Cor 8:7; Col 1:4; Eph 1:15; 3:17; 1 Thess 1:3; 3:6; 2 Thess 1:3), but here the sensory-aesthetic of "love" occurs first as the beginning of a strategic rhetorical move aimed at moving Philemon to a position guided first by love rather than by his rights as a slave owner (cf. vv. 7, 9, 16). The effect is reversed, however, as Paul anticipates a result from Philemon's faith (v. 6) and indicates his joy at having been a recipient of his love (v. 7). The balanced threefold accusative catena (homoioptoton) σου τὴν ἀγάπην καὶ τὴν πίστιν (twelve syllables) ἣν ἔχεις πρὸς τὸν κύριον Ἰησοῦν (ten syllables) καὶ εἰς πάντας τοὺς ἁγίους (eight syllables) directs the senses toward the recipients of the love and faith. The love and faith are invested in particular, real persons.

The sensory appeal of the thanksgiving and prayer forms a captatio benevolentiae,[34] because it seeks to express not only sincere prayer wishes for Philemon, but also the amenability and benevolence of Philemon to Paul's forthcoming request and argument. This kind of appeal has a strong sensory effect because it can build up Philemon with the feeling that Paul is personally interested in him. Paul is not simply far away in prison, but in that circumstance is hearing news about Philemon and is praying for him. He is eliciting receptivity.

---

33. The "zone of self-expressive speech," according to Malina, *New Testament World*, 69; see Robbins, *Exploring*, 31.
34. See Quintilian, *Inst.* 4.1.16–17.

A particularly striking sensory feature of this step is the employment of first- and second-person pronouns and verbs. The sensory emphasis is directly on Paul and Philemon individually and particularly.

Εὐχαριστῶ τῷ θεῷ μου ... ἐπὶ τῶν προσευχῶν μου ... χαρὰν γὰρ πολλὴν ἔσχον καὶ παράκλησιν πάντοτε μνείαν σου ποιούμενος ... ἀκούων σου τὴν ἀγάπην καὶ τὴν πίστιν; ἣν ἔχεις πρὸς τὸν κύριον Ἰησοῦν καὶ εἰς πάντας τοὺς ἁγίους ... ἐπὶ τῇ ἀγάπῃ σου ... διὰ σοῦ, ἀδελφέ.

I thank my God … in my prayers.… For I have much joy and comfort always making remembrance of you … hearing of the love and faith which you have for the Lord Jesus and for all the holy ones … from your love … by you, brother.

The effect may be set out like this:

I thank **MY** God,
always making remembrance of **YOU**
in[35] **MY** prayers,
HEARING of **YOUR** love and faith
which **YOU HAVE** for the Lord Jesus
and [**WHICH YOU HAVE**][36] for all the holy ones,
so that the partnership of **YOUR** faith might become energized … ;
for I have much joy and comfort from **YOUR** love,
because the viscera of the holy ones have been refreshed by **YOU**,
BROTHER.

This *sensory texture* continues throughout the letter. There is no occurrence of a plural pronoun from this step until verse 22 (ὑμῶν). By addressing Philemon with the family language of "brother" (vocative, repeated at v. 20), the sensory notion of kinship is injected into the emotional sound level.

Analysis of *sensory-aesthetic texture* shines some light on the difficult grammar of verse 6.[37] What is the connection between "partner-

---

35. Ἐπί, "at the time of."

36. Implied from the preceding clause.

37. How should ὅπως ἡ κοινωνία τῆς πίστεώς σου ἐνεργὴς γένηται ἐν ἐπιγνώσει παντὸς ἀγαθοῦ τοῦ ἐν ἡμῖν εἰς Χριστόν be translated and interpreted? On the difficulty see, for example, Cain Hope Felder, "The Letter to Philemon" in *NIB* 11:883–905, here 895. For a lengthy discussion see Markus Barth and Helmut Blanke, *The Letter to Philemon*, ECC (Grand Rapids: Eerdmans, 2000), 280–91.

ship" ("fellowship," "participation"; ἡ κοινωνία) and Philemon's faith
(τῆς πίστεώς σου)? Should it be read subjectively (Philemon's own faith)
or objectively (the partnership of people of faith, including Philemon)?
What "knowledge of every good thing among us for Christ" (ἐν ἐπιγνώσει
παντὸς ἀγαθοῦ τοῦ ἐν ἡμῖν εἰς Χριστόν) does Paul have in mind? Is it good
done *for* Paul and others *by* Philemon? Is it good done *for* Philemon *by*
Paul and his coworkers? Is it good done *for all* concerned (the holy ones,
Paul, Timothy, Philemon, the *ekklēsia*, others)?[38] *Sensory-aesthetic texture*
is instructive because it indicates the building of an aesthetic progression that emphasizes the good Philemon has done as a Christ-believer
for the holy ones, and the joy and comfort Paul (and presumably those
with him) have received from Philemon's love. There has been influence
all around. All of those concerned are, as the sensory-aesthetic, visceral
view progresses, recipients of much good. This is the "good among us," the
knowledge of which Paul prays will energize the situation. Paul seems to
have a comprehensive view. Paul is building a sensory-aesthetic (visceral,
splanchnic, joyful partnership) view of continuing and intensified good
and refreshment for the near future indicated in the quite well-balanced
lines of verses 6–7.

ὅπως ἡ κοινωνία τῆς πίστεώς σου ἐνεργὴς γένηται	18 syllables
ἐν ἐπιγνώσει παντὸς ἀγαθοῦ τοῦ ἐν ἡμῖν εἰς Χριστόν·	17 syllables
χαρὰν γὰρ πολλὴν ἔσχον καὶ παράκλησιν ἐπὶ τῇ ἀγάπῃ σου,	19 syllables
ὅτι τὰ σπλάγχνα τῶν ἁγίων ἀναπέπαυται διὰ σοῦ, ἀδελφέ.	20 syllables

Paul's prayers for Philemon are aimed toward the energizing of the partnership he imagines he and Philemon and others share (see v. 17). Paul
envisions the good occurring among all, probably including his own recent
work with the as yet unnamed Onesimus, as energizing the partnership
of faith that they hold in common. Philemon, for his part, has refreshed
viscera, the inward being of people. This known behavior suggests that he
should do this again, keep on doing it. The nearly equal lines of the progression form a sensory, *melopoeic* balance that helps make the point, to
influence Philemon, forcefully. In view is Christ, for whom ultimately the
good is done.

---

38. The variant ἐν ὑμῖν occurs in some manuscripts but is relatively weakly
attested. The sounds of the pronouns ἡμῖν and ὑμῖν are easy to confuse when they are
pronounced aloud.

Intertexture

Intertexture identifies and analyzes the "interactive world" of a text; that is, it examines "a text's representation of, reference to, and use of phenomena in the 'world' outside the text being interpreted."[39] This involves what interpreters call "intertextuality," but it also aims to consider the relationships texts have with multiple observable phenomena. Sociorhetorical interpretation argues that the study of intertextuality should be expanded to identify and analyze contact points and interconnections between the text being interpreted and as large a range of external phenomena as possible. Readers and listeners might recognize an **intertexture**, but do not necessarily need to know an allusion or interaction from a specific text or source or sociocultural feature in order for it to have rhetorical force. They may be affected from a more general knowledge.

There are no quotations or direct intertextual uses of Old Testament language or other texts in the Letter to Philemon. There are, however, many intertextural relationships with the world of texts, ideas, and phenomena outside of the letter.

The most obvious intertextures with the opening are found in the letters of the Pauline corpus, other letters of the New Testament, and with ancient Hellenistic letters more generally. The Pauline letters begin with similar but not always precisely the same introductory greeting statements that reflect usage in Hellenistic letters (see Rom 1:1, 7; 1 Cor 1:1–2; 2 Cor 1:1–2; Gal 1:1–3; Eph 1:1; Phil 1:1–2; 1 Thess 1:1; cf. 1 Pet 1:1–2; Jude 1–2). Philemon begins (vv. 1–7) by employing features of the standard Hellenistic formula (author to recipient followed by a greeting, followed in turn by a thanksgiving statement) that Paul characteristically expands to reflect his belief convictions and his concern for his audience. Timothy is named as coauthor and co-sender with Paul, an unusual practice in Hellenistic letters, but relatively common in Paul's letters (see 2 Cor 1:1; Phil 1:1; 1 Thess 1:1; 2 Thess 1:1). What is different in Philemon is that Paul does not identify himself as an apostle (ἀπόστολος, Rom 1:1; 1 Cor 1:1; 2 Cor 1:1; Gal 1:1; Eph 1:1; Col 1:1; 1 Tim 1:1; 2 Tim 1:1; Tit 1:1) or as a slave

---

39. Robbins, *Exploring*, 40. According to Robbins's taxonomy (pp. 40–68) there are four categories of **intertexture**: oral-scribal, cultural, social, and historical. There can also be **intertextures** related to material culture.

(δοῦλος, Rom 1:1; Phil 1:1; Titus 1:1),[40] but as a "prisoner of Christ Jesus" (δέσμιος, vv. 1, 9; cf. v. 13).[41] Paul reshapes and recontextualizes the rhetoric of standard Hellenistic letter style to suit his own rhetorical exigencies. This rhetorical reshaping introduces the letter as something recognizable to a Christ-believer like Philemon and to the *ekklēsia* that meets in his house. Philemon and the *ekklēsia* recognize the style of discourse and are likely to be amenable to it.

Prisoner

Paul, it is generally assumed, was an actual prisoner, incarcerated, when he prepared the letter. He also means for the term to have a dual meaning, to be understood metaphorically, that is, that he was a prisoner of, one bound to, one captive to Christ. Paul undoubtedly speaks, however, from physical incarceration.[42] This physical **intertexture** here is with the Roman (or Mediterranean) prison[43] and with the experience of one held in such a prison. Being a prisoner is an **intertexture** people understand at least in a general way, even if they have never been imprisoned themselves. Roman prisons were generally not imagined as penal or correctional institutions. They were secure places of confinement and remand, not of punishment, where prisoners awaited trial, sentencing, exile, execution, or release.[44] Paul may have been experiencing a rather light custody, possibly in a military camp or barracks, perhaps in a home, perhaps with a soldier present. It is possible only to speculate about the nature of his imprisonment, but

---

40. Some of the Pauline letter greetings do not employ a substantive to name or describe Paul (1 Thess 1:1; 2 Thess 1:1).

41. See also Acts 23:18; Eph 3:1; 4:1; 2 Tim 1:8. For δεσμός see Phil 1:13; Col 4:18. Cf. also Adolf Deissmann, *Light from the Ancient East: The New Testament Illustrated by Recently Discovered Texts of the Graeco-Roman World* (London: Hodder & Stoughton, 1910), 306–10, regarding the notion of being bound by (or released from) demonic powers, as Mark 7:35.

42. See **social and cultural texture**, below.

43. On Paul's geographical location see the introduction.

44. See Brian Rapske, *The Book of Acts and Paul in Roman Custody*, vol. 3 of *The Book of Acts in its First Century Setting*, ed. Bruce W. Winter (Grand Rapids: Eerdmans, 1994), 18–27. There were, of course exceptions, and punishment sometimes occurred. For the notion of being a prisoner of Christ extended into the patristic period see Ignatius, *Rom.* 1.

Paul does seem to have been accessible to Onesimus.[45] That Paul calls himself a "prisoner of Christ Jesus" supports the notion that he does not envision his imprisonment as penalty or punishment, but as a feature of his commitment to Christ Jesus. He seems not to consider himself a criminal who is paying for guilt. He is bound with regard to the gospel (ἐν τοῖς δεσμοῖς τοῦ εὐαγγελίου, v. 13), and employs his imprisonment as part of his rhetoric aimed at Philemon. The fact that Paul describes himself as "prisoner of Christ Jesus" indicates his commitment to the authority of Christ rather than to Caesar, the ultimate authority with regard to Roman imprisonment. Paul's rhetoric is therefore implicitly resistant to imperial imprisonment and authority. Imprisonment is described in relation to the gospel, not to Caesar or to Rome. Intertexturally this is reminiscent of the ancient biblical rhetoric of Exodus: Who will be God? Yahweh or Pharaoh? The rhetorical implication and rhetorical force of this language is that being a prisoner of Christ is an elevated role. It is Jesus Christ who is "Lord" (v. 3), not Caesar. Philemon is meant to feel the force of the idea and not be bound by the social and cultural expectations placed on him with regard to Onesimus. The notions of being bound and imprisoned is a significant part of the rhetoric.

The *Ekklēsia*

The *ekklēsia* in the New Testament and the Pauline letters is a well-known and well-studied notion, including comparative and intertextual connections. In the Septuagint ἐκκλησία represents the word קהל, "assembly" or "community" in the Hebrew Bible, particularly in Deuteronomy, the Former Prophets, and the Psalms. To Greek speakers in Asia Minor ἐκκλησία was a familiar word indicating an assembly of persons.[46] Jews of the diaspora who did not have synagogues often met in homes, as did other religious groups.[47] It is employed in Acts to refer both to the church (e.g., 8:1) and to an (out of control) assembly in Ephesus (19:32). For Paul the ἐκκλησία is the people who are Christ-believers gathered together,[48]

---

45. On the nature of Roman imprisonments see Rapske, *Book of Acts*, 24–35, 177–225.

46. In ancient Greece to an assembly of summoned citizens or to a legislative assembly (LSJ, 509).

47. Barth and Blanke, *Letter to Philemon*, 261.

48. Or the church in the world understood more generally.

typically called "church"[49] in English translation. It is "the body of Christ" that, even though composed of "many members" with differing appearances, responsibilities, and functions, remains (and is to remain) a single unit, a unified body of persons (1 Cor 12:12–28). Paul envisions this body-*ekklēsia* as a community that must not allow itself to be divided (e.g., 1 Cor 1:10–17). The *ekklēsia* is a space of wisdom where love for God, for Christ, for one another, and for all people is understood and practiced (e.g., 1 Cor 13:1–13). It is the space where humans are clothed with and identified by Christ, the new person, rather than by national or ethnic identities (see Rom 13:14; Gal 3:27; Eph 4:24; Col 3:10).[50] It is the space of freedom and mutual care in the midst of slavery, oppression, and externally imposed power (see Gal 5:1, 13–14). In addition to the letter to Philemon and the *ekklēsia* in his house, all of the letters of the Pauline corpus are addressed to or are concerned with the *ekklēsia*,[51] many of them explicitly (e.g., 1 Cor 1:2; 2 Cor 1:1; Gal 1:2; 1 Thess 1:1; 2 Thess 1:1). Those letters that address "the holy ones" (οἱ ἅγιοι), or "beloved ones" (ἀγαπητοί), or like terms are also understood to have the *ekklēsia* in mind (Rom 1:7; Eph 1:1; Phil 1:1; Col 1:2). The Pastoral Letters, while addressed to individuals, have ecclesial concerns in mind. Paraeneses and ethical exhortations in the letters are directed toward what in sociorhetorical description are wisdom concerns regarding good living and good relations between and among members of the churches. The *ekklēsia* is composed, socially, genetically, and ethnically, of males and females, Jews and gentiles, slaves and nonslaves (Gal 3:28), all of whom are portrayed as "sinners," who formerly were slaves to sin (Rom 6:6–7, 9, 12, 14; Gal 4:8) who have been freed from earthly, sinful bondage to live as the new society described in familial terms as a caring community where the needs of all are met (Gal 3:29; 4:7). Members of the *ekklēsia* are to come to know who they are: Christ-believers who live faithfully and care genuinely for all believers, regardless of risk.

The particular spatial context in Philemon is the house *ekklēsia*, the assembly in Philemon's home.[52] A leading **intertexture** is, therefore, the house (οἶκος), a locus of kinship, hospitality, and love. Philemon is a home-

---

49. From κυριακός, the Lord's.

50. On this see Roy R. Jeal, "Clothes Make the (Wo)Man," *Scriptura* 90 (2005): 685–99.

51. And ἐκκλησίᾳ, plural, e.g., Gal 1:2.

52. Philemon, however, is the only letter that mentions a house church in the letter opening. See the discussion in Barth and Blanke, *Letter to Philemon*, 260–62.

owner and a slave owner, affluent enough to be both. As a Christ-believer he has, hospitably, opened his home to the *ekklēsia*. "House churches," or house assemblies of Christ-believers, were common in early Christianity, as Acts indicates (Acts 1:13; 2:46; 5:42; 12:12; 20:20) and as Paul's letters indicate (Rom 16:5, 23; Col 4:15). Meeting in Philemon's house[53] provides this *ekklēsia* with an identity marker, at least for the purpose of the letter: it is the church in Philemon's house.[54] This intertexturing shows that Paul's request of Philemon was by no means a private affair. The house included not only Philemon and his immediate family but also others, perhaps Apphia and Archippus[55] and including, until his separation, Onesimus, likely other slaves and/or servants, perhaps additional relatives and/or other persons, and, very importantly, members of the *ekklēsia* who were present at least from time to time. In the house church slaves are to be considered full members of the believing society.

Refreshment of the Viscera

The notion of having the viscera refreshed (vv. 7, 20; cf. v. 12) is important to Paul in this letter. In the opening, where in the hearing of the *ekklēsia* he praises Philemon for his good works, Paul specifies his awareness that Philemon has refreshed the viscera of the holy ones, presumably the people of the *ekklēsia* who meet in his house. Paul is able to draw on fairly wide and wise intertextural understanding in this language that he assumes Philemon and the *ekklēsia* will understand. He draws Onesimus into the visceral scene, making it intensely personal (v. 7). He recontextualizes[56] the idea when, drawing his argumentation together at the end of the middle, he calls for Philemon to refresh his, Paul's, viscera (v. 20) by receiving the slave Onesimus as a beloved brother.

The refreshment Philemon has brought about and is requested to bring about again draws on a broad cultural understanding of ideas. The verb "I refresh" (ἀναπαύω) indicates the notion of rest and refreshment

---

53. That it is Philemon's own house is indicated by the singular pronoun σου. There is no compelling reason to think the house belonged to Archippus even if his name is closer to the word οἶκος than is Philemon's.

54. There could have been other house churches in the location.

55. Some have speculated, without evidence, that Apphia and Archippus were relatives, perhaps wife and son, of Philemon.

56. Robbins, *Exploring*, 48.

from the pressure of difficult or stressful conditions.[57] It occurs, for example, in Homer's *Iliad* (17.550) indicating rest or cessation from hard work. In the Septuagint ἀναπαύω refers to the rest and refreshment ("peace" in the NRSV) that came from the end of strife with Canaanite tribes (1 Chr 22:18), and to the refreshment that comes from having a disciplined son (Prov 29:17). Job speaks of being at rest in death (3:13). In the Synoptic Gospels ἀναπαύω describes physical, bodily rest and refreshment (Mark 6:31; 14:41) and a more spiritual and inward refreshment of the soul (Matt 11:28-29). Revelation speaks of the rest of those who have been martyred and of those who have died (6:11; 14:13), as also does Joseph and Aseneth (7.9; 15.7; 22.13). Paul himself describes the refreshment provided to his soul through the goodness of Christ-believing friends (1 Cor 16:18).

While translations of Philemon typically render τὰ σπλάγχνα (vv. 7, 12, 20) as "heart," the word more literally means "entrails," "viscera,"[58] or "bowels," and hence refers metaphorically to the affections of the heart, the emotions and feelings of concern or compassion or pity, or, a little more crassly, feeling it in one's guts.[59] It occurs eleven times in the New Testament (always in the plural), in the NRSV as "tender mercy" (Luke 1:78), the more literal "bowels" (Acts 1:18), "affections" (2 Cor 6:12),[60] "heart" (2 Cor 7:15), "compassion" (Phil 1:8; 2:1; Col 3:12), and "refuses" (literally "shuts his viscera," 1 John 3:17). In the Septuagint a similar range of meaning occurs: "mercy" (Prov 12:10), "inner parts" (Prov 26:20), "compassion" (Wis 10:5), "heartache" (Sir 30:7), "heart" (Sir 33:5), "bodies" (Bar 2:17), and "bowels" (2 Macc 9:6). In what are the most graphic and emotional usages of σπλάγχνα, 4 Maccabees describes the prospect of and actual descriptions of torture and dismemberment of humans: "entrails" (5:30; 10:8; 11:19); a mother's emotion in her "inmost parts" (14:13); and "heart" (15:23, 29). In more distant connections in Greek literature, σπλάγχνα is employed to refer to the entrails used in sacrifices and sacrificial feasts and in divination, and to the womb.[61] Paul's reference to Onesimus as his own viscera (v. 12), touches intertexturally with Philo, *De Iosepho* 25, who has

---

57. See Otto Bauernfeind, "Ἀναπαύω," *TDNT* 1:250-51.

58. See the Latin *viscera*.

59. See above on rhetography. The KJV uses "bowels" in Phlm 7, 12, 20. Cf. the verb form σπλαγχνίζομαι, "to have compassion."

60. But cf. the near synonym ἡ καρδία in 2 Cor 6:11.

61. See Helmut Köster, "Σπλάγχνον," *TDNT* 7:548-59.

Jacob describing his supposed dead son Joseph as "my viscera."[62] The first-century-CE Roman historian Quintus Curtius Rufus, in his Latin work *The History of Alexander the Great* (*Historiarum Alexandri Magnum Macedonis* 4.14.22), has Darius call his mother and children his own viscera. The second-century-CE diviner (*oneiromancer*) Artemidorus, in *Oneirocritica* 1.44 (*The Interpretation of Dreams*), employs σπλάγχνα as a synonym for παῖς (child).[63] Several passages in the Testaments of the Twelve Patriarchs use σπλάγχνα to describe the inner feelings or affections (T. Sim. 2:4; T. Zeb. 2:2, 4–5; 4:2; 7:4; 8:2, 6). The occurrences in the Testament of Zebulun describe, very interestingly, incidents from the story of the mistreatment of Joseph by his brothers.[64]

This intertextural contextualization demonstrates that, for Paul, the terminology of viscera, the refreshment of the viscera, and the parent-child notion of viscera have powerfully emotive, pathos connotations that run deeply into his own knowledge of Scripture, history, and the rhetorical use of language. He anticipates that Greek speakers like Philemon and the *ekklēsia* will, like himself, grasp the meaning and rhetorical force and be moved appropriately by his usage. The deep emotional nature of the rhetoric makes powerful and graphic (rhetographic) points. Paul draws on a range of intertextural rhetorical meaning that moves his argument along with palpable force. He is grateful for the refreshment of the holy ones and anticipates his own rest and refreshment from the tension he is experiencing with regard to Onesimus. The refreshment he anticipates is "in Christ" (ἐν Χριστῷ, v. 20), where in his mind it is complete because it is resurrection, reconciled, kinship, brotherly refreshment that reflects love and faith (v. 7). Titus had his spirit "refreshed" by the Corinthian church (2 Cor 7:13), and in response his viscera overflowed toward them (2 Cor 7:15). Paul seems to anticipate something similar from Philemon. The anticipated result is temporal, of course, of life where people are loved and get along as brothers. This is the intertextural rhetoric; it presses on Philemon to do the right thing as he has done it before, using a range of meanings from the world that he and Paul understand.

---

62. See below on the Joseph narrative (Gen 37–50) as Paul's frame for the Letter to Philemon.

63. Craig S. Wansink, "Philemon," in *The Oxford Bible Commentary: The Pauline Epistles*, ed. John Muddiman and John Barton (Oxford: Oxford University Press, 2010), 265.

64. See below, again, on the Joseph narrative.

Social and Cultural Texture

Social and cultural texture considers the "social and cultural nature," the "social and cultural location" of the language used, and the "social and cultural world" evoked and created by a text.[65] This means that interpreters must identify and analyze topoi and categories that denote social and cultural situations and creations in the rhetorical discourse in order to understand their rhetorical function and force. For the Letter to Philemon this means that interpreters must consider social topoi such as the *ekklēsia*, kinship, slavery, indebtedness, and others. Social and cultural topoi set up the rhetorical situation and the social rhetoric of the discourse.

Christ, Gospel, *Ekklēsia*

The undergirding social and cultural situation (not to mention the undergirding theology) is established and guided by the repetitive references to Christ (Christ Jesus; Jesus Christ; in Christ; Lord) and by the words *ekklēsia* (v. 1) and "gospel" (v. 13). The entire visual scene, the argumentation, and the ideology have their foundation and, consequently, their social location in the gospel convictions and community that are shared by Paul, Philemon, the *ekklēsia* that meets in his house (the members of which are called "holy ones," vv. 5, 7), specified persons—particularly Apphia and Archippus—in the introductory and concluding greetings, and, by the time Paul is preparing the letter, Onesimus the slave. Paul's imprisoned life is (literally) bound up with Christ (vv. 1, 9), and he understands himself to be "in Christ" (vv. 8, 20, 23). He understands himself to be imprisoned for, literally to be chained or bound for, the sake of the gospel (v. 13). Intertexturally we are informed that Paul identifies strongly with Christ (Gal 2:19–20), and it cannot be imagined that Paul would have any other view when he addresses Philemon. For Paul it is "in Christ" that one knows who one is and how life is properly lived. Philemon, who might live in the town of Colossae[66] and be a leader of the *ekklēsia* there, is a believer who has already been practicing and is known for behavior that is socially reordered toward faith and for love toward the Lord Jesus and all the "holy ones," and for actions that "refresh the viscera" of those holy

---

65. Robbins, *Exploring*, 71–94.

66. See introduction. See Col 4:9, where Onesimus is spoken of as living in Colossae. The connection is tenuous.

persons (v. 7). It is the gospel and faith in Christ Jesus that has brought about the trajectory of Philemon's belief and behavior. Social change has already occurred, and Philemon has become a social participant in it. This new society and behavior constitute a social realm of operation, a culture of operation, where many persons who know Philemon are, it is implied, observers who are watching him. These social topoi and the social location create a social space and rhetoric where there are expectations of continuation of beliefs and behaviors that accord with what has already taken place. This is social and cultural persuasion. Analysis of social and cultural texture shows that behavior and ethics are at the heart of what the letter aims to get at. Philemon, in sociorhetorical terms, has a wisdom intention.

Prisoner

Paul places particular rhetorical emphasis on his status as "prisoner" (δέσμιος, vv. 1, 9) and in his "imprisonment" (or chains; δεσμός, v. 10) and on the role of Onesimus, who shares a kind of imprisonment (v. 13). Paul is a prisoner as he addresses Philemon (v. 1) and as he appeals to Philemon (v. 9). There is an apparent double meaning to the terms since Paul is likely physically imprisoned while the letter is being composed and, at the same time, considers himself as Christ's prisoner, as one bound or chained to Christ and the messianic faith. This double meaning forms a social interweaving of the Roman provincial legal establishment—hence the imperial system—and Christianity. Paul, as he speaks, cannot separate himself from either Caesar or Christ. What does come through, though, is that his role as "prisoner of Christ Jesus" transcends his condition as a prisoner of civil authorities. The social status and role of prisoner is something for which Paul seems to feel no shame, fear, or deep personal concern—he is not languishing in prison—because it is directly connected to Christ Jesus and to the gospel, the things that define his life. Imprisonment for Paul is tied to Christ, not to Caesar. It extends, as we have seen, to Epaphras who is a "co-prisoner" or "co-captive" with Paul (v. 23), though the terminology indicates the idea of a "prisoner of war," of a captive who cannot get away without being released by another. During the first century CE in the Roman Empire, being a prisoner meant that one was being confined, not punished, perhaps on remand while waiting for trial, sentencing, exile, execution, or release.[67] This may

---

67. On this, see again especially Rapske, *Book of Acts*, 18–27.

be why Paul anticipates his release and envisions the need for hospitality (a room, hospitality space, ξένια, v. 22) from Philemon and being restored to face-to-face social contact. Prisons were usually places for confining "common, not high status criminals."[68] They were unhygienic, unhealthy places where day-to-day existence was very stressful and threatening on multiple levels.[69] Paul can appeal to Philemon from such a position of social and cultural weakness, an old man and a prisoner, without concern for the culture of shame that would be associated with it. He is actually a prisoner of a much greater authority than Rome and Caesar. Paul does not refer to himself as "slave" (δοῦλος) in the Letter to Philemon as he does in other letters (e.g., Rom 1:1), though he does use the term to describe Onesimus (v. 16). Like prisoners, though, slaves can be released only by others.

Thanksgiving, Prayer, Faith, Love, Fellowship, Refreshment (Verses 4–7)

Standing in some contrast to Paul's social and cultural condition of shame, Philemon appears as an honorable and honored social character. The immediate cultural context of this honor is the *ekklēsia*, the assembly of Christ-believers who have been the recipients of Philemon's faith and love and who have been refreshed in inner, personal, visceral ways—one might say in their souls—by him (v. 7). Philemon has been affected morally by his faith in Christ Jesus. Paul is, of course, arranging his rhetorical stage with a kind of *encomion*, setting Philemon up as an honored person so that he can make a request of him that might affect his honorable status in the *ekklēsia* and in the larger community.[70] Nevertheless, the **social and cultural textures** of thanksgiving, prayer, faith, love, fellowship, and refreshment work to move Philemon toward amenability to the request that is to come to him shortly.[71]

68. Ibid., 25.
69. Ibid., 196–255.
70. "An exposition of the good qualities of a person or thing, in general or individually" (*Progymnasmata* attributed to Hermogenes, 7).
71. "The outstanding characteristic of Christianity is its placing the highest value on love, not only for one's family or group, but for everyone—including people who chew with their mouths open" (Margaret Visser, *Beyond Fate*, 2002 Massey Lectures [Toronto: House of Anansi, 2003], 50).

Sacred Texture

Sacred texture is the rhetoric of God, of the divine, in a text. Analysis of sacred textures involves identifying where texts speak of God and "finding insights into the nature of the relation between human life and the divine."[72] The rhetoric of sacred spaces and texturing speaks of holy things, why they are important, and how people who are cognizant of holy things should order their lives. This is the texture of the relationships between and among humans, the created order, and the divine. It gets at the relationships between the profane and the sublime. It addresses redemption, commitment, worship, community, ethics, holy living, spirituality, and personal and social formation. It can be eschatologically directed, or it can be aimed at life in the present. **Sacred texture** is distinct from other textures, but the other textures are woven together with and move toward the sacred as the locus of lived reality.[73] It is most like **ideological texture** because it *is* ideological.[74] The language of **sacred texture** relates closely to that of wisdom rhetorolect, but links also with other modes of rhetorical discourse. The sacred is properly understood in relation to how the world and life are understood. The recognition or perception or "feel" of sacred textures moves out obliquely into human belief and action. This is the realm of discipleship and spiritual formation. Paul the apostle claims that the wisdom of God is revealed by God through the Spirit (1 Cor 2:6–16), and some things are understood "because they are discerned spiritually" (1 Cor 2:14). **Sacred texture** is like that: it is analyzed and appraised when sacred things are discerned in and from the text by minds attuned to and seeking holy relationships. When the sacred texturing in the texts is grasped it can be lived out in real life. It fills in religious understanding of how life should be lived in relation to God, Christ Jesus, the church, people in the world, indeed to the entire cosmos.

---

72. Robbins, *Exploring*, 121.

73. See ibid., 130. Rosemary Canavan, in *Clothing in the Body of Christ at Colossae*, WUNT 334 (Tübingen: Mohr Siebeck, 2012), 66, describes **sacred texture** as "an encompassing cloud" that surrounds the other textures. I think this is inadequate because rhetoric persuades, it moves people to belief and action, so it is *more than* a context like a cloud. **Sacred texture** has cloud-like characteristics, but it also has trajectories, geometric outward forces, that move people in multiple directions toward multiple holy actions.

74. See below on **ideological texture**.

In Philemon, the sacred is everywhere and is pervasive. It has to do with how life is now understood and actually lived "in Christ" by people like Philemon, who can and do "refresh the viscera" of the holy ones. Sacred texturing aims to influence Philemon's religious understanding and behavior, that is, his faithfulness. Influencing someone's faithfulness is a sacred activity and goal. In particular, the sacred texturing indicates much about the nature of the new life in the new society where Onesimus's enslavement cannot continue. The sacred life of and in relationship with God through Christ and "in Christ" exists in a sacred space of freedom. It is not possible, as Paul presents it, for slavery to stand in the new society of the *ekklēsia*.

Step One (Verses 1–7)

From its outset the Letter to Philemon is focuses on the sacred. Paul presents himself as a "prisoner of Christ Jesus" (v. 1). By placing "Christ" before "Jesus" as a kind of divine title, a sacred trajectory is already set into the rhetorical environment. The rhetorical implications of who Christ Jesus is along with Paul's clear statement about his own relationship to Christ establish a deeply religious sense of faith and faithfulness.[75] Naming Timothy as "the brother," Philemon as "beloved" and "fellow worker," Apphia as "sister," Archippus as "fellow soldier," and the *ekklēsia* that meets in Philemon's house extends the sacred trajectory to a significant number of persons who form a holy community. This language also confirms to the letter recipients that they share together, with Paul, in the Christ-believing fellowship and in the reception and force of the letter. Paul ties these connections together in his greeting: "grace to you and peace from God our father and Lord Jesus Christ" (v. 3).

Paul offers thanks to God and intercedes for Philemon ("you," σου, singular) in his prayers. Philemon loves and has faith in the Lord Jesus (v. 5). Together with the grace and peace greeting, these things indicate the assumption that God and Jesus Christ are personal, present, and active. God and Jesus Christ convey grace and peace, can be observed as divine, can be thanked, can be addressed in prayer, and can be believed in by people. Philemon's good works for "the holy ones" (vv. 5, 7) show his commitment to others, to the people of the *ekklēsia*. Philemon is a faithful

---

75. On the repetitions of Christ, Jesus, and Lord see above on *repetitive texture*.

man ("the fellowship of your faith," v. 6) who is conscious of who he is and wishes to do good things as a Christ-believer. Paul is himself encouraged by Philemon's faithfulness. It is clear that Philemon is an honest and active disciple of Christ. The way in which this first rhetorical step in the letter is shot through with the sacred is striking, though it accords with what is observed in other Pauline letters. The sacred connections are the foundation on which the theological views and the appeal of the letter are made.

Rhetorical Force as Emergent Discourse

The letter emerges into the polyvalent worlds of Philemon, the *ekklēsia* in his house, the new society of Christ-believers more generally, and ancient Mediterranean cultures and societies. The opening makes this entrance in a distinctly Christ-believing fashion, where Paul focuses on his own situation and space as "prisoner of Christ" and prophetic letter writer, and on Philemon's situation and space as a host to the *ekklēsia* and "refresher" of believers. Both characters are motivated by "love" (vv. 5, 7). Paul has in mind an emerging and challenging situation that he does not mention in the opening, but his rhetoric, by praising Philemon's good works, subtly insists that Philemon continue doing good things as a Christ-believer. There is already a hint in the narrational story line of an emerging moral and behavioral realm. Paul employs topoi and conceptual frames in his language that are intended to move Philemon intellectually, emotionally, and behaviorally in his messianic faith. Others around Philemon will be similarly affected by Paul's letter.

As is described in the section on rhetography, the letter has an overall wisdom intention, envisioning a wisdom and household space where Philemon, other named persons, and the *ekklēsia* are located and functioning (v. 2), and employs overall blended wisdom rhetorolect.[76] There is, there-

---

76. Recall the earlier discussion of wisdom. See Vernon K. Robbins, *The Invention of Christian Discourse* (Dorset, UK: Deo, 2009), 1:121–74. Wisdom rhetorolect and space blends "human experiences of the household, the geophysical world within God's cosmos, and the intersubjective body in which people live. In this conceptual blending, God functions as heavenly Father over God's children in the world. The blending of these spaces conceptually presents a goal for people's intersubjective bodies to produce goodness and righteousness.... Wisdom rhetorolect emphasizes 'fruitfulness' (productivity and reproductivity)" (ibid., 1:121). See also Robert H. von Thaden Jr., *Sex, Christ, and Embodied Cognition: Paul's Wisdom for Corinth* (Dorset, UK: Deo, 2012), chap. 2, "Wisdom," 76–108.

fore, an overall wisdom cultural frame. Paul has in mind the social formation of Philemon with regard to the slave Onesimus throughout his letter.
An apocalyptic, gospel change has occurred that has familial, kinship,
gospel, and eternal implications (vv. 10, 13, 15–16). These implications
are deeply personal for Paul and Philemon and, to be sure, for Onesimus
(vv. 10–12, 16, 17, 18–20). They are personally observed by people in the
rhetographic description such as Apphia, Archippus, and the *ekklēsia*. Philemon has already been practicing the new wisdom life in the new community (vv. 4–7), and is being urged to extend it. Paul the prisoner is the
wise person who is encouraging the new wisdom conditions. In contrast
to usual household operations and to the larger economy (οἰκονομία, the
management of a household;[77] administration, the orderly way in which
things are usually done[78]) of the Mediterranean world, Christ-believers
function in a new economy located, in this specific circumstance, in Philemon's house.

What occurs rhetorically in the emergent structure of the letter opening is the conceptual blending of multiple frames or spaces that begin to
produce the cognitive and mentally/intellectually and emotionally understood new space of Philemon's household and the *ekklēsia*, where all persons, regardless of status, are free and equal.[79] New and emergent cognitive
structures are formed when topoi from particular and clear input frames
are set together and elicit understanding of new concepts and conditions
not previously understood in the input frames alone (so A + B can evoke a
new structure and a new understanding, C).[80] This is the interplay of conceptual frames and topoi that produces and evokes ideas, thoughts, and
behaviors. There are several rhetorical frames in the opening that blend
together to move Philemon toward an unexpected social life relationship
in Christ.

---

77. LSJ, 1204; BDAG, 559–60. The word is obviously cognate with οἶκος, "house."
78. See MM 442.
79. For discussion of conceptual blending see Robbins, *Invention*, 77–120, and
von Thaden, *Sex, Christ, and Embodied Cognition*, 37–75. For theory of conceptual
blending see Gilles Fauconnier and Mark Turner, *The Way We Think: Conceptual
Blending and the Mind's Hidden Complexities* (New York: Basic Books, 2002). See also
my article "Starting before the Beginning: Precreation Discourse in Colossians," *R&T*
18 (2011): 287–310, here 287–89.
80. As explained by von Thaden, *Sex, Christ, and Embodied Cognition*, 46 (see
pp. 44–50).

Frame One

The first input frame presents Paul, in prophetic and priestly roles, speaking directly to Philemon (though others are observing and listening).
Paul calls himself a prisoner of Christ Jesus, the one in whom both he
and Philemon are believers. Paul's life, particularly now in imprisonment, is shaped by Christ, not by the physical imprisonment of Roman or
local incarceration. This itself is a significant rhetorical force: Paul is constrained by Christ Jesus, not by his civil and sociocultural circumstances.
He does not indicate concern for his physical imprisonment.[81] He is also,
in this frame, a knowledgeable and experienced old man (v. 9), who, for
this reason alone, deserves a hearing. Paul's assumption is that Philemon is
listening to all this. While Paul is, when viewed from outside of the Christ-
believing community, socially inferior because he is a prisoner, he knows
he is completely acceptable to Philemon because of their apocalyptic connection in Christ.

Frame Two

This input presents Philemon in wisdom space, where he is a well-known
householder who is recognized by a number of interested people, and
who hosts the *ekklēsia* in his house. He practices the wisdom role of love
and faith for the Lord Jesus and all the holy ones (v. 5). He refreshes their
viscera, functioning in a priestly role. Paul hopes that Philemon's priestly
function will continue (v. 6). He is unlikely to reject Paul due to Paul's
imprisonment, and he is amenable to Paul's letter. The wisdom behavior
he already practices seems likely to continue.

Frame Three

The *ekklēsia* functions as a topos within its own frame. This is household
space apparently occupied by Apphia the sister and Archippus the fellow
soldier, and by a number of persons not named in the letter. They are the
holy ones for whom Philemon has done much good, and they are, in the
rhetoric of the letter, located in Philemon's house. They are listening and
watching. The presence of these people and the assumption that they are

---

81. Though he anticipates his release; see v. 22.

observing the situation indicates significant external rhetorical pressure on Philemon.

The Middle, Philemon 8–20

Middle Texture

The middle is where there is a major shift to the central concern and to the central argumentation. Identifying the central argument, hence the central point and objective of Philemon, indicates the location of the middle. The word διό indicates the transition to the middle, where Paul makes his actual argumentative appeal to Philemon. The transition sequence links the opening view of Philemon and his good and faithful works to Paul's urging for those things to continue in the future. His first employment of the word "I urge" (παρακαλῶ, v. 9), along with his insistence that he urges through love and does not issue a command, indicates his method of appeal and moves thought ahead, but Paul inserts a structural parenthesis, or anacoluthon, into his sentence in the self-referring and self-effacing "an old man" (πρεσβύτης) and "prisoner of Christ Jesus" (δέσμιος Χριστοῦ Ἰησοῦ, v. 9). The second use of παρακαλῶ (v. 10) indicates the substance of Paul's appeal. Here the central concern and person at its focus, Onesimus, are identified.[1] With the second παρακαλῶ statement,[2] Paul shifts attention from himself (v. 9) to Onesimus and makes an appeal to action.[3] Philemon should receive and accept his slave, Onesimus, who was once "useless" but is now "useful" (v. 11), no longer as his slave (δοῦλος), but as a "beloved brother" (ἀδελφὸν ἀγαπητόν, v. 16). Paul regards Onesimus as his own viscera (τὰ ἐμὰ σπλάγχνα, v. 12) and calls on Philemon to provide him the refreshment Philemon has given to others (ἀνάπαυσόν μου τὰ σπλάγχνα ἐν Χριστῷ, v. 20). Paul wishes Philemon to receive Onesimus as if he were Paul himself (προσλαβοῦ αὐτὸν ὡς ἐμέ, v. 17).

---

1. Verse 10 (not 8–9) may thus be a *propositio*, a feature typically following a *narratio* and functioning to provide a short summary of what a speaker is addressing.
2. See the discussion of παρακαλῶ in **intertexture**, below.
3. And hence presents a new idea, certainly a new clause or even sentence.

The middle intensifies the rhetoric that began in the opening by focusing Paul's appeal and argumentation on how Philemon is expected to receive Onesimus. A way of understanding how this works and thus of the nature of the shifts of thought in our document is by considering Daniel Kahneman's description of "cognitive ease" and "cognitive strain."[4] There is cognitive ease when "things are going well—no threats, no major news, no need to redirect attention or mobilize effort."[5] When there is cognitive strain, "a problem exists, which will require increased mobilization," that is, increased effort to meet demands.[6] For Philemon and others in the opening of the rhetograph, there is a high level of ease. Philemon is strongly praised for his good works. This situation of cognitive ease starts to shift in the middle (vv. 8–9), where Philemon begins to be pressed to engage in as yet unnamed and unfocused behavior. It is in verses 10–20, however, that the cognitive strain is applied. Philemon here must remember, reenvision, and engage in deepened thought to consider change that has already occurred, evaluate social and relational situations and realities, consider the possibility of some kind of debt owed to him and whether it requires payment, and consider the presentation of a benefit to Paul. This places significant cognitive strain on Philemon and indicates Paul's central concerns for the letter. This is what middle sections of texts do: they elicit the cognitive strain and increased energy, including moral and social tension, that must be faced and on which thought, decision, and action will be based.

Progressive Texture

In the central rhetoric of the letter there are eleven progressions.

1. Verse 8
    [8] Διό, πολλὴν ἐν Χριστῷ παρρησίαν ἔχων ἐπιτάσσειν σοι τὸ ἀνῆκον

    [8] Therefore, having much boldness in Christ to command your obedience

---

4. Daniel Kahneman, *Thinking Fast and Slow* (New York: Farrar, Straus, & Giroux, 2011), 59–70.

5. Ibid., 59.

6. Ibid.

The inferential conjunction διό creates a link between Paul's knowledge of Philemon's past good works for others and his move toward making a specific request of Philemon for the future. Paul's apparently very close knowledge has given him enough confidence to be authoritative toward Philemon by issuing a command for his obedience. This sequence is Paul's way of building on an interrelationship with a view to more and particular behavior.

2. Verse 9
⁹ διὰ τὴν ἀγάπην μᾶλλον παρακαλῶ,
    τοιοῦτος ὢν ὡς Παῦλος πρεσβύτης
    νυνὶ δὲ καὶ δέσμιος Χριστοῦ Ἰησοῦ

⁹ I appeal, rather, through love—
    I do this as Paul, an old man,
    but now also a prisoner of Christ—

Now the adverb μᾶλλον with the first-person verb παρακαλῶ ("I appeal, rather") moves thought ahead from the notion of command, effectively overturning or refuting its necessity[7] by shifting completely to love as the means of persuasion. While Paul would rather use love than force, he nevertheless continues to move the sequence forward with strong personal, pathetic appeal by adding that he is an "old man" and a prisoner.

3. Verses 10–11
¹⁰ παρακαλῶ σε περὶ τοῦ ἐμοῦ τέκνου
    ὃν ἐγέννησα ἐν τοῖς δεσμοῖς Ὀνήσιμον
¹¹ τόν ποτέ σοι ἄχρηστον νυνὶ δὲ σοὶ καὶ ἐμοὶ εὔχρηστον

¹⁰ I appeal to you for my child—
    whom I have birthed in chains—*Onesimus*,
¹¹ who formerly was *useless* to you, but now is *useful*—to you and to me—

This progression is marked by the repeated "I appeal" (παρακαλῶ), which now functions to move toward defining Paul's request of Philemon regarding his "child." This step moves ahead internally by identifying the child

---

7. On refutation (ἀνασκευή), see "*Progymnasmata* Attributed to Hermogenes" 5 in George A. Kennedy, trans., *Progymnasmata: Greek Textbooks of Prose Composition and Rhetoric* (Atlanta: Society of Biblical Literature, 2003), 79.

as Onesimus, to whom Paul has dramatically given birth in his chains of imprisonment. The child Onesimus, who is here implicitly known to Philemon and whose name means "useful," was, according to another internal step, formerly (ποτέ) "useless" to Philemon but is now (νυνί) "useful" to both Philemon and Paul. This progression moves the discourse and Philemon toward thinking about a specific person and implies, but does not state, that some action with regard to Onesimus will be in order.

4. Verse 12
    12 ὃν ἀνέπεμψά σοι αὐτόν,
        τοῦτ' ἔστιν τὰ ἐμὰ σπλάγχνα

    12 whom I send back to you,
        this one who is my own viscera—

The relative pronoun and verb move the discourse forward, not yet by calling for Philemon's action, but by indicating what Paul is doing and what he is thinking. He sends Onesimus to Philemon. But he sends him with a rhetorical statement full of pathos: "this one who is *my own* viscera." In this way he raises the stakes for Onesimus. Onesimus, whom Paul has metaphorically brought forth as if he were his own child, is metaphorically his own flesh. Paul will be aware that it will be very difficult for Philemon to resist the pressure to agree to what is being put to him "through love."

5. Verse 13
    13 ὃν ἐγὼ ἐβουλόμην πρὸς ἐμαυτὸν κατέχειν
        ἵνα ὑπὲρ σοῦ μοι διακονῇ ἐν τοῖς δεσμοῖς τοῦ εὐαγγελίου

    13 whom I strongly wish to keep to myself,
        so that he might serve me on your behalf in the chains of the gospel

The discourse progresses here by the relative pronoun ὅν together with the first-person verb ἐβουλόμην emphasized by the first-person pronoun ἐγώ. Paul is strongly emphatic in this step and indicates continuing pathos. His deep wish is that Onesimus could stay with him serving in place of Philemon himself in gospel work. Paul portrays himself and Philemon as being bound to the gospel. It is something that neither he nor Philemon can escape even if they wished it. Paul wants Onesimus to participate in this work.

6. Verse 14
    ¹⁴χωρὶς δὲ τῆς σῆς γνώμης οὐδὲν ἠθέλησα ποιῆσαι

    ¹⁴ But apart from your consent I wish to do nothing

The prepositional phrase "but apart from your consent" moves the argument ahead by placing the responsibility for action on Philemon.

7. Verse 14
    ἵνα μὴ ὡς κατὰ ἀνάγκην τὸ ἀγαθόν σου ᾖ ἀλλὰ κατὰ ἑκούσιον

    so that you do not do the good thing out of necessity, but voluntarily

This ἵνα statement importantly advances the discourse by playing the rhetorical game of claiming that there is no pressure on Philemon when it is actually enormous. Paul claims that he does not aim to coerce Philemon. Philemon should act voluntarily of his own free will. But of course the pressure *is* on Philemon very powerfully in this kind of rhetorical discourse. No pressure, Paul seems to say, while the good Philemon, who has done so much for many people, has just been told that Onesimus is a child to Paul and Paul's own viscera. This progression moves the rhetoric ahead by politely claiming there is no pressure while in fact adding pressure.

8. Verses 15–16
    ¹⁵τάχα γὰρ διὰ τοῦτο ἐχωρίσθη πρὸς ὥραν
        ἵνα αἰώνιον αὐτὸν ἀπέχῃς
            ¹⁶οὐκέτι ὡς δοῦλον ἀλλὰ ὑπὲρ δοῦλον, ἀδελφὸν ἀγαπητόν,
    μάλιστα ἐμοί, πόσῳ δὲ μᾶλλον σοὶ καὶ ἐν σαρκὶ καὶ ἐν κυρίῳ

    ¹⁵ For perhaps this is why he was separated from you for a while,
        so that you might have him back forever,
            ¹⁶ no longer as a slave, but more than a slave, a beloved brother—
    certainly to me, but more to you, as in the flesh also in the Lord

This step employs the notion of possibility (τάχα γάρ, "for perhaps") and the passive voice "he was separated" (ἐχωρίσθη) to suggest that there was divine purpose and action behind the separation of Philemon and Onesimus. Internally the ἵνα clause suggests an "eternal" reason. This divine and eternal purpose is expanded by the "no longer" (οὐκέτι) statement that argues from the negative to positive (not this but that) and by the μάλ-

(μάλιστα; μᾶλλον) statements meant to advance the notion of Onesimus as a "beloved brother."

9. Verse 17
    ¹⁷ Εἰ οὖν με ἔχεις κοινωνόν, προσλαβοῦ αὐτὸν ὡς ἐμέ

    ¹⁷ If therefore you have me as partner, receive him as me

While this progression uses the first-class conditional "if therefore" (εἰ οὖν) to point out that there is a partnership between Paul and Philemon, its effect is to advance the rhetorical discourse by drawing Philemon more deeply into the argument. The protasis, "If therefore you have me as a partner," is actually not in doubt, and Philemon knows it. What is in doubt is the apodosis, whether Philemon will receive Onesimus as Paul wishes. Philemon is meant to respond mentally with the thought "Of course, we are partners" and "Yes, I will accept Onesimus as if he were you, Paul." Paul's conditional "if" is a lead-in to his polite command, "Receive him as me." Paul is conceding to his own argument that Onesimus now stands in a different relationship both to himself and to Philemon. Philemon recognizes that there is a Christ-believer's partnership of himself and Paul, particularly with regard to Onesimus. Paul and Philemon are friends.[8] This means that Onesimus the slave must be received as Paul, as a partner in the gospel. This progression solidifies the very personal connection between Philemon and Paul.

10. Verses 18–19
    ¹⁸ εἰ δέ τι ἠδίκησέν σε ἢ ὀφείλει, τοῦτο ἐμοὶ ἐλλόγα
    ¹⁹ ἐγὼ Παῦλος ἔγραψα τῇ ἐμῇ χειρί, ἐγὼ ἀποτίσω·
    ἵνα μὴ λέγω σοι ὅτι καὶ σεαυτόν μοι προσοφείλεις

    ¹⁸ But if he has wronged you or owes you anything, charge it to me.
    ¹⁹ I Paul, I write this in my own hand: I will repay it
    —not that I say that you owe yourself to me!

---

8. How could they have actually known each other personally? If Philemon lived in Colossae or nearby in the Lycus Valley and if Paul had not been there (Col 1:8–9; 2:1), could they be personally known to each other? Or had Paul traveled in the Lycus Valley? Or could a partnership in the gospel be imagined between people who had never met face-to-face?

This progression employs another conditional statement, this time with the conjunctions εἰ δέ and ἤ. It progresses by playing off of the partnership between Paul and Philemon, with Paul offering to pay himself for some kind of offense committed by Onesimus or some kind of cost or debt owed. Paul, Philemon's partner and Onesimus's metaphorical parent, accepts the debt. Paul writes this with his own hand, literally signing his name to guarantee what is owed. This progression clearly intensifies the personal nature of the discourse. While on its face this progression serves to relieve the pressure of responsibility for an apparent outstanding debt owed by Onesimus to Philemon by placing it on Paul, in fact it functions to increase the pressure on Philemon. The progression advances internally with Paul's rather less than subtle counter ἵνα statement, "not that I say that you owe yourself to me." This progression is designed to cause Philemon to feel pathos pressure, to think and perhaps to say, "No, No, Paul. Don't worry about it!"

11. Verse 20
    ²⁰ ναί, ἀδελφέ, ἐγώ σου ὀναίμην ἐν κυρίῳ· ἀνάπαυσόν μου τὰ σπλάγχνα ἐν Χριστῷ

    ²⁰ Yes, brother, might I possibly have this benefit from you in the Lord? Refresh my viscera in Christ!

With the polite familial but high-pressure "Yes, brother, might I possibly have this benefit from you in [the] Lord? Refresh my viscera in Christ!" Paul corroborates what he has just said and presses hard on Philemon to accept Onesimus and do the right thing. Philemon has refreshed the viscera of holy people before; he can and should do it again.

Narrational Texture

Step three (vv. 8–9) is a transitional narrative sequence that links the story between past, present, and future. Readers and listeners—including Philemon and the named recipients—by now grasp the most basic lines of thought and are open to moving ahead. The initial διό of verse 8 naturally leads them along. Philemon, the loving, faithful, praiseworthy person who does good for others, is quite clearly being requested, indeed more than requested, he is being pushed by a very strong rhetoric, to do another good, but not yet named, thing. The nuancing of the narrative language puts

pressure on the scene: "Therefore, having much boldness in Christ to command your obedience ..." (v. 8). The narrator places himself, apparently
righteously, in an authoritative position. Philemon, though highly praised,
is not above Paul in status—though Paul is currently imprisoned and old,
and narrates these facts to his advantage—Philemon can be given orders
to perform. But Paul takes a subtle "pressure on/pressure off," authoritative then humble encouragement approach, saying he would rather operate by love. It seems obvious that the old man plays a rather obsequious,
self-effacing role in order to get his way: "I could command you, but I
prefer to encourage you by love." This narration moves the situation along
toward what Paul actually wants Philemon to do. The word παρακαλῶ ("I
appeal" or "I encourage") sets up a linkage for the transit to Paul's hope for
the future, because he will immediately, in step four, use it again to specify
what he wants Philemon to do.

It is in step four (vv. 10–11) that the narration reveals its central concern and the circumstance of the character who has brought about the issue
of concern in the letter. A request is made of the highly praised and set up
Philemon. The repeated παρακαλῶ (from v. 9) specifies that Paul's request
to Philemon through love (rather than a command) is about Onesimus,
whose name means "useful." Onesimus, whose name will be immediately
recognizable to Philemon, Apphia, Archippus, and the *ekklēsia*, has had a
change of status and role: he has become, during Paul's current imprisonment, his "child." This is a significant thought, logically in the context to
be understood as a development connected with the faith both Paul and
Philemon have in Jesus Christ. Onesimus, too, has become a believer in
Jesus and is Paul's "child" in this sacred, ideological, and theological sense.
It is understood that Paul is not describing Onesimus as his natural child.
The metaphorical yet genuinely felt faith development of kinship between
Paul and Onesimus is connected directly to an additional development
presented in a dramatic play on words: Onesimus ("useful") was formerly
"useless" to Philemon, but has now, as Paul's "child," become "useful" to
both Paul in his imprisonment and to Philemon at home with the *ekklēsia*.
The circumstances that would indicate just what "useless" and "useful"
mean are not described, but it is clear that Philemon knows what they
are. Attempts at reading a precise metanarrative regarding Onesimus in
either category are unproductive. The narrational change from "useless to
you" to the doubled "useful to you and to me" is suggestive of the practical
change Onesimus has undergone. This information is completely fundamental to the argument being presented and to the narrative as a whole,

and it is situated exactly in the middle at the turning point of the narration. This is the central idea Paul wishes Philemon to grasp: things are different now. Onesimus has become a believer just like Philemon himself, he has become a useful person, and Paul views him as his own child.

Step five (vv. 12–14) presents Paul's voice narrating a carefully crafted argumentation aimed at supporting his case and making the case persuasive by adding deeply personal and moving statements intended to have a pathos effect. Paul states that he now is sending Onesimus back to Philemon, the first hint we get that they are separated, embellished by the emotion-arousing statement that Onesimus is Paul's "own viscera," his own inward emotion and being. Onesimus represents Paul in an emotional-physical way; this is an extension of the notion of Onesimus as Paul's child. The level of pathos is thick and palpable. Listeners will not miss the description of the deep, emotive connection between Paul and Onesimus. With Onesimus coming back to Philemon, the onus is now on Philemon to respond to the good faith Paul has shown to him regarding Onesimus. The narration points out Paul's wish to keep Onesimus with him so he might serve him, but his concern for Philemon's voluntary consent is important to him and, moreover, important to the rhetorical pressure placed on Philemon. Philemon is not being directly forced to do anything at all. Paul is seeking his free agreement. Nevertheless, by stating it as he does, Paul places enormous pressure on Philemon that will be recognized by Philemon and by those with him. The persuasive effect of Paul's narration is clear, and Philemon would have a difficult time turning down Paul's request. To deny Paul's request would have the force of directly denying Paul himself.

Next, step six (vv. 15–16) narrates a suggested logic. Perhaps (τάχα) Onesimus was separated from Philemon for a divinely directed purpose. This idea proposes that Onesimus was a quite passive party in the separation (ἐχωρίσθη, third-person-passive verb) and that there is an eternal purpose in the separation: "so that you might have him back forever" (ἵνα αἰώνιον αὐτὸν ἀπέχῃς).[9] Paul inserts a fact into his narrative for the first time, a fact that restructures much of the context of the narrative and understanding of the relationship between Philemon and Onesimus: Onesimus is a slave (δοῦλος). This was certainly known by Philemon and those near him, but not necessarily by other early audiences and certainly

---

9. See below on **intertexture** and the Joseph cycle of stories.

not by modern audiences until this point in the story. This injects into the narrative implicit understandings of ownership and property with all their social and legal implications. It raises questions about how the separation actually took place, even if it was divinely directed. Paul addresses only the question of the reason for the separation, nothing else,[10] positing that it may have been caused by God so that Onesimus could now be received "no longer as a slave, but more than a slave, a beloved brother." This entire narrator's suggestion about the nature of the situation simultaneously proposes a dramatic alteration of the normal ancient Mediterranean narrative. The social metanarratives are subverted. Law is effectively ignored. Slavery is effectively abolished at least in this particular instance. Onesimus is not a slave any longer.[11] He is coming back, Paul suggests, as a family member in kinship, in a brotherly relationship with Philemon. This is to be understood as brought about by divine and rather sudden intervention into Philemon's affairs. Paul plays on the possibility in direct address to Philemon, arguing that since this new relationship with Onesimus is actually now true for himself, how much more will it be so for Philemon both "as in the flesh also in the Lord" (καὶ ἐν σαρκὶ καὶ ἐν κυρίῳ)? This narration simply does not let Philemon get away from its argument and the new story of himself and Onesimus. Philemon and Onesimus are brothers (metaphorically) in the flesh and in the Lord (in faith in Christ).

Step seven (vv. 17–20) moves from the suggestion regarding divine intervention to the anticipated application of the argument. Paul, as narrator, uses his own voice and now his own hand to place himself, once again, directly into the story as part of the narrational, rhetorical appeal. He says, "If therefore you have me as partner, receive him as me." This draws on and emphasizes the narrational points made earlier regarding Philemon as Paul's coworker and his love for the holy ones and his desire for refreshing actions for them. It also draws on the logic and emotion

---

10. Though there have been many suggestions about why Philemon and Onesimus were separated. Was Onesimus a runaway? Had he stolen from Philemon? Had he overstayed a trip as messenger from Philemon to Paul? And why had Philemon not already previously proclaimed the gospel message to Onesimus? Or had he? The letter simply does not say, and speculation does not help. See the introduction.

11. Implicit is the view that slavery is not a righteous condition for Philemon to continue to impose on Onesimus or, again implicitly, for anyone, since all believers are brothers (or sisters) in Christ the Lord. This seems to me to be a feature of the larger New Testament narrative. See below on **intertexture**.

of Paul's highly rhetoricized, stated desire that Philemon would freely and voluntarily accede to his request regarding Onesimus. Paul wants, in this context, to be viewed as Philemon's partner (κοινωνός). While the statement sounds slightly tentative because of the use of the particle εἰ, Paul is confident of the partnership. This partnership narrative has made an opening for the imperative "receive him as me." This emphasizes a point already made implicitly. Receiving Onesimus as if he were Paul himself would be, in Paul's thinking, the same thing as receiving Paul himself. Onesimus, too, is to be understood as a partner, not as a slave. Paul extends the partnership relationship to its logical yet, in the circumstances and context of slavery, rather surprising level. He is prepared to cover Onesimus's debts if there are any. The narration makes clear that Paul boldly and personally takes charge of his double partnership with Philemon and Onesimus by saying, "I, Paul, I write this with my own hand: I will repay it!" He will be the responsible party and do the right thing regardless of the cost. He signs his name to it. Having taken charge this boldly, the force of the story is dramatically deepened even more with Paul pressing hard on his personal relationship with Philemon: "not that I say to you that you owe yourself to me!" Paul is willing to pay the price for Onesimus, but Philemon, to whom the debt would be paid, actually owes Paul everything. The power of the storytelling has become clear. Philemon is simply expected to do the right thing. Philemon is again called "brother" (ναί, ἀδελφέ, vocative), drawing out again the kinship relationship between Paul, Philemon, and Onesimus and simultaneously pressuring Philemon to behave in the anticipated brotherly manner. While the narrator makes the request again in a mood of possibility, he presumes that Philemon will indeed once again refresh the viscera of another person, in this case Paul's viscera, by receiving Onesimus as requested (ἀνάπαυσόν μου τὰ σπλάγχνα ἐν Χριστῷ). By closing the clause with "in Christ" the narration presses home a final, strong, and significant point. All that is requested and done is done in the shared context and understanding of faith in Christ.

Argumentative Texture

The focused "me"/"you" argumentation of the opening continues in the middle section. As was noted in the section on *repetitive texture*, the requests are made by one person, Paul; and only one person, Philemon, is expected to grapple with the ethical, social, and gospel connections of the requests and with Onesimus's future. The repetitive texturing of first- and second-person-singular verbs and pronouns forms the foundation for the *argumentative texturing*. The argument employs a repetitive pattern of I-you-me-with-regard-to-him. The "him," of course, is Onesimus, who is now introduced into the argument for the first time and becomes the focus for Philemon's thinking and action. In his overall argumentation Paul calls for Philemon to receive the separated slave Onesimus as a beloved brother on the argumentative rationale he began using subtly in the opening (vv. 4–7). The loving and faithful Philemon has "refreshed the viscera" of many holy ones. Paul now calls on Philemon to refresh Paul's viscera by receiving Onesimus (v. 20). Paul explicitly ties his argument to the topos of Christ (ἐν κυρίῳ; ἐν Χριστῷ). Paul and Philemon and now Onesimus are "in Christ" and must behave toward one another with this reality in mind.

> Case: Philemon has, because he is a believer in Jesus Christ and in his loving, faithful, and frankly praiseworthy way, done much good for the holy ones. He has refreshed their viscera. His history in this regard is impressive and has brought Paul "much joy" and "comfort."

> Rationale: As this good "brother" in Christ and in the same way he has behaved toward the holy ones, Philemon should, when Onesimus arrives, refresh Paul's viscera by receiving Onesimus as a brother.

> Anticipated result: On his return, Onesimus will be received by Philemon not as a slave but as a beloved brother in Christ, that is, "in the flesh and in the Lord" (v. 16).

Other arguments in the middle are placed within the frame and the argumentative parameters of this overall argument.

Supporting *argumentative textures* flow through the middle to make the point. Signaling a step three, Paul begins with the inferential διό ("therefore," "so"), followed by the "I could but will not" approach claiming the authority to command Philemon, but quickly refusing it in favor of an appeal to love (vv. 8–9). This strategy is *permissio* (cf. *concessio*), where argument is made by appearing to leave something to the judgment of the listener (Quintilian, *Inst.* 9.2.25). In the brief digression or anacoluthon, Paul points out, rather artfully and obsequiously, that he is both an old man and a prisoner of Christ Jesus (v. 9), thereby adding a level of drama and personal appeal to his argument. The socially low-level person—a prisoner—who may also be considered past his prime because of his age, argues his case to the socially high-level home- and slave owner Philemon.[12] Paul is not making a woeful, whining argument, but he is willing to appeal to his personal circumstances as an argumentative point.[13] This is an emotional, pathos argument probably meant to touch Philemon in his own viscera. With the first occurrence of παρακαλῶ ("I appeal," v. 9) and the claim that he speaks through love, not command, Paul indicates his approach but does not yet make his request explicit.

> Case: Paul has authority to issue an order to Philemon but, with a strongly emotional component, chooses to appeal by love, not by command.

> Rationale: Employing an "I could but will not" argument with an appeal to personal circumstances will likely push Philemon toward an agreeable response that is better than a forced acquiescence.

> Anticipated Result: Philemon will get the idea about receiving Onesimus and will actually do so.

Following the anacoluthon, Paul resumes his direct appeal in step four (vv. 10–13) by repeating the first-person παρακαλῶ and completing his thought: "I appeal to you for my child—whom I have birthed in chains—Onesimus" (v. 10). The argument names the person of concern, Onesimus, for the first time. The argument continues to be focused directly on Philemon ("I appeal to you"), but Paul brings in himself again with more pathos appeal in a series of emotionally touching statements: "my child"; "whom I have birthed in chains"; "who formerly was useless [worthless] to you, but now is useful [valuable]—to you and to me"; "my viscera"; "whom I strongly

---

12. Perhaps an implicit synkrisis, comparison of lesser to greater or greater to lesser; See Hermogenes, Progymnasmata 8.

13. It is fascinating to note again that Paul does not appeal to his status and role as an apostle for his authority as he does in other letters such as 1 and 2 Corinthians. Perhaps he assumes that Philemon recognizes his apostolic authority without being explicit about it for rhetorical reasons.

wish to keep to myself, so that he might serve me on your behalf in the chains of the gospel" (vv. 11–13). Here Paul comes closer to explicating the precise appeal he wishes to make, but does not do so yet. What he does say, however, argues again dramatically and personally, if also circumstantially, that compelling changes have taken place. In an oppositional "then"/"now" (ποτέ/νῦν) argument he says, euphonically, that Onesimus is changed, that the useless has become useful. This new usefulness takes on a gospel and apocalyptic rhetoricizing when Paul states that Onesimus now might serve (διακονῇ, subjunctive) him, in Philemon's stead, in the chains or bonds of the gospel. The change in Onesimus is a gospel change and is a major turning point. Onesimus, metaphorically birthed by Paul, is now one of "the holy ones"; like Philemon, he is a believer in Christ Jesus[14] who can serve the purposes of the gospel in the same way Paul does. The topos "gospel," implicitly present before, now becomes an explicit and powerful piece of the reasoning, because it is central to what has happened. Onesimus is not the person he used to be in Philemon's experience and memory, because he has been affected apocalyptically by the gospel message of Christ and his life is reoriented to it. The implications are that Philemon should be happy with this turn of events and that Onesimus should now be a beneficiary of his love, faith, and refreshing actions.

> Case: Paul makes a personal and emotional appeal to Philemon on behalf of Onesimus. He does not (yet) state the exact nature of the appeal.

> Rationale: Things are different now for Onesimus. There has been a gospel change. Paul considers himself to be in a figurative parent-child relationship with Onesimus. Onesimus has become knowledgeable of, affected by, and committed to the gospel and can work with Paul in gospel service. He has become "useful," though formerly he was "useless."

> Anticipated result: Philemon will be persuaded by Paul's report of the changes in Onesimus and will consequently have an altered view of him.

---

14. Whom Paul and Philemon believe to exist in the present, that is, as the raised and living Christ Jesus.

The next argumentative move, step five, is indicated by "but apart from your consent" (v. 14) and is strategically astute, because it places the possibility of Onesimus's service with Paul (and on behalf of Philemon) distinctly under Philemon's authority. Paul states that he will not move on the matter without Philemon's consent and this, argumentatively, "so that you do not do the good thing out of necessity, but voluntarily." This echoes Paul's earlier choice to appeal to Philemon through love rather than through command. Paul remains the self-effacing prisoner, not the authoritative apostle, again using the "I could but will not" texturing. The choice for gospel service is up to Philemon, who will recall that he has just been described as one who loves and has faith in the Lord Jesus and does good things for other believers (vv. 4–7). The argumentative pressure is on Philemon, certainly not on Paul or on Onesimus, to produce the still unspoken but anticipated result. While the choice belongs to Philemon, it is Paul who, ironically, retains the actual power position.

> Case: Paul wishes to keep the changed Onesimus with him for participation in gospel service. He will not do this without Philemon's consent. The situational context is emotionally charged.

> Rationale: It is up to Philemon to make a freewill choice regarding Onesimus's gospel service rather than be coerced into allowing Onesimus to serve with Paul. In fact Paul's move makes it extremely difficult for Philemon to refuse consent.

> Anticipated result: Philemon will consent.

Argumentation comes finally to the main point in step six, the central request and the crux of Philemon's social, ecclesial, and gospel formation (vv. 15–16). A shift in reasoning is signaled by the words "for perhaps" (τάχα γάρ) followed by argumentation that clarifies the entire situation involving Paul, Philemon, and Onesimus in at least a limited way and that also explicates what Paul wants from Philemon. Paul argues for quite specific action in a blend of prophetic and wisdom rhetorolects; the expected action will demonstrate Philemon's social formation. The central request identifies Onesimus's social status and relationship to Philemon and Paul's proposal for a new understanding and practice of the relationship and injects divine purpose along with eternal and apocalyptic perspectives as rationales for argumentation. The case being presented here for argument is that

Onesimus may have been separated from Philemon for a period of time for a divine purpose. This offers to readers (but not to the characters in the rhetograph) the new information that Philemon and Onesimus have been separated and that they were themselves passive in the divine action of separation. The argument, in an ἵνα clause, is set in terms of two notions: of possibility (in the subjunctive ἀπέχῃς) and of eternal existence (αἰώνιος): "For perhaps this is why he was separated from you for a while, so that you might have him back forever." The topos of eternal existence points back to the suggested divine (apocalyptic) intervention and forward to continuing relationship. The expected result from this argument on the part of Philemon is that he would do what Paul himself has already done (v. 10): receive and treat Onesimus as a family member, as a "beloved brother" (ἀδελφὸν ἀγαπητόν, v. 16). A second piece of new information now is that Onesimus is here identified explicitly as a slave (δοῦλος). The separation, the possibility of the return and restoration of Onesimus, and the denotation of his identity as Philemon's slave bring clarity to the reasons why the letter was written. Strikingly, Paul states that Onesimus is to be received "no longer as a slave" (οὐκέτι ὡς δοῦλον). The negative adverb μηκέτι would be expected to occur here, because the verb ἀπέχῃς is in the subjunctive mood in order to express the notion of possibility ("so that you might have him back"). Paul uses οὐκέτι, however, to make the indicative point that Onesimus is in fact now not a slave but a freeperson and brother in Christ.[15] The central argument is extended by an additional rationale when Paul adds to his call for Philemon to receive Onesimus as a beloved brother by saying, "certainly to me, but more to you, as in the flesh also in the Lord" (v. 16). This is argumentation by *synkrisis*, comparison,[16] where the kinship relationship Paul has with Onesimus is presented as comparatively of much more significance to Philemon. This comparison is offered to impress Philemon with the power and importance of his reception of Onesimus. Onesimus is, at the time of writing and sending of the letter, Philemon's slave, his legal property, subject to Philemon's decisions and treatment. As a beloved brother, however, in a family-type relationship—both in the flesh (i.e., the human kinship context of familial care and affection) and in "the Lord" (Christ-*ekklēsia*-gospel-*aiōn*, i.e., Christian faith)—Philemon's relationship to Onesimus is

---

15. See various commentaries, particularly Markus Barth and Helmut Blanke, *The Letter to Philemon*, ECC (Grand Rapids: Eerdmans, 2000), 414–20. See also below on **intertexture** and **social and cultural texture**.

16. Hermogenes, *Progymnasmata*, 8.

intensified. The new relationship is dramatically different, a point Paul uses to intensify his argumentation. This is apocalyptic change brought about by Christ and the gospel. It has a view toward eternity, not only to the present.

> Case: Onesimus has been separated from Philemon. Philemon should now receive him back in the new ecclesial space in familial and eternal relationship.

> Rationale: While the exact details of the separation are not explained, Paul suggests that divine intervention has brought it about. He argues that a divinely caused separation might bring about eternal good results in the form of reconciliation. The overall argument is that Philemon the Christ-believer should, as such, now do the right thing by receiving Onesimus. The rationale is made on the basis of the possibility of a loving, brotherly relationship for eternity where Onesimus will not be a slave and, implicitly, Philemon will not be his owner. The eternal, apocalyptic understanding of the present and future forms the basis for the reception and relationship with the Christ-believer Onesimus. The argument for the reception of Onesimus as such a brother is extended by a comparative "more to you than to me" rationale that intensifies the thrust of the loving and eternal new relationship.

> Anticipated result: Philemon will accept Onesimus the slave as a "beloved brother" for eternity, no longer as slave. Onesimus is not treated as slave, hence is de facto free.

Step seven of the argumentation (v. 17) draws on Paul's own relationship with Philemon: "If, therefore, you have me as partner, receive him as me" (v. 17). Paul has already portrayed himself as one who cares deeply for Philemon and sees him as a coworker (v. 1). Paul is very much aware of Philemon's good, ecclesial works. Philemon will quite clearly recognize Paul's affection for him, his current status as prisoner, and his age. Philemon will recognize participation with Paul in the gospel (v. 13). While there may be more to a partnership between Paul and Philemon than is indicated and than we can possibly know, Paul uses the idea to advance his case and to persuade Philemon. This is an "if"/"then"[17] form of argumen-

---

17. The word "then" is implicit.

tation that plays off of something Philemon knows and will undoubtedly grant is true. It assumes Philemon's agreement that a partnership exists, even if only implicitly. Based on it, the reception of Onesimus follows naturally. It is as if Paul had said, "In the same way you receive me, receive Onesimus, my 'child.'" Receiving Onesimus is equivalent to receiving Paul himself. This argument, interestingly, suggests a *dependence* of Philemon on Onesimus. The ongoing partnership of Paul and Philemon seems now to hinge on Philemon's reception of Onesimus. If Philemon does not (or if he in fact did not) receive Onesimus, then his relationship with Paul—who, again, sees Onesimus as his child—will be damaged, perhaps irretrievably. It would suggest that Philemon does not or will not continue in the partnership. Maintenance of the partnership, which we may assume Philemon values, depends, subtly but clearly, on the relationship between Philemon and Onesimus. Philemon should understand his relationship with Onesimus in the same way he understands his relationship with Paul. To receive Onesimus is to receive Paul. This has the effect of turning the tables on Philemon. Onesimus is Philemon's partner. The slave owner is dependent on the slave in his Christ-believing faith and practice. It is known, certainly, that owners did sometimes become dependent on slaves in a way similar to how slaves were dependent on the will of their owners. For Philemon, however, this partnership and dependence is likely a striking surprise.

> Case: Paul and Philemon have an implicit, if strikingly conditional (εἰ), brotherly partnership in Christ, in the *ekklēsia*, in the gospel, and in an eternal perspective.

> Rationale: Philemon should, in view of and because of the partnership, receive Onesimus in the same way he would receive Paul. Onesimus is implicitly Philemon's partner.

> Anticipated result: Philemon will receive Onesimus as brother and partner in the gospel.

The next *argumentative texture*, step eight, is an unexpected shift to what might at first glance appear to be a tangential notion, but is an important and rhetorically forceful move. The argument employs the "if"/"then" form of the preceding verse.[18] "But if he has wronged you or owes you

---

18. With "then" once more implicit.

anything, charge it to me. I Paul, I write this in my own hand: I will repay it—not that I say that you owe yourself to me!" (vv. 18–19). This posits the possibility, but not, it is important to notice, the certainty, that Onesimus has wronged Philemon in some way. The separation itself is not in mind here. Many interpreters have read the statement to mean that Onesimus was a thief who had stolen money or some sort of tangible goods from Philemon. Others have suggested that Onesimus owes Philemon for the loss of labor during the time of the separation.[19] There is insufficient evidence for these suggestions. What Paul *does* argue is that "if" Onesimus owes Philemon something tangible that he will pay for it, presumably in some sort of cash value, himself. The conditional "if" assumes something for the sake of argument, not necessarily as an actual reality.[20] The hypothetical rationale is founded on the "if" statement. If there is a debt, Paul will repay it. Paul's own rationale, however, functions at a deeper level. Paul wants, still, Philemon to receive Onesimus as a beloved brother. Paul is prepared to indemnify Philemon against any loss that may stand in the way of the reception. That is, Paul himself is willing to bring about Onesimus's reception. This would mean a considerable sacrifice for Paul for the sake of another. This is the argument of a parent such as Paul is to Onesimus. Paul the partner of Philemon and prisoner of Christ and the gospel will do what he can to bring about good for Philemon and Onesimus even by covering a blamable action, if such exists. Paul intensifies his argument in favor of Onesimus's reception by making his willingness personal: by his own mark, his handwritten name or signature. This is starkly emphasized by the inclusion of the first-person pronoun ἐγώ. Paul in this way insists on his participation in Onesimus's reception by Philemon. Then

---

19. See the discussion in, e.g., Douglas J. Moo, *The Letters to the Colossians and Philemon*, PNTC (Grand Rapids: Eerdmans, 2008), 427. See also James D. G. Dunn, *The Epistles to the Colossians and to Philemon*, NIGTC (Grand Rapids: Eerdmans, 1996), 338.

20. A first-class conditional; see BDF §§371–72; Daniel B. Wallace, *Greek Grammar beyond the Basics: An Exegetical Syntax of the New Testament* (Grand Rapids: Zondervan, 1996), 690–94. See also Brook W. R. Pearson, "Assumptions in the Criticism and Translation of Philemon," in *Translating the Bible: Problems and Prospects*, ed. Stanley E. Porter and Richard S. Hess (Sheffield: Sheffield Academic, 1999), 268–71. See also especially Clarice J. Martin, "The Rhetorical Function of Commercial Language in Paul's Letter to Philemon (Verse 18)," in *Persuasive Artistry: Studies in New Testament Rhetoric in Honor of George A. Kennedy*, ed. Duane F. Watson (Sheffield: JSOT Press, 1991), 330–34.

follows the clincher for the argumentative rationale: "not that I say that you owe yourself to me!" This rationale takes the form of paralipsis (or, more broadly defined, apophasis),[21] the rhetorical figure that addresses a subject by denying that it is addressed. The personal argumentative intention of Paul to pay for any debt owed by Onesimus is placed equally personally on Philemon. By claiming he does not say what he actually says, Paul pressures Philemon by indicating that he owes his own self, his life, his loving, faithful, and refreshing actions, to the prisoner-partner Paul. Thus by implication Philemon owes Paul much more than Paul is asking of him. This is a major piece of Paul's rationale; in effect he says, "Do what I ask because you owe me more than I ask of you." Wisdom living in the *ekklēsia* that is shaped by Christ, the gospel, and eternity calls to Philemon. The wisdom of the forgiveness of debts is implicit. Philemon must do it. This is why Paul can say, shortly, that he is confident of Philemon's obedience. This argument also implicitly ends Onesimus's slavery.

> Hypothetical case: Onesimus owes Philemon something valuable. The debt is here hypothetically mentioned so the exact nature of the valuable, whether money or goods or labor or some other thing(s), is unknown. Whether there is an actual debt owing is not directly relevant. The *rhetoric* of debt and payment is relevant to Paul's case. Paul will himself cover any debt owed. He guarantees the debt by signing his own name.

> Rationale: Paul is concerned deeply enough about Onesimus being received as a beloved brother by Philemon that he is prepared to cover any hypothetical costs involved; indeed he rationalizes with the force of his signature. Paul believes Philemon will be persuaded by this rhetoric. He also rationalizes that Philemon will be moved by the logic (presented in a rhetorical paralipsis) that Philemon actually owes Paul more than anything possibly owed by Onesimus. The rationale of forgiveness of debts (surely a theological gospel motive and topos) is implicit.

---

21. Apophasis mentions by not mentioning. See apophatic theology, where God is described in terms of what God is not. Paralipsis (also spelled *paraleipsis*) is known by a number of terms including *praeteritio, cataphrasis, antiphrasis, occupatio, permissio,* and others.

THE MIDDLE, PHILEMON 8–20

Anticipated result: Philemon will receive Onesimus as a beloved brother in Christ.

This one is Paul taking a shot to drive the point home. By the way, Philemon, do you think Onesimus owes you? Well, Get over it!

The rhetoric of verse 20, step nine, forms the ending to the central argument by bringing the thought of the letter and of Philemon himself back to memory of his refreshing actions: "Yes, brother, might I possibly have this benefit from you in the Lord? Refresh my viscera in Christ!" These clauses repeat features of the language and ideas of verse 7, where Paul had said, "because the viscera of the holy ones have been refreshed by you, brother." The overall argument of the letter is closed by the recurring topoi of viscera, refreshment, and brotherhood. The actions anticipated already in verse 7 are explicitly requested in the positive call to Philemon in verse 20. Paul appeals to Philemon with the vocative "brother" (ἀδελφέ), evoking the familial connection he wishes for Philemon and Onesimus. This texturing argues by placing the currently socially low Paul, a prisoner, in kinship relationship with the socially prominent home- and slave owner. The socially low points out to the socially high the nature of the Christian relationship. Philemon will recognize, of course, the high, intellectual, gospel, and "in the Lord" nature of Paul's reasoning. Paul the prisoner calls for Philemon's refreshing action of receiving the slave Onesimus, who can no longer be a slave. Philemon has refreshed before, and he should now refresh again. In a remarkably subtle play on words that may or may not have been intentional, but does appear to be natural rhetoric, Paul employs the second-aorist-middle optative verb form ὀναίμην, a *hapax legomenon* in the New Testament, which means to benefit, to help, to assist, and to be useful and which sounds like the name Onesimus. The effect is rather like saying, "Onesimus is truly Onesimus, Philemon. The useful one is now genuinely useful. Let me have something useful out of this." Perhaps Paul's rhetoric is subtly calling for the double benefit: Onesimus is a brother to Philemon forever and a servant with Paul in the chains of the gospel (v. 13).

Case: Paul calls finally and movingly for the benefit of brotherhood between Philemon and Onesimus.

Rationale: Philemon is a brother and refresher of viscera. He is with Paul "in the Lord." Paul the prisoner calls for Philemon to

recognize these relationships and, consequently, do the beneficial, useful thing. Because Philemon has refreshed the holy ones
before, he should now do it again.

Anticipated result: Philemon will receive Onesimus no longer as a
slave but as a beloved brother.

Sensory-Aesthetic Texture

The *sensory-aesthetic texture* of the middle can be set out and analyzed in
the five steps of the following pattern:

Step three (vv. 8–9)
> [8] Διό, πολλὴν ἐν Χριστῷ παρρησίαν ἔχων ἐπιτάσσειν σοι τὸ ἀνῆκον,
>   [9] διὰ τὴν ἀγάπην μᾶλλον παρακαλῶ
> —τοιοῦτος ὢν ὡς Παῦλος πρεσβύτης
>   νυνὶ δὲ καὶ δέσμιος Χριστοῦ Ἰησοῦ—

> [8] Therefore, having much boldness in Christ to command your obedience,
>   [9] I appeal, rather, through love
> —I do this as Paul, an old man,
>   but now also a prisoner of Christ—

Step four (vv. 10–11)
> [10] παρακαλῶ σε περὶ τοῦ ἐμοῦ τέκνου,
> ὃν ἐγέννησα ἐν τοῖς δεσμοῖς, Ὀνήσιμον,
>   τόν ποτέ σοι ἄχρηστον
>   νυνὶ δὲ σοὶ καὶ ἐμοὶ εὔχρηστον

> [10] I appeal to you for my child
> —whom I have birthed in chains—*Onesimus*,
>   [11] who formerly was *useless* to you,
>   but now is *useful*—to you and to me—

Step five (vv. 12–14)
> [12] ὃν ἀνέπεμψά σοι αὐτόν,
>   τοῦτ᾽ ἔστιν τὰ ἐμὰ σπλάγχνα·
> [13] ὃν ἐγὼ ἐβουλόμην πρὸς ἐμαυτὸν κατέχειν,
>   ἵνα ὑπὲρ σοῦ μοι διακονῇ
>   ἐν τοῖς δεσμοῖς τοῦ εὐαγγελίου,
> [14] χωρὶς δὲ τῆς σῆς γνώμης οὐδὲν ἠθέλησα ποιῆσαι,

ἵνα μὴ ὡς κατὰ ἀνάγκην τὸ ἀγαθόν σου ᾖ
　　ἀλλὰ κατὰ ἑκούσιον

¹² whom I send back to you,
　　this one who is my own viscera—
¹³ whom I strongly wish to keep to myself,
　　so that he might serve me on your behalf
　　in the chains of the gospel.
¹⁴ But apart from your consent I wish to do nothing,
　　so that you do not do the good thing out of necessity,
　　　but voluntarily.

Step six (vv. 15–16)

¹⁵ τάχα γὰρ διὰ τοῦτο ἐχωρίσθη πρὸς ὥραν
　　ἵνα αἰώνιον αὐτὸν ἀπέχῃς,
¹⁶ οὐκέτι ὡς δοῦλον
　　　ἀλλὰ ὑπὲρ δοῦλον,
　　　ἀδελφὸν ἀγαπητόν,
　μάλιστα ἐμοί,
　πόσῳ δὲ μᾶλλον σοὶ
　　　καὶ ἐν σαρκὶ καὶ ἐν κυρίῳ.

¹⁵ For perhaps this is why he was separated from you for a while,
　　so that you might have him back forever,
　　¹⁶ no longer as a slave,
　　　but more than a slave,
　　　a beloved brother—
　　certainly to me,
　　but more to you,
　　　as in the flesh also in the Lord.

Step seven (vv. 17–20)

¹⁷ Εἰ οὖν με ἔχεις κοινωνόν,
　　προσλαβοῦ αὐτὸν ὡς ἐμέ.
¹⁸ εἰ δέ τι ἠδίκησέν σε ἢ ὀφείλει,
　　τοῦτο ἐμοὶ ἐλλόγα
　　　¹⁹ ἐγὼ Παῦλος ἔγραψα τῇ ἐμῇ χειρί,
　　　ἐγὼ ἀποτίσω
　　ἵνα μὴ λέγω σοι ὅτι καὶ σεαυτόν μοι προσοφείλεις.
²⁰ ναί, ἀδελφέ, ἐγώ σου ὀναίμην ἐν κυρίῳ·
ἀνάπαυσόν μου τὰ σπλάγχνα ἐν Χριστῷ.

¹⁷ If therefore you have me as partner,
    receive him as me.
¹⁸ But if he has wronged you or owes you anything,
    charge it to me.
       ¹⁹ I Paul, I write this in my own hand:
       I will repay it
     —not that I say that you owe yourself to me!
²⁰ Yes, brother, might I possibly have this benefit from you in the Lord?
Refresh my viscera in Christ!

Step three functions as transitional rhetoric linking the thanksgiving, step two, with the middle and the central argumentative rhetoric. The initial διό, an inferential conjunction, has the force "for this reason," indicating a continuation of idea from what precedes rather than a final or concluding notion. Philemon has been doing much good, and by stating it Paul has set Philemon up for an exhortation through love, not command. The sensory-aesthetic texturing is set out as follows:

⁸ Διό, πολλὴν ἐν Χριστῷ παρρησίαν ἔχων ἐπιτάσσειν σοι τὸ ἀνῆκον,
⁹ διὰ τὴν ἀγάπην μᾶλλον παρακαλῶ,
    —τοιοῦτος ὢν ὡς Παῦλος πρεσβύτης
    νυνὶ δὲ καὶ δέσμιος Χριστοῦ Ἰησοῦ—

⁸ Therefore, having much boldness in Christ to command your obedience,
⁹ I appeal, rather, through love
    —I do this as Paul, an old man,
    but now also a prisoner of Christ—

The physical sensory-aesthetic is focused again in Paul, with Philemon being the recipient of Paul's own sensory situation, love, and the behavioral and moral encouragement Paul is shortly to present. Paul makes a dramatic, emotional, personal sensory appeal: he is an old man and a prisoner. It is instructive that this rhetoric is composed of three virtually equal-length, melopoeic statements that convey this sensory-aesthetic vision ("I exhort"; "I am old"; "I am a prisoner"):

διὰ τὴν ἀγάπην μᾶλλον παρακαλῶ	12 syllables
τοιοῦτος ὢν ὡς Παῦλος πρεσβύτης	10 syllables
νυνὶ δὲ καὶ δέσμιος Χριστοῦ Ἰησοῦ	11 syllables

While he places himself on the side of strength in the relationship as one who could command Philemon to action, he simultaneously sets himself on the weak side of the relationship. He calls for Philemon to be moved to obey as someone who, he has already made emotionally clear, loves the Lord Jesus and all the holy ones, including, to be sure, old men and prisoners. The emphasis on Christ by repetition (ἐν Χριστῷ ... δέσμιος Χριστοῦ Ἰησοῦ) provides a sense of the positional authority of Christ. The authority clearly is Christ, not Paul himself, who in aesthetic terms is portrayed bodily in straitened position. Also, Paul is not a young, inexperienced, naive person. He is mature, knowledgeable, and fully engaged. His exhortation is difficult if not impossible to refuse. How can Philemon turn down an old man who is, it is implied, unfairly in prison for, what he must agree, is doing right and good things? The rhetoric plays on Philemon's knowledge of Paul, on his already strongly praised sense of love, and on his emotions. Still, Paul has not yet specified what he wants Philemon to do. Part of the sensory rhetoric is Paul's tactic of delay. He has not yet mentioned Onesimus. Paul has worked through the entire opening and transitional sections setting the sensory stage, persuading Philemon to recall his goodness toward people and his love for and faith in God. It is an honest setup. But Philemon knows Paul wants something, even if he is amenable to it. The παρακαλῶ of this transitional step is a feature of the sensory-aesthetic rhetoric that anticipates the repeated παρακαλῶ and the specific call of the middle and central argument of the letter.

Paul has played strongly on his own sensory condition. The repetition of the sound and imagery of δέσμιος Χριστοῦ Ἰησοῦ (vv. 1, 9) gives a level of primacy to the sound, image, and thoughts of both Paul and imprisonment since repeated words tend to be remembered. This is a major sensory-aesthetic feature of the letter. The sound and aesthetic texturing of Paul as a prisoner, indeed, as a prisoner of Christ, in whom Paul knows Philemon and those around him are also believers, presents a dramatic rhetoric. Paul is in a felt condition of suffering for what and for whom all concerned are connected by faith.

Through the entire middle section, as in the opening, first- and second-person personal pronouns and first- and second-person verbs stand out strongly. The sensory force is focused on Paul and Philemon. Onesimus with his own body and senses is crucial and central to the argument, but Paul's discourse places sensory pressure on the relationship between himself and Philemon. Philemon in his own body, in his own intellect, by his own judgment, and in good conscience should hear Paul's appeal and refresh Paul's viscera.[22]

Step four repeats the emotional appeal to the senses with παρακαλῶ, now employed to make his specific call[23] to Philemon. Paul plays his pitiable, self-effacing best by placing himself and Onesimus in a stressed situation. He is, as he has already stated (vv. 1, 9), a prisoner in chains, bound.[24] This uncomfortable status continues to have a powerful sensory appeal; Paul addresses Philemon as a prisoner and now appeals to Philemon from those chains. Paul strategizes that his situation will be part of what will move Philemon to do what he wishes. Significantly, Paul continues in this step as a "prisoner of Christ," not explicitly of civil authorities.[25] The rhetoric emphasizes the notion of being bound, imprisoned, chained, tied. The repetition reinforces the sensibility of the appeal. Now assuming he has obtained Philemon's goodwill, Paul raises the name of Onesimus—the first and only time he is named in the letter—as the person for whom he wishes Philemon to be concerned. In his chains, Paul has birthed "his child," Onesimus. The feminine imagery of giving birth, begetting (ἐγέννησα, from γεννάω), evokes a dramatic family and biological aesthetic and elicits the memory of the already employed "brother" kinship idea. The parallelism of the lines presents the aesthetic. The child (τοῦ ἐμοῦ τέκνου) is Onesimus (useful), who was useless (ἄχρηστον) but is now useful (εὔχρηστον). The lines of this step have a balanced rhythm (τοῦ ἐμοῦ τέκνου, genitive homoioteleuton; Ὀνήσιμον, ἄχρηστον, εὔχρηστον, accusative homoioteleuton). The ποτέ/νυνί, then/now structure brings out the before-and-after notion, indicating that former sensory situations with regard to Onesimus have changed for the better.

---

22. Affecting the "zone of emotion-fused thought," Bruce J. Malina, *The New Testament World: Insights From Cultural Anthropology*, 3rd ed. (Louisville: Westminster John Knox, 2001), 69; Vernon K. Robbins, *Exploring the Texture of Texts: A Guide to Socio-rhetorical Interpretation* (Valley Forge, PA: Trinity Press International, 1996), 30–31.

23. A "call" since παρακαλέω is built on the root word καλέω ("call").

24. The "zone of purposeful action," Malina, *New Testament World*, 69; Robbins, *Exploring*, 31.

25. Though we assume he is actually imprisoned. Compare this with Paul's statement about Epaphras, συναιχμάλωτός μου ἐν Χριστῷ Ἰησοῦ (v. 23, "captive with me in Christ Jesus") from αἰχμάλωτός ("prisoner of war") a miserable person who needs God's help (Gerhard Kittel, "Αἰχμάλωτός," *TDNT* 1:195–97). They are seen as captives, imprisoned. See below on **intertexture**. See the introduction.

Step five continues to press on the you/me discourse that places personal pressure on Philemon while emphasizing Onesimus in bodily form being sent by Paul to Philemon. The one "whom" (repetitive ὅν) Paul sends is described in sensory, bodily terms by the repeated τὰ ἐμὰ σπλάγχνα ("my viscera"). In this way Paul indicates again the particularly close connection between himself and Onesimus. The pathos is deep and personal, and the rhetoric is therefore powerful.[26] Onesimus is to be imagined as the emotionally presented Paul himself. Philemon is meant to "get" this emotional connection and to react positively to it. Philemon would have to be a hard man to refuse this kind of sensory appeal. The first-person verbs (ἀνέπεμψά ... ἐβουλόμην ... ἠθέλησα, "I send ... I wish ... I wish"), the second one emphasized by the personal pronoun (ἐγὼ ἐβουλόμην, "I strongly wish"), show Paul taking the initiative. It is Paul's mental, emotional, and physical action that is observed, in anticipation of a similar response from Philemon. Paul wants Onesimus to stay with him, to function aesthetically as his servant, tied emotionally with Paul to the very thing to which Philemon has been faithful, namely, the gospel of the Lord Jesus (see step two). The melopoeic force of the lines of this step builds up toward sensory resolution in two ἵνα statements:

> ¹²ὃν ἀνέπεμψά σοι αὐτόν,
> 　τοῦτ᾽ ἔστιν τὰ ἐμὰ σπλάγχνα
> ¹³ὃν ἐγὼ ἐβουλόμην πρὸς ἐμαυτὸν κατέχειν,
> 　ἵνα ὑπὲρ σοῦ μοι διακονῇ
> 　ἐν τοῖς δεσμοῖς τοῦ εὐαγγελίου,
> ¹⁴χωρὶς δὲ τῆς σῆς γνώμης οὐδὲν ἠθέλησα ποιῆσαι,
> 　ἵνα μὴ ὡς κατὰ ἀνάγκην τὸ ἀγαθόν σου ᾖ
> 　ἀλλὰ κατὰ ἑκούσιον·

> ¹²whom I send back to you,
> 　this one who is my own viscera—
> ¹³whom I strongly wish to keep to myself,
> 　**so that** he might serve me on your behalf
> 　in the chains of the gospel.
> ¹⁴But apart from your consent I wish to do nothing,
> 　**so that** you do not do the good thing out of necessity,
> 　but voluntarily.

26. The NRSV translation (and others) "my own heart" conveys a modern view of the idea, for emotions are, popularly, felt "in the heart."

Two major action points are indicated in the parallel pronoun plus first-person verb lines (ὃν ἀνέπεμψά and ὃν ἐγὼ ἐβουλόμην) with their corresponding sound effects (e.g., pronouns of the same sound and form; ὅν/ὅν; αὐτόν/ἐμαυτόν). This is enhanced by the cadence of -α and -ν word endings. This flow of sound coming out of Paul's viscera along with the vision of his imprisonment is turned back on Philemon by the contrasting "apart from you" line. This sets Philemon in sensory contrast to Paul, implying that Philemon is the person in control when both know that Paul is controlling the discourse. Paul turns his gut feelings back on Philemon for response. The question is palpable: will Philemon do what Paul the emotive prisoner wants? Paul appeals for cooperation and will not move ahead without Philemon's consent. The emotional pressure is on Philemon. The sensory resolution for Philemon, or at least what points toward resolution, comes out in those ἵνα statements:

> ἵνα ὑπὲρ σοῦ μοι διακονῇ
> ἐν τοῖς δεσμοῖς τοῦ εὐαγγελίου
>
> so that he might serve me on your behalf
> in the chains of the gospel.
>
> ἵνα μὴ ὡς κατὰ ἀνάγκην τὸ ἀγαθόν σου ᾖ
>   ἀλλὰ κατὰ ἑκούσιον
> so that you do not do the good thing out of necessity,
>   but voluntarily.

It is for the sake of the gospel that Paul makes his appeal to Philemon. Philemon must make the decision regarding this matter by his own free will. The sensory-aesthetic, pathos message for Philemon is that the underlying issue is about the gospel and the answer to it is up to him. The pressure on Philemon is not, to be sure, entirely emotional. It has a logical, intellectual component that requires Philemon to think about the situation and what he will do. But this does not detract from the sensory, emotional rhetoric of the language.

Step six appeals to the senses by suggesting (τάχα, "perhaps," "possibly") a gospel understanding for what has happened.

> τάχα γὰρ διὰ τοῦτο ἐχωρίσθη πρὸς ὥραν
>   ἵνα αἰώνιον αὐτὸν ἀπέχῃς,
>   οὐκέτι ὡς δοῦλον

ἀλλὰ ὑπὲρ δοῦλον,
ἀδελφὸν ἀγαπητόν,
μάλιστα ἐμοί,
πόσῳ δὲ μᾶλλον σοὶ
καὶ ἐν σαρκὶ καὶ ἐν κυρίῳ.

[15] For perhaps this is why he was separated from you for a while,
so that you might have him back forever,
[16] no longer as a slave,
but more than a slave,
a beloved brother—
certainly to me,
but more to you,
as in the flesh also in the Lord.

The word τάχα indicates that the ideas of this step are for Philemon to ponder, to penetrate the "zone of emotion-fused thought" so that they can have effect. Perhaps Onesimus was separated from Philemon for a period of time for a particular purpose. Paul does not here indicate or even suggest any other reason for Onesimus's departure and current separation. Rather, he plays off of the felt knowledge that Philemon knows (and Paul knows he knows) that Onesimus is gone and off of the sensory and faith notion that God may have been involved in it. This sensory effect has a forward-looking view: "so that you might have him back forever" (ἀπέχῃς, second-person aorist subjunctive, "have him back"; from ἀπέχω), and at that future moment Onesimus will no longer be a slave, but more than (beyond, above, exceeding) a slave, a beloved brother. Paul has moved Onesimus along in terms of kinship from being his "child" now to Philemon's "beloved brother." Paul has already used the appellative "brother" to refer to Philemon (v. 7) and will shortly do so again (v. 20). Philemon can hardly miss the emotional kinship connections of brotherhood. This is, of course, subversive of the usual aesthetic of slavery of the Roman period and undoubtedly goes against Philemon's own sensibilities.[27] Paul gives the clear sensory impression that as a Christ-believer he stands against slavery and that those who are in fact enslaved are to be seen as slaves no longer but as loved family members. Paul is an abolitionist certainly on

---

27. See sections below on **intertexture** and **social and cultural texture**. If there was no conflict with Philemon's sensibilities Paul might not have written the letter.

the emotional, sensory, and gospel level of his thinking.[28] Being a slave does not matter now; what matters is reconciliation and brotherhood. According to Paul's sensory, gospel approach slaves are implicitly free brothers. How things are under the gospel is how things should be in the world, with eternal implications. The decision, though, is now up to Philemon. The rhetorical force is placed directly on him. Paul intensifies this rhetorical effect with the superlative μάλιστα and contrasting comparative μᾶλλον, both forms of μάλα ("very much, exceedingly"). Onesimus is "certainly" considered by Paul to be his brother and, Paul stressing his point, to be considered *"much more"* as a brother to Philemon "in the flesh and in the Lord." By these coordinated prepositional dative phrases (καὶ ἐν σαρκὶ καὶ ἐν κυρίῳ), Paul presses home the sensorially physiological, theologically locative, gospel notions with which he is working. Philemon is meant to recognize intellectually and emotively that Onesimus is now his beloved brother in superlative terms. These points are conveyed in the sound orchestration of the language. In the previous step Paul indicated he would do nothing "apart from" (χωρίς) Philemon's consent and in this step uses the cognate form and sound "apart from" (ἐχωρίσθη) to describe the current situation. The notion of this double separation from Philemon is thus crucial to the sensory progression. The melodic and balanced progression οὐκέτι ὡς δοῦλον ... ἀλλὰ ὑπὲρ δοῦλον ... ἀδελφὸν ἀγαπητόν with its accusative endings and six-syllable form sends a subtle euphonic message. The sounds and dative pronoun endings of the final statement of the step reinforce the ideas.

Step seven moves the senses and emotions back to the relationship between Paul and Philemon. This *sensory-aesthetic texturing* is direct and probably uncomfortable for Philemon. He is left no room to maneuver without appearing to be something much different from the loving and faithful man he has been described to be.[29] Paul the old man, prisoner, father, brother, sufferer, worker, praiser of Philemon, friend of the loving faithful Philemon—the one who always remembers Philemon in his prayers—makes a direct, personal request: "If, therefore, you have me

---

28. See his employment of the metaphor of slavery in, e.g., Rom 6:15–23. See also 1 Cor 7:20–24; Gal 3:28.

29. The later references to someone named Onesimus as a bishop in Ephesus (d. c. 90 CE) in Ignatius, *Eph* 1.3 (see nn. 48 and 78 in the introduction, above), if the same person—apart from having the same name there is no evidence for it—suggests that the letter may have had its intended effect.

as partner, receive him as me." Paul seems certain that Philemon knows and will be touched by the nature of their relationship as partners. He has already spoken of the "partnership" of Philemon's faith (κοινωνία, v.6, cognate of κοινωνός), picking up on the relational notion again here in sound and aesthetic meaning. Paul and Philemon are partners in gospel faith and interests. The notion of partnership implies honesty, trust, sharing, and cooperation. Paul is keeping his side of the partnership and places the pressure on Philemon to keep his side. If Paul now trusts Onesimus, then his partner Philemon should also trust Onesimus. In this sensory and personal context, Philemon is called to engage in a personal, deeply emotive action: "receive him as [if he were] me." When Philemon sees Onesimus, he should imagine him as if he were his partner, Paul, present. The sound coordination, or melopoeia, is perceptible in the beat and measure,[30] even if not directly worked out by ordinary listeners. The statements beginning with εἰ are coordinated together to make the point rhythmically.

> Εἰ οὖν με ἔχεις κοινωνόν,
>   προσλαβοῦ αὐτὸν ὡς ἐμέ.
> εἰ δέ τι ἠδίκησέν σε ἢ ὀφείλει,
>   τοῦτο ἐμοὶ ἐλλόγα

[17] **If** therefore you have me as partner,
    receive him as me.
[18] But **if** he has wronged you or owes you anything,
    charge it to me.

The lines of the first colon are balanced with eight syllables each. The pronouns με, ἐμέ, σε, and ἐμοί play on similarity of sound and meaning and keep the sensory focus on Paul and Philemon. The encouragement to "receive" Onesimus is enhanced by the second colon, which suggests the possibility that Onesimus has done something against Philemon or owes something to him. We imagine Paul raising his hand in a defensive gesture that appeals to Philemon's sense of sight. Paul wishes whatever it is to be charged to himself. Onesimus might have done something wrong, but Paul does not hold it against him and is willing to pay for it—no doubt being fairly certain that he will not have to pay. The force is enhanced by

---

30. On the connection between grammar and music, see Quintilian, *Inst.* 1.10.17–20.

the pronouns: "**me** your partner?" then "charge **me**." The future verb "I will repay" (ἐλλόγα) stands in contrast to the aorist verb "he has wronged" (ἠδίκησέν) and the present verb "he owes" (ὀφείλει), bringing the sense of time to mind. Whatever Onesimus might have done in the past will be covered by Paul in the future. Philemon will recognize that Paul is playing on their sense of partnership. Paul and Philemon will both recognize that the potential future benefit is to be refused.

Yet Paul continues, expands, and intensifies the rhetorical aesthetic by emphasizing his personal commitment.

> ἐγὼ Παῦλος ἔγραψα τῇ ἐμῇ χειρί,
> ἐγὼ ἀποτίσω

> [19] I Paul, I write this in my own hand:
> I will repay it

The first-person pronouns and first-person verbs press on the partnership and on the personalities of Paul and Philemon. Paul is pushing hard on their relationship and on the implicit memory of himself as prisoner, old man, and proclaimer of the gospel. He makes it directly physiological and sensory by emphatically inserting his own hand in the action of writing into Philemon's emotional space: "I Paul, I write with **my** own hand." It is as if Philemon can see Paul's hand forming the letters he is reading. There is a direct connection between Paul's hand and Philemon's eyes (and/or ears) as the words come to him. But then, Paul dramatically throws the sensory-aesthetic pressure from his own hand and from his declaration of intent to repay onto Philemon's physiology and sense of honor in a subtle yet remarkably powerful subordinate clause: "not that I say that you owe yourself to me!" (ἵνα μὴ λέγω σοι ὅτι καὶ σεαυτόν μοι προσοφείλεις). This is the subordinate clause that kills, the coup de grâce that surely Philemon could not refuse. Philemon owes Paul everything, certainly from a gospel point of view. The one whom Paul promises to pay is the very one who owes Paul his own soul. Philemon has, metaphorically, burning coals heaped on his head (Rom 12:20). Paul does not need to spell out why Philemon owes himself to Paul; Philemon already knows and so understands Paul's implication. There is nothing left except for Philemon to do the right thing vis-à-vis Onesimus *and* Paul. The sensory figure is paralipsis (or apophasis; *occupatio*), where a speaker invokes a topic by denying it should be invoked ("not that I say").³¹ Paul closes and draws his appeal together with an apparently friendly, soothing, kinship appeal to good works: "Yes, brother, might I possibly have this benefit from you in the Lord?" and the more imperative "Refresh my viscera in Christ!" Paul addresses Philemon as his brother, as a family member and an equal in the Lord, as one with some level of power in contrast to the apparently powerless Onesimus, whom he previously called his "child." The optative mood of the first-person-singular verb ὀναίμην must be consciously and intentionally employed³² as a means of making a polite request while anticipating a positive response.³³ By calling on Philemon to refresh his viscera, or, more literally, "to give rest"³⁴ for his viscera, Paul employs a sensory double metaphor (rest and viscera) that tells Philemon that if he receives Onesimus and treats him as a brother ("receive him as me," v. 17) rather than as a slave, he will be simultaneously making life better for old Paul, his friend who prays for him. The shift to the imperative, with the verb ἀνάπαυσόν, pushes Philemon to make the decision, to perform the action, to give Paul some relief and some benefit regarding this matter. The refreshment Paul expects to experience will be both emotional and physiological. These two lines flow together in a neat balance of thirteen and eleven syllables.

ναί, ἀδελφέ, ἐγώ σου ὀναίμην ἐν κυρίῳ·
ἀνάπαυσόν μου τὰ σπλάγχνα ἐν Χριστῷ.

²⁰ Yes, brother, might I possibly have this benefit from you in the Lord?
Refresh my viscera in Christ!

Both end, poetically, with ἐν followed by dative -ῳ sound endings that convey the same apparently locative sensory "in Christ" meaning and implication.³⁵ They emphasize the distinctly gospel context of the entire letter and the entire appeal being made. When the initial words are sepa-

---

31. See above on *argumentative texture*.

32. Wallace, *Greek Grammar*, 480. The optative form of the verb ὀνίνημι (ὀναίμην), "might I possibly have this benefit," is found elsewhere in biblical literature only in Sir 30:2.

33. Ibid., 481.

34. See Barth and Blanke, *Letter to Philemon*, 297–301.

35. Perhaps Paul has "body of Christ" notions in mind since he addresses, along with Philemon, "the church in your house" (v. 2; cf., e.g., 1 Cor 12:12–27).

rated off, the poetry is quite clearly measured and balanced in the parallelism of sound.

ἐγώ σου ὀναίμην ἐν κυρίῳ·
ἀνάπαυσόν μου τὰ σπλάγχνα ἐν Χριστῷ.

might I possibly have this benefit **from you in the Lord**?
Refresh **my** viscera **in Christ**!

The sensory-aesthetic effect is obvious.

Intertexture

The Appeal

Paul employs the word παρακαλῶ (παρακαλέω) to make his appeal to Philemon (9, 10).[36] This common verb occurs frequently in the Pauline Letters, particularly in moral discourse.[37] It is used in Eph 6:22 and Col 4:8 in a way rhetorically similar to what is observed in Philemon to indicate an appeal to the heart (παρακαλέσῃ τὰς καρδίας ὑμῶν). In Acts 9:38; 14:22; Heb 10:25; and Jude 3, it is used to urge people to behave in ways that accord with faith and proclamation. This intertexturality of appeal was familiar to Greek speakers and so to Philemon. Paul does not command Philemon, as he makes clear (v. 8); he appeals to him, urges him persuasively, to receive Onesimus. It is clear intertexturally that Paul understands how to act and speak with "boldness" (παρρησία, v. 8; cf. 2 Cor 3:12; 7:4; Phil 1:20), but here he appeals implicitly to Philemon's own σπλάγχνα, a pathos appeal, for the reception he believes is right. This approach is textured in a way similar to Pliny's letter to Sabinianus[38] where Pliny says, "I am afraid you will think I am using pressure, not persuasion" (Pliny, *Ep.* 9.21).[39] This indicates that such careful approaches to appealing to and

---

36. Παρακαλέω has a broad semantic range ("appeal," "exhort," "urge," "encourage," "comfort"). For a thorough discussion of this word, see C. J. Bjerkelund, *Parakalō, Form, Funktion und Sinn der parakalō-Sätze in den paulinischen Briefen* (Oslo: Universitetsforlaget, 1967).

37. E.g., Rom 12:1; 15:30; 16:17; 1 Cor 1:10; 4:16; 16:15; 2 Cor 2:7–8; 8:6; 9:5; 10:1; 13:11; Phil 4:2; 1 Thess 2:12; 4:18; 5:11; Eph 4:1; 1 Tim 2:1; Tit 1:9.

38. On which see below.

39. As in Dunn, *Colossians and Philemon*, 326.

appealing for people were well understood and often employed. Appealing "through love" (διὰ τὴν ἀγάπην) is foundational to all relationships among believers.[40] The pressure added by Paul stating that he makes his appeal as "an old man, but now also as a prisoner of Christ" (v. 9) suggests intextural connections about Paul's age from Philo's description of "seven ages."

> Solon therefore thus computes the life of man by the aforesaid ten periods of seven years. But Hippocrates the physician says that there are seven ages of man, infancy, childhood, boyhood, youth, manhood, *middle age* [πρεσβύτου, "elder, senior"], old age [γέροντος, from γέρων]; and that these too, are measured by periods of seven, though not in the same order. And he speaks thus; "In the nature of man there are seven seasons, which men call ages; infancy, childhood, boyhood, and the rest. He is an infant till he reaches his seventh year, the age of the shedding of his teeth. He is a child till he arrives at the age of puberty, which takes place in fourteen years. He is a boy till his beard begins to grow, and that time is the end of a third period of seven years. He is a youth till the completion of the growth of his whole body, which coincides with the fourth seven years. Then he is a man till he reaches his forty-ninth year, or seven times seven periods. He is a middle aged man (elder) till he is fifty-six, or eight times seven years old; and after that he is an old man. (Philo, *Opif.* 105 [Colson, LCL])[41]

The πρεσβύτης is the sixth of the seven age categories. This intertexturality suggests that Paul was fifty to fifty-six years old when his appeal to Philemon was made. Certainly this feature is meant to persuade Philemon to have appropriate respect for an older person (see Lev 19:32; Sir 8:6; see also Luke 1:18; Titus 2:2–3; Mart. Pol. 7.2).

With the second occurrence of παρακαλῶ, old Paul the prisoner refers to Onesimus as his child (cf. 1 Cor 4:14, 17), whom he has himself "birthed" (ὃν ἐγέννησα, v. 10). The same verb form is employed in the Septuagint in Isa 1:2, where God is described as having birthed sons and raised them. Paul himself states that he birthed the members of the church in Corinth through the gospel (1 Cor 4:15; see also Gal 4:19). The language suggests

---

40. E.g., Rom 5:8; 12:9–10; 1 Cor 13; Gal 5:13–14.

41. On this, see Barth and Blanke, *Letter to Philemon*, 321–22; Dunn, *Colossians and Philemon*, 327. See Philo, *Opif.* 103–106. See also the stages described by Seneca in *Ep.* 12.6. See also Censorinus, *De Die Natali* 14 (third century CE), who describes persons from forty-six to sixty as seniors, "because the human body then commences to grow old" (*senescere*).

that Paul thinks of believers he knows in very close, relational ways, though he refers only to Onesimus, Timothy, and Titus by the term "child" (τέχνον, 1 Cor 4:17; Phil 2:22; 1 Tim 1:2, 18; 2 Tim 1:2; 2:1; Titus 1:4). This idea and language is, then, part of the emotional, cultural, and rhetorical milieu in which Paul thinks and lives, and it flows into the rhetoric of Philemon.[42] Paul's concern that Philemon "consent" to the appeal "voluntarily" (κατὰ ἑκούσιον, v. 14) stands in the fairly wide intertextural milieu of usage of the noun γνώμη. This word has to do with the mind and with knowing.[43] It is employed in classical Greek literature to describe thought, judgment, intelligence, understanding, opinion, and disposition.[44] It indicates the result of careful thought, hence intention, consent, and agreement with an idea or action. Paul uses γνώμη a number of times (1 Cor 1:10; 7:25–26, 40; 2 Cor 8:10),[45] indicating agreement, opinion, or consent. The word is also used with the same notion in mind in Acts 20:3 and Rev 17:13, 17, and in the Septuagint in 2 Macc 4:39 and Wis 7:15. This intertexturality shows that, although Paul has made a strong pathos appeal, playing on Philemon's emotions (vv. 8–13, to which he returns, vv. 17–20), he wishes Philemon to come to his own carefully considered, critical understanding of the situation and what should be done.

Partnership

Paul visualizes Philemon as his "partner" (κοινωνός) and calls on him to receive Onesimus as if he were Paul himself, thus also as a partner. While the term "partner" has a commercial tone, Paul here imagines himself and Philemon—and by extension Onesimus—as partners in things related to the gospel and the *ekklēsia*. He portrays Philemon as having the same understanding of their relationship. The notion of partnership demonstrates that the situation regarding Onesimus is not simple, it is not just about receiving the separated person back again, nor is it only about slavery or about welcoming a slave as a brother. It is about the complex relationship between Paul and Philemon.

---

42. For extensive detail, see "Excursus: Inclusive Language of Procreation" in Barth and Blanke, *Letter to Philemon*, 329–35.

43. LSJ 354.

44. See LSJ 354; MM §864; Josephus, *Ant.* 7.60.

45. Cf. the compound noun συγγνώμη in 1 Cor 7:6, "concession," with knowledgeable, reasoned consent.

The intertextural complexity and force of κοινωνός are striking in the way they reveal much about the scope of partnered relationships. The word has a broad semantic range in the New Testament. James, John, and Simon Peter were partners in a fishing business according to Luke 5:10. According to Matt 23:(29–)30, Jesus claims that hypocritical scribes and Pharisees state that they would not have been "partners" with their ancestors who shed the blood of prophets. Paul, according to 1 Cor 10:18, 20, urges members of the church in Corinth to avoid idolatry, arguing that those who (as in Israel) eat the sacrifices in idolatrous worship are "partners" of the altar (v. 18). This argument shows that Christ-believers should not participate in idolatrous worship because they would thereby become "partners" of demons (vv. 20–21). Paul speaks of Corinthian believers as "partners in our suffering" (2 Cor 1:7) and of Titus as his "partner" for the benefit of the Corinthians (2 Cor 8:23). Hebrews 10:33 points out that some faithful persons had been persecuted and were sometimes "partners" of others who were persecuted. The elder (author) of 1 Pet 5:1 speaks of being the "partner" in the glory to be revealed. Second Peter 1:4 envisions becoming "partners" in the divine nature. In the Septuagint, κοινωνός is employed in similar ways. It describes persons who steal from their parents, thinking it no crime, as "partners with thugs" (Prov 28:24). Isaiah 1:23, somewhat similarly, speaks of corrupt princes who have become the "partners of thieves." Malachi 2:14 complains about those who have been unfaithful to the wives of their youth even though the wives were their partners. Sirach 41:19 calls immoral persons to be ashamed of their behavior, including those who have treated their "partners" and friends unjustly. People should avoid shame by keeping correct accounts with their "partners" (Sir 43:2). Some "friendly partners" will dine with people whom they will abandon in times of trouble (Sir 6:10).

These uses of κοινωνός imply sharing among people who are bound together in various positive ways (business, friendship, faith, proclamation, persecution, the expectation of glory) and in various negative ways (thugs, thieves, unfaithful husbands, immoral behavior). Partnered relationships in the ancient Mediterranean were in general, however, made between persons considered to be equals. Partnerships were not normally formed between owners and slaves or, it would be imagined, between homeowners like Philemon and imprisoned and itinerant preachers like Paul (on this see Plato, *Leg.* 756e–757a; Aristotle, *Eth. nic.* 8.11.6–7; Seneca, *Ep.* 47).

These intertexts demonstrate that partnerships were formed between and among persons who had affinities of social or ethical status. Partnership between Philemon and Paul and between Philemon and Onesimus would therefore have been socially unexpected and socially questionable. The letter in this way turns out to be not only, perhaps not even primarily, about Philemon's reception of Onesimus, but about the relationship between Paul and Philemon. Philemon is imagined both by himself and by Paul as Paul's partner. This is not about business or commerce, but about two persons who have been affected by the gospel. It is a gospel partnership, not a commercial one. Philemon is requested to respond as a Christ-believing partner, one on an equal footing, with Paul, not as a slave owner, householder, or as the injured party in the separation. It does have the scent of binding relationships of the commercial world, but it is, despite the debt and payment notions of verses 18–19, about following up on and maintaining the relationship between Paul and Philemon.

Debt

The notion of debt touches on a range of **intertextures**. Paul, obviously, understands the idea of being in debt (ὀφείλω, "owe, be in debt, be obligated to pay"; ἐλλογέω, "charge to one's account"; ἀποτίνω,[46] "repay"). The term "charge" (ἐλλογέω) was common in accounting procedures. Debt can be understood as money owed or as something owed of a more moral or behavioral nature. Paul's foundational view seems to be that, apart from the sacred and moral obligation to love, debts of all kinds should be avoided: "Owe no one anything, except to love one another; for the one who loves another has fulfilled the law" (Rom 13:8). Debt in the Roman Mediterranean could be incurred from borrowing, tax arrears, theft, or failure to perform an expected function.[47] Paul will also have understood debt in a clear relation to the forgiveness of or freedom from debt. According to the Torah, Hebrew slaves could be kept for six years, but in the seventh year

46. Used only here in the New Testament.
47. According to Jean Andreau, there was no real public debt during the Greco-Roman era. Personal debt, however, led to a number of financial crises. Law regarding usurious loans was sometimes ignored, but later revived when it led to civil unrest (Tacitus, *Ann.* 6.16). Overwhelming taxation burdens were occasionally reduced or written off (Tacitus, *Ann.* 1.76.4; 2.42). See Jean Andreau, "Personal Endebtment and Debt Forgiveness in the Roman Empire," Committee for the Abolition of Third World Debt website, 17 December 2012, http://cadtm.org/Personal-endebtment-and-debt; Andreau, *Banking and Business in the Roman World* (Cambridge: Cambridge University Press, 1999).

they were to be freed without debt (Exod 21:2; Deut 15:1).[48] David, after he had escaped from threats made by King Saul and was hiding in the cave of Adullam, became the leader of "everyone who was in distress, and everyone who was in debt, and everyone who was discontented" (1 Sam 22:2). Debt, a great stressor for people, was something from which there was some hope of freedom. Paul may have been familiar with the proverb that says, "Do not be one of those who give pledges, who become surety for debts" (Prov 22:26). The right thing to do is to forgive debts. During the Hasmonean period, after Jonathan became high priest, the Seleucid king Demetrius II issued the decree absolving some persons from debt: "All who take refuge at the temple in Jerusalem, or in any of its precincts, because they owe money to the king or are in debt, let them be released and receive back all their property in the kingdom" (1 Macc 10:43). Later, King Antiochus VII made a similar decree of cancellation of debts (1 Macc 15:8). Fourth Maccabees 2:8 points out that when the law is learned and observed carefully even one who loves money will act against what seems natural by lending to the needy without interest and by canceling debts during the seventh year. In a not altogether dissimilar description, Jesus, in the parable of the unforgiving slave (Matt 18:23–35), speaks of a compassionate king who forgave the debt of a slave who appealed to him. This slave, in his turn, refused the same forgiveness to another slave. Serious punishment resulted. According to Luke 7:41–43, Jesus used the example of a creditor who canceled the debts of debtors who could not pay. On a more behavioral and moral level, Paul speaks of what wives and husbands "owe" each other sexually (1 Cor 7:3). Paul understands the concept of the forgiveness of debts. Debt and the forgiveness of debt parallels the slavery and freedom that he requests for Onesimus. There is an intertextural dyadic paradigm of debt/forgiveness, slavery/freedom in Paul's thinking.

In this cultural and intertextural milieu, Paul says he is prepared to pay for any debt Onesimus owes to Philemon (vv. 18–19). He signs his name to it.[49] He lives in an intertextural realm where debts that are not forgiven are understood as things to be paid (see Eccl 5:4–5). One could offer to pay for debts that were not, strictly speaking, one's own. Josephus, for example, who had received twenty pieces of gold taken from a Jewish

---

48. Under specified circumstances a slave could choose to stay with an owner for life. A pierced ear was the physical indication of this commitment (Exod 21:3–6).

49. On Paul personally signing his name as a sign of greeting or good faith, see 1 Cor 16:21; Gal 6:11; Col 4:18.

palace in Galilee during the first Jewish revolt and had given the money to ambassadors going to Jerusalem, undertook to repay it himself.

> Well, if I did wrong in paying your deputies out of public money, you need have no further cause for resentment; I will pay the twenty pieces of gold myself. (Josephus, *Life* 57 [Thackeray, LCL])

Intertexture shows that in judgment there is (will be) an equalizing of creditors and debtors as also there is (will be) an equalizing of masters and slaves.

> And it shall be, as with the people so with the priest;
>   as with the slave, so with his master,
>   as with the maid, so with her mistress;
>   as with the buyer, so with the seller;
>   as with lender so with the borrower;
>   as with the creditor, so with the debtor. (Isa 24:2)

A righteous person restores the pledges made by debtors (see Ezek 18:5–9).

For Paul, then, it follows implicitly that any debt—if there actually was any real debt—owed by Onesimus was to be forgiven by Philemon. Elevation to brotherhood for Onesimus means, for Paul and for Philemon, the dyadic condition of freedom/forgiveness. Paul surely does not anticipate that his signed statement will be called, that he will be required to pay off, presumably in cash, some debt allegedly owed by Onesimus. He anticipates the cancellation of debt and of slavery. The foundational **intertexture** for Paul, Philemon, and Onesimus is the gospel, that is, that "Christ died for our sins" (1 Cor 15:3). All debts/sins have been canceled. Ironically, it turns out that Philemon, morally speaking, is the debtor: "not that I say that you still owe [προσοφείλεις] yourself to me!" (v. 19).[50]

Slave and Slavery

Onesimus is described as and was a slave (δοῦλος, v. 16). His exact status as a slave—indeed whether he even was a slave—when the Letter to Philemon was composed is widely discussed, and a number of scenarios have

---

50. The word προσοφείλω (a compound form of ὀφείλω) is used only here in the New Testament.

been proposed.[51] The questions typically posed by interpreters are: What is the specific (historical) situation of the slave Onesimus? What specific (historical) situation with regard to slavery is in view in Philemon? What intertextual resources clarify the situation? The fact is that we do not have certain and clear answers to these questions. While many interpreters analyze the available information, the letter itself does not say whether Onesimus was a *fugitivus*, a messenger, on an errand, or that he sought out Paul as an intercessor. Since he is explicitly called δοῦλος, it is difficult to understand how the letter could mean he was an actual genetic brother to Philemon.[52] The letter makes clear only the basic information that Paul is imprisoned, that Onesimus and Philemon are separated (v. 15), that Onesimus has become a believer in Christ Jesus, and that Paul is sending Onesimus back to Philemon. There is also the suggestion that Philemon is displeased with the "useless" Onesimus (v. 11) and that Onesimus might not be graciously received on his return to Philemon (vv. 11–20). Intertextural analysis sheds little if any light on the *actual* situations of Onesimus, Philemon, and Paul. What it does provide is information about the general contexts and conditions for assessing the institution and conditions of slaves and slavery in the Mediterranean world and for assessing the change from slavery to brotherhood in the *ekklēsia*. Intertextural analysis also provides rhetorical context and imagery for assessing Paul's language and for how the letter functions.

Since the letter comes from Paul, the nearest **intertextures** are found where he discusses slavery in other letters. Paul seems to think, as a matter of principle as a Christ-believer, that there is an equality of slaves and freepersons in Christ ("there is no longer slave or free … for all of you are one in Christ Jesus," Gal 3:28; "For just as the body is one and has many members, and all the members of the body, though many, are one body, so it is with Christ. For in the one Spirit we were all baptized into one body—Jews or Greeks, slaves or free—and we were all made to drink of one Spirit," 1 Cor 12:13; "In that renewal there is no longer … slave and free; but Christ is all and in all!" Col 3:11). Paul advises believers not to be concerned about having been called to faith as slaves and that slaves themselves are freepersons who belong to Christ as his slaves ("Were you a slave when called? Do not be concerned about it.… For whoever was called in

---

51. See the introduction for a survey of views.

52. As Allen Dwight Callahan, *Embassy of Onesimus: The Letter of Paul to Philemon* (Valley Forge, PA: Trinity Press International, 1997). See the introduction.

the Lord as a slave is a freed person belonging to the Lord, just as whoever
was free when called is a slave of Christ," 1 Cor 7:21–23). People in Christ
are, to Paul, by definition free ("For freedom Christ has set us free. Stand
firm, therefore, and do not submit again to a yoke of slavery," Gal 5:1); yet
at the same time they are to be intentional, as freepersons, about becoming
slaves to each other ("For you were called to freedom, brothers and sisters;
only do not use your freedom as an opportunity for the flesh, but through
love become slaves to one another," Gal 5:13). He refers to the incarnation
as Christ Jesus himself becoming a slave ("who … emptied himself, taking
the form of a slave, being born in human likeness," Phil 2:6–7). Using slavery as a powerful metaphor, Paul describes believers' former lives as slaves
to sin leading to death and how they have been set free to become slaves of
righteousness with a view to eternal life.

> Do you not know that if you present yourselves to anyone as obedient
> slaves, you are slaves of the one whom you obey, either of sin, which
> leads to death, or of obedience, which leads to righteousness? But thanks
> be to God that you, having once been slaves of sin, have become obedi-
> ent from the heart to the form of teaching to which you were entrusted,
> and that you, having been set free from sin, have become slaves of righ-
> teousness.… For just as you once presented your members as slaves to
> impurity and to greater and greater iniquity, so now present your mem-
> bers as slaves to righteousness for sanctification. When you were slaves
> of sin, you were free in regard to righteousness.… The end of those
> things is death. But now that you have been freed from sin and enslaved
> to God, the advantage you get is sanctification. The end is eternal life.
> (Rom 6:16–22)

While the Pauline Letters recognize slaves and slavery (see Eph 6:5–10;
Col 3:22–4:1; 1 Tim 6:1–2; Titus 2:9–10), it is clear that Paul envisions and
proclaims freedom. This intertextural analysis means that Paul views, and
his rhetoric argues for, Onesimus the slave as a freeperson.

The Hebrew Bible and the Septuagint were major features of Paul's
interactive and intertextural world. He would have been very aware of the
texts that addressed the topics of slaves and slavery, and Paul himself is
conscious that the stories and events provided in Scripture serve as examples to Christ-believers.

> These things happened to them to serve as an example and they were
> written down to instruct us, on whom the ends of the ages have come.
> (1 Cor 10:11)

Certainly he would know that Deuteronomy regularly pointed out that Israelites themselves had a background in Egyptian slavery from which Yahweh had delivered them.

> Remember that you were a slave in the land of Egypt, and the Lord your God brought you out from there with a mighty hand and an outstretched arm. (Deut 5:15; see also 6:20–21; 15:15; 16:12; 24:18, 22)

This sets a general context for Paul's thinking about slaves and slavery. He believed that his Israelite ancestors were slaves who had been saved from oppression by the power of God. This sets in place and reinforces the paradigm of release from the oppression of slavery.[53] God's people are by definition not, or are no longer, slaves. Paul also knew that observance of the Torah was a matter of Jewish identity and holy living.

> So now, O Israel, what does the Lord your God require of you? Only to fear the Lord your God, to walk in all his ways, to love him, to serve the Lord your God with all your heart and with all your soul and to keep the commandments of the Lord your God and his decrees that I am commanding you today, for your own well-being. Although heaven and the heaven of heavens belong to the Lord your God, the earth with all that is in it, yet the LORD set his heart in love on your ancestors alone and chose you, their descendants after them, out of all the peoples, as it is today. Circumcise, then, the foreskin of your heart, and do not be stubborn any longer. For the Lord your God is God of gods and Lord of lords, the great God, mighty and awesome, who is not partial and takes no bribe, who executes justice for the orphan and the widow, and who loves the strangers, providing them food and clothing. You shall also love the stranger, for you were strangers in the land of Egypt. You shall fear the Lord your God; him alone you shall worship; to him you shall hold fast, and by his name you shall swear. He is your praise; he is your God, who has done for you these great and awesome things that your own eyes have seen. Your ancestors went down to Egypt seventy persons; and now the Lord your God has made you as numerous as the stars in heaven.
>
> You shall love the Lord your God, therefore, and keep his charge, his decrees, his ordinances, and his commandments always. (Deut 10:12–11:1)

---

53. See the section below "Brotherhood: The Joseph Stories." See also Luke 4:16–21.

Observing the Torah was how life was understood and how it was lived by one trained as a Pharisaic Jew of the diaspora, as Paul had been. Serving God with one's entire being ("with all your heart and with all your soul ... for your own well-being") was, similarly, Paul's way of living as a Christ-believer. This is the way of life of people whom God has saved from slavery.

Paul knew that the directives of the Torah including the Sabbath and festivals were to be observed by entire Israelite households, including and involving slaves.

> You shall not covet your neighbor's house; you shall not covet your neighbor's wife, *or male or female slave*, or ox, or donkey, or anything that belongs to your neighbor. (Exod 20:17, emphasis added)

> Observe the sabbath day and keep it holy, as the Lord your God commanded you. Six days you shall labor and do all your work. But the seventh day is a sabbath to the Lord your God; you shall not do any work—you, or your son or your daughter, *or your male or female slave*, or your ox or your donkey, or any of your livestock, or the resident alien in your towns, *so that your male and female slave may rest as well as you.* (Deut 5:12–14, emphasis added)

> And you shall rejoice before the Lord your God, you together with your sons and your daughters, *your male and female slaves*, and the Levites who reside in your towns. (Deut 12:12, emphasis added)

> Rejoice before the Lord your God—you and your sons and your daughters, *your male and female slaves*, the Levites resident in your towns, as well as the strangers, the orphans, and the widows who are among you— at the place that the Lord your God will choose as a dwelling for his name. *Remember that you were a slave in Egypt*, and diligently observe these statutes. You shall keep the festival of booths for seven days, when you have gathered in the produce from your threshing floor and your wine press. Rejoice during your festival, you and your sons and your daughters, *your male and female slaves*, as well as the Levites, the strangers, the orphans, and the widows resident in your towns. Seven days you shall keep the festival for the Lord your God at the place that the LORD will choose; for the Lord your God will bless you in all your produce and in all your undertakings, and you shall surely celebrate. Three times a year all your males shall appear before the Lord your God at the place that he will choose: at the festival of unleavened bread, at the festival of weeks, and at the festival of booths. They shall not appear before the Lord

empty-handed; all shall give as they are able, according to the blessing of the Lord your God that he has given you. (Deut 16:11–17, emphasis added)

Slaves in Israel were certainly restricted and were the property of other humans, but they were also to be participants in the religious life of the elect people.

Paul knew that Israelites had possessed slaves and that slavery was regulated by the Torah.

These are the ordinances that you shall set before them: When you buy a male Hebrew slave, he shall serve six years, but in the seventh he shall go out a free person, without debt. If he comes in single, he shall go out single; if he comes in married, then his wife shall go out with him. If his master gives him a wife and she bears him sons or daughters, the wife and her children shall be her master's and he shall go out alone. But if the slave declares, "I love my master, my wife, and my children; I will not go out a free person," then his master shall bring him before God. He shall be brought to the door or the doorpost; and his master shall pierce his ear with an awl; and he shall serve him for life. When a man sells his daughter as a slave, she shall not go out as the male slaves do. If she does not please her master, who designated her for himself, then he shall let her be redeemed; he shall have no right to sell her to a foreign people, since he has dealt unfairly with her. If he designates her for his son, he shall deal with her as with a daughter. If he takes another wife to himself, he shall not diminish the food, clothing, or marital rights of the first wife. And if he does not do these three things for her, she shall go out without debt, without payment of money. (Exod 21:1–11)

If any who are dependent on you become so impoverished that they sell themselves to you, you shall not make them serve as slaves. They shall remain with you as hired or bound laborers. They shall serve with you until the year of the jubilee. Then they and their children with them shall be free from your authority; they shall go back to their own family and return to their ancestral property. For they are my servants, whom I brought out of the land of Egypt; they shall not be sold as slaves are sold. You shall not rule over them with harshness, but shall fear your God. As for the male and female slaves whom you may have, it is from the nations around you that you may acquire male and female slaves. You may also acquire them from among the aliens residing with you, and from their families that are with you, who have been born in your land; and they may be your property. You may keep them as a possession for your children after you, for them to inherit as property. These you may treat as slaves, but as for your fellow Israelites, no one shall rule over the other with harshness. (Lev 25:39–46)

Slaves were, the Torah indicates, to be freed after specified periods of time, during the seventh year or, in the case of indentured slave laborers, at the Jubilee year. What this indicates is that the notion of the freeing of slaves was an attribute of Paul's Israelite/Jewish interactive worldview. It was part of what informed his life. It becomes a feature of his rhetoric in the Letter to Philemon. Slaves are also God's "servants, whom I brought out of the land of Egypt"; they are now brothers, also elect persons who may not be treated harshly. Paul would also have known that according to the Torah escaped slaves (*fugitivi*) were not to be sent back to their owners.

Slaves who have escaped to you from their owners shall not be given back to them. They shall reside with you, in your midst, in any place they choose in any one of your towns, wherever they please; you shall not oppress them. (Deut 23:15–16)[54]

This regulation might suggest—though it certainly does not prove—that Onesimus was not a *fugitivus* since Paul was indeed sending him back to Philemon (v. 12). Paul may well also have known that Essenes, as Philo points out, did not practice slavery.[55]

These biblical **intertextures** are part of the contexts that inform Paul's view of slaves and slavery. The notion of freedom for people was embedded in Paul's thinking and character. His ethic held that slaves are to be part of the Christ-believing community and that they are freepersons in Christ who should not be treated as slaves. While in ancient Mediterranean context slaves did not have independence or self-determination, in Christ and in the *ekklēsia* things are different: they are freepersons. The Deuteronomistic paradigm applies to all: God with a mighty hand and an outstretched arm has redeemed enslaved humans. Just as Israel was to love and serve the LORD God and keep the commandments, so should Philemon refresh Paul's viscera by receiving Onesimus as a brother.

---

54. See Isa 16:3–4. The Torah directive may not often have been followed (see 1 Sam 25:10–12; 30:11–15).

55. Philo, *Prob.* 79; see Neil Elliott and Mark Reasoner, eds., *Documents and Images for the Study of Paul* (Minneapolis: Fortress, 2011), 290. See also Barth and Blanke, *Letter to Philemon*, 354.

Greco-Roman texts are regularly cited in the discussions about slavery and Philemon. Many interpreters note the letter from Pliny the Younger (61–ca. 113 CE) to Sabinianus[56] in which Pliny pleads for the merciful reception of a fugitive (but not a slave; a freedman).

> The freedman of yours with whom you said you were angry has been to me, flung himself at my feet, and clung to me as if I were you. He begged my help with many tears, though he left a good deal unsaid; in short, he convinced me of his genuine penitence. I believe he has reformed, because he realizes he did wrong. You are angry, I know, and I know that your anger was deserved, but mercy wins most praise when there was just cause for anger. You loved the man once, and I hope you will love him again, but it is sufficient for the moment if you allow yourself to be appeased. You can always get angry again if he deserves it, and will have more excuse if you were once placated. Make some concession to his youth, his tears, and your own kind heart, and do not torment him or yourself any longer—anger can only be a torment to your gentle self.
>
> I am afraid you will think I am using pressure, not persuasion, if I add my prayers to his—but this is what I shall do, and all the more freely and fully because I have given the man a very severe scolding and warned him firmly that I will never make such a request again. This was because he deserved a fright, and is not intended for your ears; for maybe I shall make another request and obtain it, as long as it is nothing unsuitable for me to ask and you to grant. (Pliny, *Ep.* 9.21 [Radice, LCL])

Sabinianus is angry with cause, but Pliny states that "mercy wins most praise when there was just cause for anger." The contact points with Paul, Philemon, and Onesimus are obvious. So, while unusual in a slaveholding society, it is possible to conceive that a request like Paul's could be made, and it could be done without compulsion but through appeal to goodwill. Less frequently noted is another letter to Sabinianus where Pliny indicates his pleasure that the fugitive was well-received.

> You have done the right thing in taking back into your home and favor the freedman who was once dear to you, with my letter to mediate between you both. You will be glad of this, and I am certainly glad, first because

---

56. For example Dunn, *Colossians and Philemon*, 304–5, 326; Marianne Meye Thompson, *Colossians and Philemon*, Two Horizons Commentary (Grand Rapids: Eerdmans, 2005), 196; Barth and Blanke, *Letter to Philemon*, 86–87.

I see you are willing to be reasonable and take advice when angry, and then because you have paid me the tribute of bowing to my authority, or, if you prefer, granting my request. So accept my compliments as well as my thanks, but, at the same time, a word of advice for the future: be ready to forgive the faults of your household even if there is no one there to intervene for them. (Pliny, *Ep.* 9.24 [Radice, LCL])

Here Pliny points out that one can be "reasonable and take advice when angry," that people can comply with requests sent by letter, and that the same kinds of things can be done again. Philemon, similarly, is requested to provide refreshment of the viscera again as he had done before and to receive Onesimus as if he were Paul himself, rather than with anger.

Pliny also addressed a letter to Statius Sabinus in which he speaks of a slave who was to be manumitted according to the will of the deceased Sabina.[57] While apparently not legally bound to free the slave, Pliny advises it be done.

I understand from your letter that Sabina in making us her heirs left us no instructions that her slave Modestus was to be given his freedom, but even so left him a legacy with the words: "To Modestus whom I have ordered to be set free"; and you would like to hear my view. I have consulted the legal experts, and it was their unanimous opinion that Modestus should receive neither his freedom, as it was not expressly granted, nor his legacy, as it was bequeathed to him while his status was that of slave. But it seems to me obvious that it was a mistake on Sabina's part, and I think we ought to act as if she had set out in writing what she believed she had written. I am sure you will agree with me, for you are always most scrupulous about carrying out the intention of the deceased. Once understood, it should be legally binding on an honest heir, as honor puts us under obligation as binding as necessity is for other people. Let us then allow Modestus to have his liberty and enjoy his legacy as if Sabina had taken every proper precaution. She did in fact do so by her wise choice of heirs. (Pliny, *Ep.* 4.10 [Radice, LCL])

Manumitting a slave is here perceived as good and honorable, indeed in this case morally required.

---

57. On manumission according to a will, see below on **social and cultural texture**.

According to Roman law, people were categorized either as freepersons or slaves (*Digest* 1.5.4).[58] Slaves were simply not seen as equal to owners or to other freepersons.[59] The foundation for this is seen already in Aristotle's writing about slaves and slavery (Aristotle, *Pol.*, book 1), which provides an important **intertexture** for the Letter to Philemon. His famous discussion was mainly for the benefit of slave owners and household management and reflects the general view of slavery in the Greco-Roman world. To Aristotle some persons are naturally slaves who should be dominated. They were effectively "nonpersons."[60] The lines of authority are clear, for "a slave is a live article of property" to work for the benefit of the household (Aristotle, *Pol.* 1.4).

> The slave is not merely the slave of the master but wholly belongs to the master. These considerations therefore make clear the nature of the slave and his essential quality: one who is a human being belonging by nature not to himself but to another is by nature a slave, and a person is a human being belonging to another if being a man he is an article of property. (Aristotle, *Pol.* 1.4 [Rackham, LCL])

Masters of the household are to exercise their authority while slaves are to exercise obedience.

> It is proper for the one party to be governed and for the other to govern by the form of government for which they are by nature fitted, and therefore by the exercise of mastership, while to govern badly is to govern disadvantageously for both parties (for the same thing is advantageous for a part and for the whole body or the whole soul, and the slave is part of the master—he is, as it were, a part of the body, alive yet separated from it; hence there is a certain community of interest and friendship between master and slave in cases when they have been qualified by nature for these positions, although when they do not hold them in that way but by law and constraint of force the opposite is true. (Aristotle, *Pol.* 1.6 [Rackham, LCL])

Aristotle considered slaves to be unable to engage intellectually.

---

58. The *Digest* is a compendium of Roman law drawn together from laws long in force by (Eastern) Emperor Justinian in the sixth century.

59. See Dunn, *Colossians and Philemon*, 338.

60. John G. Nordling, *Philemon*, ConC (Saint Louis: Concordia, 2004), 53–54.

> For the slave has not got the deliberative part at all, and the female has it,
> but without full authority, while the child has it, but in an undeveloped
> form. (Aristotle, *Pol.* 1.13 [Rackham, LCL])

Slaves were perceived to be such by nature. The slave was considered to be
part of the master, a living but bodily separate part of the master. Masters
were the source of all direction for slaves.

> For the slave is a partner in his master's life, but the artisan is more
> remote, and only so much of virtue falls to his share as of slavery—for the
> mechanic artisan is under a sort of limited slavery, and whereas the slave
> is one of the natural classes, no shoemaker or other craftsman belongs to
> his trade by nature. It is manifest therefore that the master ought to be
> the cause to the slave of the virtue proper to a slave, but not as possessing
> that art of mastership which teaches his slave tasks. Hence those persons
> are mistaken who deprive the slave of reasoning and tell us to use com-
> mand only; for admonition is more properly employed with slaves than
> with children. (Aristotle, *Pol.* 1.13 [Rackham, LCL])

On this view slaves, though they could relate to their masters, deserved
their enslavement and had no independent or natural life apart from masters. Paul stands against, indeed he counters and subverts, this established
understanding and practice of slavery.[61] He stands for freedom, equality,
brotherhood, and full fellowship in Christ. Very important is his understanding that this freedom in Christ is located in the household, the space
of wisdom. He shapes his rhetoric with this in mind.

The thoughtful Seneca (ca. 4 BCE–65 CE) had a more moderating
view than others in the Greco-Roman world. In his Letter to Lucilius on
master and slave (*Ep.* 47), Seneca recognizes the popular view that slaves
are not "men" but mere "slaves" with whom one must not share table fellowship, but he nevertheless stands against the Roman, Aristotelian, and
commonly perceived view of slaves. Seneca argues that the practices of
slavery are self-defeating. Slaves are in practice made into the enemies of
masters precisely because they can see the actions and immorality of their
masters. He argues that slaves should be treated as "unpretentious friends"
and that people recognize the obvious truth that both slaves and freepersons "sprang from the same stock." Slaves should be treated kindly and
affably. Friends of masters, he says, may be found at home among, it is

---

61. Nordling, *Philemon*, 60.

implied, the slaves. The long letter, in its own powerful and practical rhetoric, makes its own point clearly and is worth including here.

> I am glad to learn, through those who come from you, that you live on friendly terms with your slaves. This befits a sensible and well-educated man like yourself. "They are slaves," people declare. Nay, rather they are men. "Slaves!" No, comrades. "Slaves!" No, they are unpretentious friends. "Slaves!" No, they are our fellow-slaves, if one reflects that Fortune has equal rights over slaves and free men alike.
>
> That is why I smile at those who think it degrading for a man to dine with his slave. But why should they think it degrading? It is only because purse-proud etiquette surrounds a householder at his dinner with a mob of standing slaves. The master eats more than he can hold, and with monstrous greed loads his belly until it is stretched and at length ceases to do the work of a belly; so that he is at greater pains to discharge all the food than he was to stuff it down. All this time the poor slaves may not move their lips, even to speak. The slightest murmur is repressed by the rod; even a chance sound,—a cough, a sneeze, or a hiccup,—is visited with the lash. There is a grievous penalty for the slightest breach of silence. All night long they must stand about, hungry and dumb.
>
> The result of it all is that these slaves, who may not talk in their master's presence, talk about their master. But the slaves of former days, who were permitted to converse not only in their master's presence, but actually with him, whose mouths were not stitched up tight, were ready to bare their necks for their master, to bring upon their own heads any danger that threatened him; they spoke at the feast, but kept silence during torture. Finally, the saying, in allusion to this same high-handed treatment, becomes current: "As many enemies as you have slaves." They are not enemies when we acquire them; we make them enemies.
>
> I shall pass over other cruel and inhuman conduct towards them; for we maltreat them, not as if they were men, but as if they were beasts of burden. When we recline at a banquet, one slave mops up the disgorged food, another crouches beneath the table and gathers up the left-overs of the tipsy guests. Another carves the priceless game birds; with unerring strokes and skilled hand he cuts choice morsels along the breast or the rump. Hapless fellow, to live only for the purpose of cutting fat capons correctly—unless, indeed, the other man is still more unhappy than he, who teaches this art for pleasure's sake, rather than he who learns it because he must. Another, who serves the wine, must dress like a woman and wrestle with his advancing years; he cannot get away from his boyhood; he is dragged back to it; and though he has already acquired a soldier's figure, he is kept beardless by having his hair smoothed away or plucked out by the roots, and he must remain awake throughout the

night, dividing his time between his master's drunkenness and his lust; in the chamber he must be a man, at the feast a boy. Another, whose duty it is to put a valuation on the guests, must stick to his task, poor fellow, and watch to see whose flattery and whose immodesty, whether of appetite or of language, is to get them an invitation for tomorrow. Think also of the poor purveyors of food, who note their masters' tastes with delicate skill, who know what special flavours will sharpen their appetite, what will please their eyes, what new combinations will rouse their cloyed stomachs, what food will excite their loathing through sheer satiety, and what will stir them to hunger on that particular day. With slaves like these the master cannot bear to dine; he would think it beneath his dignity to associate with his slave at the same table! Heaven forfend!

But how many masters is he creating in these very men! I have seen standing in the line, before the door of Callistus, the former master, of Callistus; I have seen the master himself shut out while others were welcomed,—the master who once fastened the "For Sale" ticket on Callistus and put him in the market along with the good-for-nothing slaves. But he has been paid off by that slave who was shuffled into the first lot of those on whom the crier practises his lungs; the slave, too, in his turn has cut his name from the list and in his turn has adjudged him unfit to enter his house. The master sold Callistus, but how much has Callistus made his master pay for!

Kindly remember that he whom you call your slave sprang from the same stock, is smiled upon by the same skies, and on equal terms with yourself breathes, lives, and dies. It is just as possible for you to see in him a free-born man as for him to see in you a slave. As a result of the massacres in Marius's day, many a man of distinguished birth, who was taking the first steps toward senatorial rank by service in the army, was humbled by fortune, one becoming a shepherd, another a caretaker of a country cottage. Despise, then, if you dare, those to whose estate you may at any time descend, even when you are despising them.

I do not wish to involve myself in too large a question, and to discuss the treatment of slaves, toward whom we Romans are excessively haughty, cruel, and insulting. But this is the kernel of my advice: Treat your inferiors as you would be treated by your betters. And as often as you reflect how much power you have over a slave, remember that your master has just as much power over you. "But I have no master," you say. You are still young; perhaps you will have one. Do you not know at what age Hecuba entered captivity, or Croesus, or the mother of Darius, or Plato, or Diogenes?

Associate with your slave on kindly, even on affable, terms; let him talk with you, plan with you, live with you. I know that at this point all the exquisites will cry out against me in a body; they will say: "There is nothing more debasing, more disgraceful, than this." But these are the very persons whom I sometimes surprise kissing the hands of other men's slaves. Do you not see even this, how our ancestors removed from masters everything invidious, and from slaves everything insulting? They called the master "father of the household," and the slaves "members of the household," a custom which still holds in the mime. They established a holiday on which masters and slaves should eat together,—not as the only day for this custom, but as obligatory on that day in any case. They allowed the slaves to attain honours in the household and to pronounce judgment; they held that a household was a miniature commonwealth.

"Do you mean to say," comes the retort, "that I must seat all my slaves at my own table?" No, not any more than that you should invite all free men to it. You are mistaken if you think that I would bar from my table certain slaves whose duties are more humble, as, for example, yonder muleteer or yonder herdsman; I propose to value them according to their character, and not according to their duties. Each man acquires his character for himself, but accident assigns his duties. Invite some to your table because they deserve the honor, and others that they may come to deserve it. For if there is any slavish quality in them as the result of their low associations, it will be shaken off by intercourse with men of gentler breeding. You need not, my dear Lucilius, hunt for friends only in the forum or in the Senate-house; if you are careful and attentive, you will find them at home also. Good material often stands idle for want of an artist; make the experiment, and you will find it so. As he is a fool who, when purchasing a horse, does not consider the animal's points, but merely his saddle and bridle; so he is doubly a fool who values a man from his clothes or from his rank, which indeed is only a robe that clothes us.

"He is a slave." His soul, however, may be that of a freeman. "He is a slave." But shall that stand in his way? Show me a man who is not a slave; one is a slave to lust, another to greed, another to ambition, and all men are slaves to fear. I will name you an ex-consul who is slave to an old hag, a millionaire who is slave to a serving-maid; I will show you youths of the noblest birth in serfdom to pantomime players! No servitude is more disgraceful than that which is self-imposed.

You should therefore not be deterred by these finicky persons from showing yourself to your slaves as an affable person and not proudly superior to them; they ought to respect you rather than fear you. Some may maintain that I am now offering the liberty-cap to slaves in general and toppling down lords from their high estate, because I bid slaves respect their masters instead of fearing them. They say: "This is what he plainly means: slaves are to pay respect as if they were clients or early-morning callers!" Anyone who holds this opinion forgets that what is

enough for a god cannot be too little for a master. Respect means love,
and love and fear cannot be mingled. So I hold that you are entirely right
in not wishing to be feared by your slaves, and in lashing them merely
with the tongue; only dumb animals need the thong.

That which annoys us does not necessarily injure us; but we are
driven into wild rage by our luxurious lives, so that whatever does not
answer our whims arouses our anger. We don the temper of kings. For
they, too, forgetful alike of their own strength and of other men's weakness, grow white-hot with rage, as if they had received an injury, when
they are entirely protected from danger of such injury by their exalted
station. They are not unaware that this is true, but by finding fault they
seize upon opportunities to do harm; they insist that they have received
injuries, in order that they may inflict them.

I do not wish to delay you longer; for you need no exhortation. This,
among other things, is a mark of good character: it forms its own judgments and abides by them; but badness is fickle and frequently changing,
not for the better, but for something different. Farewell. (Seneca, *Ep.* 47
[Gummere, LCL])

Seneca calls for the enslaved "nonpersons" to be respected and treated
equally and fairly, even though this behavior stands against social conventions. He is pleased to have heard that Lucilius already engages in such
practices with slaves. Seneca calls for the highest form of fellowship—
eating with people, table fellowship, being nourished together—to be
practiced with slaves. He deplores the ways in which slaves were regularly
mistreated by their owners. Their dignity is seriously wounded. He calls
for treatment that is very like the plea of the Golden Rule: "Treat your inferiors as you would be treated by your betters. And as often as you reflect
how much power you have over a slave, remember that your master has
just as much power over you." Paul's rhetoric calls for the slave Onesimus
to be accepted and treated in similar ways, effectively as a freeperson who
is not a beast of burden but is a brother in Christ. For Philemon to accept
Onesimus as a beloved brother would be to stand against and subvert the
social conventions of the day.[62]

---

62. For very helpful information and discussion, see G. François Wessels, "The
Letter to Philemon in the Context of Slavery in Early Christianity," in *Philemon in
Perspective: Interpreting a Pauline Letter*, ed. D. François Tolmie (Berlin: de Gruyter,
2010), 143–68.

Brotherhood: The Joseph Stories (Gen 37–50)

A leading and important **intertexture** with Philemon is the Joseph cycle of stories. Many interpreters—by no means all—refer to Gen 45:5 and 50:20 as "parallels" to Phlm 15–16.[63] They do not, however, follow up with intertextural and rhetorical analysis of the connections. Close reading indicates that Gen 37–50 and the Letter to Philemon share multiple and dramatic **intertextures**. We cannot know if the story of Joseph was known to Philemon or the *ekklēsia* in his house.[64] We can be sure, though, that it was well-known by Paul and Timothy. The stories of Genesis are part of Paul's interactive world, of his location as a Jew and as a Christ-believer. The Joseph cycle of stories are a feature of Paul's framework for understanding God and God's actions performed for the good of humans.[65] The famous stories speak of sinful actions, oppression, loss, separation, reconciliation, and restoration or salvation by God's grace. The **intertextures** are allusive, and there are no direct (oral-scribal) connections in the way of quotations, recitations, or reconfigurations of actual language from Genesis.[66]

Joseph was the favored son of his father Jacob (Gen 37:3) and, to say the least, the annoying younger brother of his male siblings (Gen 37:4–20). He might have seemed to be useless to his brothers, like Onesimus had

---

63. E.g., Dunn, *Colossians and Philemon*, 333, who refers briefly to Gen 50; Joseph A. Fitzmyer, *The Letter to Philemon: A New Translation with Introduction and Commentary*, AB 34C (New York: Doubleday, 2000), 113; Barth and Blanke, *Letter to Philemon*, 56–57 nn. 152–54; 64 n. 185; 403; Moo, *Colossians and Philemon*, 419; Thompson, *Colossians and Philemon*, 223; Nordling, *Philemon*, 254. Connections with the Joseph cycle of stories have been noted at least since John Chrysostom in the fourth century CE.

64. Readers and listeners do not always need to recognize an allusion or interaction with a specific text or source or sociocultural feature. They may understand in a more general and implicit way even if an author or speaker has particular things in mind. Indeed an author/speaker does not need to have a specific text or feature in mind, but may have a "frame" or "constellation" of ideas in mind that have their own textual connections. See Jerry L. Sumney, "Writing in 'the Image' of Scripture: The Form and Function of References to Scripture in Colossians," in *Paul and Scripture: Extending the Conversation*, ed. Christopher D. Stanley (Atlanta: Society of Biblical Literature, 2012), 186–89.

65. Although Paul never mentions Joseph in his letters, he does mention Jacob, Joseph's father, and features of Jacob's life (Rom 9:11–13). Paul knew the Genesis stories thoroughly.

66. See Robbins, *Exploring*, 40–50.

seemed "useless" as a slave to Philemon. The brothers sold Joseph as a slave, and he was transported to Egypt (Gen 37:25–28). He was separated from (passive voice; cf. Phlm 15) his father, who mourned for him (Gen 37:29–35). In Egypt he was falsely accused, imprisoned (Gen 39), and forgotten by a fellow prisoner whom he had helped (Gen 40:23). There is, however, despite the oppression Joseph encountered, an overarching notion in the story: the providence of God. God loved Joseph (Gen 39:21). God blessed Joseph, and God had the eventual restoration of Joseph in mind (see Gen 39:5, 21–23; 41:16, 37–41, 51–52; 45:5–10; 48:3–4; 50:20).[67] The rhetorical climax occurs in Gen 45:1–15, when Joseph is overcome with emotion and reveals his identity to his brothers. Joseph and all his brothers are restored and reconciled to one another, and much effort is expended to ensure the continuation of the brotherly relationship (Gen 50:15–21). All of this, including the separation of Joseph from his father and brothers, is described as being intended and brought about by God.

> God sent me before you to preserve for you a remnant on the earth, and to keep you alive for many survivors. So it was not you who sent me here, but God. (Gen 45:7–8)

> Even though you intended to do harm to me, God intended it for good, in order to preserve a numerous people as he is doing today. (Gen 50:20)

The father and brothers of Joseph prosper in Egypt, living as shepherds in the best part of the land (Gen 47:1–12). By contrast, Egyptian people affected by famine exchange their livestock and land for food, and Joseph reduces them to slavery (Gen 47:13–26).[68]

Genesis 37–50 quite powerfully employs a *repetitive texture* in the word "brother" (and the plural "brothers"), so much so that it becomes part of the underlying framework or metanarrative and, hence, a rhetorical driver of ideas. The older brothers—who are a kind of counterpart to Philemon—eventually do bow and do obeisance to their younger brother (Gen 42:6; 43:26, 28) just as Joseph's dreams had predicted (Gen 37:5–11). Joseph, through his steward, refreshed the brothers by providing water,

---

67. Indeed, the salvation of Jacob's family and descendants, in accord with the promises to Abraham (Gen 46:1–4).

68. In another interesting reversal, Joseph's younger and genetically fraternal brother, Benjamin, comes under threat himself of being Joseph's slave (Gen 44:10, 17).

foot-washing, and fodder for their donkeys (Gen 43:24).[69] Joseph is eventually overcome by emotion for Benjamin, his younger and heretofore unknown brother (Gen 43:30). Perhaps Paul hopes that Philemon will have a similar emotional recognition for the brother Onesimus. That is, that the new gospel-influenced situation will move Philemon to do the right thing.

While the intertextural relationships between these narrations do not align at every point, they nevertheless stand out strongly. Onesimus parallels Joseph as a slave and as someone separated from another important person (Joseph from his father; Onesimus from Philemon). Onesimus may not himself be imprisoned, but Paul is imprisoned, and Onesimus seems to be conscious of that situation. Just as Joseph was restored and reconciled to his brothers, becoming a brother again, so also Paul sends Onesimus to be restored to Philemon, to be reconciled, and for Onesimus to be treated as a "beloved brother" because that is what he now *is*. Joseph the annoying dreamer was eventually reconciled, and Onesimus the useless slave is to be reconciled. Paul the "old man" and metaphorical parent to Onesimus (Phlm 9, 10) corresponds to the elderly Jacob, who longs for his separated and apparently dead son and who rejoices when the son is restored to him. This intertexturality is foundational to Paul's ideology and quite clearly stands in the purview of his rhetoric. The similarity of ideas, circumstances, and language is striking. Paul knows that reconciliation of separated parties and the consequent brotherhood are integral to the gospel message he proclaims (see Phlm 13).[70] The Joseph stories are part of his scriptural heritage of ideas that inform him about how things should be done in the new society of the *ekklēsia* and in the world. It is hard to imagine that Paul could advise Philemon otherwise. It is not something to be denied or ignored or overpowered by Philemon, who possesses power to resist Paul. God has brought it about. The underlying ethos is about God's apocalyptic activity that defeats evil and brings about wisdom living. To put all this another way, the **intertexture** forms a paradigm or metanarrative or "frame" for understanding and for action. It reflects the implicit biblical story of existence where humans affected by the vicissitudes of

---

69. The refreshment may be understood as having an intertextural relationship with the good works of Philemon, who has "refreshed" the holy ones (Phlm 7, 20).

70. Compare Paul's frequently stated interest in gospel reconciliation (Rom 5:10; 2 Cor 5:17–20; Eph 2:15–17) and the unity in Christ of Jews and gentiles, slaves and freepersons, males and females (Gal 3:28).

life must nevertheless do the right thing, even if it is difficult or socially awkward. People become oppressed, separated, enslaved, and, eventually, restored and reconciled. The **intertexture**, then, is much like the rhetorical feature literary critic Ezra Pound referred to as *logopoeia*, the implicit meaning or allusions of words.[71] The *logopoeia* exists in Paul's memory and knowledge of the Joseph story. He can draw on the implicit meaning of the story to make his case. Onesimus can no longer be imagined, rhetoricized, and treated as a slave. In the *ekklēsia* and in Christ the refresher of viscera, Philemon, will need to practice the restoration of brotherhood as did Joseph and his brothers.

Social and Cultural Texture

Urging, Exhortation, Old Man, Request

Although Paul understands he has the social and cultural authority to command Philemon to do what he wants him to do, he chooses the much more rhetoricized approach of urging him and encouraging him (παρακαλῶ σε, vv. 9–10) regarding Onesimus the slave. In the parenthesis between the occurrences of the verb παρακαλῶ, Paul plays his own socially construed condition of being an old man and a prisoner of Christ Jesus. The sociocultural implication is that old men deserve respect and their instruction should be followed, because they are experienced graybeards who know what is right. This small social scenario sets up a challenge-riposte situation,[72] because Paul is entering Philemon's space and crossing personal boundaries. "I could command you to obey! Through love, rather, I urge—and I'm an old man and a prisoner—I urge you concerning ... Onesimus." Paul certainly has no legal authority over Philemon, though he seems to have significant moral authority. Paul and Philemon do not inhabit the same social spaces. But old Paul barges in brashly (v. 8) with his loving encouragement thinly laid over his (un)authoritative claim. Philemon, at least at this point in his reception of Paul's discourse, could conceivably oppose the challenge, though he might be conscious of the people of the *ekklēsia* looking over his shoulder.

---

71. Ezra Pound, "How to Read," in *Literary Essays of Ezra Pound*, ed. T. S. Eliot (London: Faber & Faber, 1954), 25–26.

72. See Robbins, *Exploring*, 80–81.

Kinship, Parent, Child, Brother

These familial metaphors are topoi that inject an emotion into the social context that is meant to draw Philemon into a kinship mind-set where Paul and Philemon's currently absent slave Onesimus stand, interwoven with Christ, gospel, and *ekklēsia* social context, in a parent-child relationship. Paul imagines Onesimus the slave as his own child, begotten in imprisonment (v. 10), apparently meaning that he and Onesimus have come into contact with each other during his current incarceration, that he has taught the gospel message to Onesimus, and that Onesimus has become a believer. Now Paul imagines Onesimus as his own child, as one whom he has (re)produced himself, thereby taking on a parental role. The kinship emotion is intensified with Paul stating that he considers Onesimus to be his own viscera, metaphorically his own flesh or heart or self (v. 12). The family-like attachment between Paul and Onesimus is deeply felt, palpable. There is, of course, no actual blood relationship between Paul and Onesimus, but Paul sets up a quasi-consanguine family that constitutes a new sociocultural, Christ-, gospel-, and *ekklēsia*-connected relationship. It is extended to Philemon, for Paul hopes for a kinship relationship between Philemon and Onesimus, where Philemon will accept the slave Onesimus as a "brother," not as a slave. This implies that Paul also imagines Philemon as his child, his own viscera, a notion supported by how Paul makes fleshly along with explicitly Christian ties between Philemon and Onesimus (v. 16) and how he calls Philemon to "refresh" his "viscera in Christ" (v. 20). This, again, is a new and quite sharply featured social and cultural construct, because the slave owner, who has full legal rights over the slave, is called by a prisoner to disregard implicit Roman legalities and various sociocultural understandings and expectations to take on and practice Christian ("in Christ") family morality.

Slavery

Onesimus is a slave.[73] This immediately injects the institution and practices of slavery during the Roman period into the analysis of **social and**

---

73. There are many studies of slavery and its connection to the New Testament and early Christianity. Virtually all commentaries on Philemon contain discussions of slavery. Among the most helpful studies are those by Barth and Blanke, "The Social Background: Slavery at Paul's Time," in *The Letter to Philemon*, 1–103; Dale B. Martin,

cultural texture. Slavery was, of course, completely embedded in Roman
and Mediterranean life. Slaves lived virtually everywhere, and everyone
knew it. It should not be imagined, however, that slavery was monolithic or
that it was established according to some evenly operated system throughout the region. There was significant variation, and changes legally and
practically were occurring during the first century CE. Slavery was not,
as at other times and in other places, related directly to race, skin color,
or national background. Some were born into slavery, and some became
slaves through war or piracy. There were many kinds of slaves who experienced a range of conditions and treatment. House slaves, for example,
were in a much different category than those who worked in harsh conditions in mines, industry, or agriculture. Slaves were ordinarily paid a
fixed amount of money (the *peculium*), though these funds and all property held by slaves in reality belonged to the slave owner. The boundaries
between slaves and freepersons (*libertini*) were often quite fluid (see Matt
24:45–51). Slaves sometimes married into the families of owners. Some
owned various kinds of property; some owned other slaves (see Matt
18:23–35; 25:14–30). Some invested in their owner's business. They might
join religious or other voluntary associations, and they might attend festivals, celebrations, and the theater. Most owners avoided extremely harsh
or unhealthy treatment or excessively heavy physical work (such as mining
or quarrying), because slaves obviously provided labor and were a cash
commodity, hence related to financial profit and loss. It was in owners'
interests to keep their slaves healthy and productive. At the same time,
there were complaints about slaves who seemed to owners not to produce
adequately. This might be indicated in Paul's paronomasic comment about

---

Slavery as Salvation: The Metaphor of Slavery in Pauline Christianity (New Haven:
Yale University Press, 1990); J. Albert Harrill, *Slaves in the New Testament: Literary,
Social and Moral Dimensions* (Minneapolis: Fortress, 2006); Norman R. Petersen,
Rediscovering Paul: Philemon and the Sociology of Paul's Narrative World (Philadel-
phia: Fortress, 1985); S. Scott Bartchy, *Mallon Chresai: First-Century Slavery and the
Interpretation of 1 Corinthians 7:21*, SBLDS 11 (Missoula, MT: Scholars Press, 1973;
repr., Eugene OR: Wipf & Stock, 2003); Jennifer Glancy, *Slavery in Early Christianity*
(Minneapolis: Fortress, 2006). Much information here is drawn from these sources.
See also William L. Westermann, *The Slave Systems of Greek and Roman Antiquity*
(Philadelphia: American Philosophical Society, 1955); John Byron, "The Epistle to
Philemon: Paul's Strategy for Forging the Ties of Kinship," in *Jesus and Paul: Global
Perspectives in Honor of James D. G. Dunn for his 70th Birthday*, ed. B. J. Oropeza, C. K.
Robertson, and Douglas C. Mohrmann (London: T&T Clark, 2010), 205–16.

Onesimus, "who then was *useless* but now is *useful* to you and to me" (v. 11). Still, slaves were the legal property of other humans. They were not free, had no legal rights, and had to do what the owner required of them, and whatever level of quality of life slaves had depended on the owner. The owner or paterfamilias had complete power to control then lives of slaves. They could be and were threatened, beaten, abused, maimed, sold, or killed, even if public opinion often stood against these treatments.[74] They could not leave without the owner's permission. They could be and were sexually exploited and abused, and they could be required to have children in order to provide more slaves. They could be hired out for prostitution. While there were laws, certainly from the time of Augustus onward, that indicated slaves were humans and should be treated as such, they were probably regularly ignored. Membership in religious and other voluntary associations could provide some relief from difficult conditions since slaves could be treated in more humane, even familial ways there. Owners were not forced to free slaves, but could manumit them after they reached the age of thirty years; sometimes the will of an owner provided for freedom at the owner's death. Slaves who ran away could seek help from a protector, though that could result in nothing more than trading a bad owner for a somewhat better one. Slaves could seek asylum at a temple to Asclepius, the Greek god of medicine and healing. There was a temple to Asclepius at Pergamon, a location not far from Ephesus. It might be imagined—though there is no evidence for it—that Onesimus had in mind to go there for asylum and a negotiated manumission.

It is important to ask whether Paul was socially and culturally informed and constrained with regard to slavery by the Torah, by Roman law, or by known practices.[75] Clearly he was a well-informed Jew who knew the Torah, and the reality of living in the Roman Mediterranean world indicates that he would have had some level of social and cultural awareness of the existence and function of Roman law regarding slavery. Certainly the Torah addressed slavery and the treatment of slaves (e.g., Exod 21:1–11, 20–32; Lev 25:39–46; Deut 5:12–18; 23:15–16). Ancient Israelites and Jews were regularly reminded that they themselves had been slaves in Egypt whom God rescued ("We were Pharaoh's slaves in Egypt, but the Lord brought us

---

74. There was some amount of social concern for slaves. According to Aristotle, *Pol.* 1.4–6, a master should rule a slave like the soul controls the body, and a slave is part of his master, a separate but living part of the master's body.

75. See above on **intertexture**.

out of Egypt with a mighty hand," Deut 6:21; see also 5:15). Slaves in Israel were to be participants in religious and social life (Exod 20:10, 17; Deut 5:14–15; 12:12, 18; 16:11–14). Paul surely would have been aware of these instructions and with the tradition of slavery in Israel. He would undoubtedly have known of the directive of Deut 23:15–16, that escaped slaves were not to be returned to their owners but were to be given residence in the land and freedom from oppression. This point is sometimes thought to be significant for Paul on the hypothesis that Onesimus was a runaway. At best only strained speculation—not likelihood—is possible since clear evidence is lacking. Paul does not indicate any direct knowledge of Roman law concerning slavery, nor does he indicate any particular concern for it. Still, as an informed person, he must have known such law existed, including law regarding the manumission of slaves. While we may assume that Paul was generally legally informed, the Letter to Philemon does not offer evidence indicating that he viewed himself to be legally constrained or even concerned about legal constraints in Roman law regarding the needs or rights of Onesimus or Philemon.

We must also ask whether Paul was making an oblique request that Philemon manumit Onesimus. He does not make such a request explicitly. Slaves were frequently manumitted informally rather than de jure (legally). We do know that Paul wishes Philemon to receive Onesimus, on his return, "no longer as a slave, but more than a slave, a beloved brother—certainly to me, but more to you, as in the flesh also in the Lord" (v. 16). As was observed in the analysis of *argumentative texture* above, Paul employs the negative adverb οὐκέτι, used normally with the indicative mood, rather than μηκέτι which would be expected with the subjunctive mood verb (ἀπέχῃς) in verse 15. He is in this way making the indicative point that Onesimus is in fact (de facto) no longer a slave, but is a freeperson and brother in the Lord (Christ). By stating that he is a brother "in [the] flesh," Paul includes Onesimus in human, familial relationship with Philemon. This in itself precludes slavery.[76] Onesimus may no longer be treated as a slave, so he is implicitly and necessarily free.

Additional analysis of **social and cultural texture** is instructive regarding Paul's intentions. As we have seen, in Paul's wisdom understanding and presentation there is a new social and cultural relationship centered on Christ, the gospel, and the *ekklēsia* that has created and established a new

---

76. See above on **intertexture**.

society and a new cultural purview. Life has been changed by Christ, and things are different now; the social situation has been altered in ways that transcend the cultural understandings of the eastern provinces. There has also been a practical social change: the "useless" one has become "useful." This alters the exchange system. Onesimus is not a person who may be disciplined, punished, or sold as a commodity. There is now a different purpose, a gospel purpose, for his life and for Philemon's life. There are at least two adversarial social domains, the domain of Christ, gospel, and *ekklēsia*, and the domain of Roman, Asian, and polis culture.[77] Both domains have their cultural expectations and social and moral worldviews. Both, interestingly, are faith domains where their inhabitants trust in the culture as the sustainer of life, honor, community, and self-esteem. In the society of the new Christ culture slaves are considered to be brothers. This is a dramatic and structural change, and Paul, of course, considers the new society to be superior.[78] Philemon is being called to recognize this and to conform to the new social conditions (vv. 16–17). This means that in the society and culture of the *ekklēsia* Onesimus is completely free. Philemon and Onesimus (and Paul and all members of the *ekklēsia*) are equals. Slavery for Christ-believers, those who have faith and love for Christ and all the holy ones and who refresh the viscera of others, is destroyed. All are brothers and sisters in the family where God is the good Father (v. 3). Notions of superior and inferior are removed, despite whatever social and cultural expectations there may be from the outside. If Philemon and Onesimus are brothers then they should not, must not, relate to each other as owner and slave.[79] It is useful to note Paul's "much more" language; he states, regarding Onesimus being a brother, "certainly to me, but *much more* to you as in the flesh also in the Lord" (v. 18). Philemon's sense of community honor as a slave owner and master (and a homeowner), thus as someone who was likely relatively wealthy with power over other people, has been deconstructed and reconstructed by the gospel. He will feel the pressure.

But was Paul calling implicitly for formal de jure manumission? First-generation *libertini*, persons who had either purchased their freedom or had been manumitted, had very low and restricted social status. Former owners functioned as patrons and retained a level of control over *liber-*

---

77. See Petersen, *Rediscovering Paul*, 90.

78. Ibid., 90, 95–96.

79. Petersen (ibid., 135) states that it is "logically and socially impossible to relate to one and the same person as both one's inferior and as one's equal."

tini, who might need significant assistance from their patrons in order to move ahead. If owners who possessed Roman citizenship provided formal de jure manumission, it was possible for freed slaves to become citizens. Second-generation *libertini* became full citizens. Manumission, whether formal or informal, for Onesimus would place him only one step above the lowest level of Roman society. First-generation freed slaves were not of equal social standing with *plebs* (common people or *vulgi*). Former slaves, whether manumitted formally or informally, were obligated to former owners and did not share equal, familial status with them. In other words, manumission was not necessarily much of an improvement for slaves. Paul likely knew this and envisioned the *ekklēsia* as the physical and moral space where persons of all classes, including slaves, former slaves, and former owners were brothers and sisters. In this new society Philemon is challenged to move beyond his familiar sociocultural and ideological world to a revolutionary situation where social status is ignored in favor of love and partnership.[80] It is hard to imagine that Paul was not implying that Philemon manumit Onesimus, at least informally, even if this freedom meant relatively little outside of the Christ-believing community.[81]

Was Paul then an abolitionist? There is, again, no indication in the Letter to Philemon that he was constrained by Roman law regarding slavery, and he was willing to subvert, certainly with regard to Philemon and Onesimus, social and cultural expectations. He seems not to have been a public abolitionist in the modern politicized sense of the term.[82] He was, though, an abolitionist in the context of gospel, *ekklēsia*, *aiōn* (eternity, v. 15), and Christ. What Paul was interested in was social formation, in wisdom living in Christ. His central concern in the letter is that Onesimus be treated as a loved sibling, as one's own viscera. Slavery, to Paul, can have no part in the social thinking and behavior for Christ-believers, even

---

80. Paul in fact speaks of making himself a slave of all (1 Cor 9:19).

81. For very helpful sociocultural information, see Max Lee, "More Pastoral Reflections on the Life of a Slave and Paul's Letter to Philemon," *Paul Redux: The Gospel of Jesus Christ in the Greco-Roman World* (weblog), 26 February 2014, http://paulredux.blogspot.ca/2014_02_01_archive.html; and Barbara F. McManus, "Social Class and Public Display," *VROMA: A Virtual Community for Teaching and Learning Classics*, 2009, http://www.vroma.org/~bmcmanus/socialclass.html.

82. That is, he did not function as a public abolitionist like, say, nineteenth-century leaders such as William Wilberforce, Frederick Douglass, John Brown, and Abraham Lincoln. But he could scarcely have disagreed with their cause.

though they lived within the imperial context. He would no doubt have rejoiced if the imperial institution of slavery was abolished. What he says in Galatians (e.g., 3:28; 5:1) and Romans (about freedom from slavery in sin, 6:5–22) is made socially active, made real, in Philemon.[83]

We might wonder why this letter and its social rhetoric was needed. Since Philemon had already done so much to refresh the viscera of the holy ones, why would he not have already known to treat the now Christ-believing Onesimus as a brother? Were the institution of slavery or local sociocultural pressures or Onesimus's separation from Philemon such powerful influences that Philemon could not or would not deal with them as a Christian without Paul's admonition? Or was Paul simply interfering? Once again, there is much we do not know and cannot know about the situation. In the letter Paul aims to address and influence and correct a human situation, not to explain historical circumstances to audiences he could not have imagined.

The entire **social and cultural texture** is fundamentally about Paul and Philemon, not about Onesimus, slavery, and manumission. The separation of Onesimus from Philemon is the precipitating social event. It is enlarged by Onesimus becoming a gospel believer. But the rhetoric is about Paul and Philemon. Many interpreters spend much time addressing slavery and concomitants like manumission, the sociology of slavery, asking why Paul is not more direct about slavery as a social evil, about the history of slavery and freedom, and other things. Much is interesting, but it often does not get at the **social and cultural texture**: Paul wants Philemon to receive Onesimus as a brother. It is clear, however, that if Onesimus is a brother, he cannot be a slave.

Onesimus

Still, the **social and cultural texture** must also be considered from the side of Onesimus.[84] Onesimus has, by the time the letter is being composed,

---

83. See above on **intertexture**. See also Richard B. Hays, "Crucified with Christ: A Synthesis of the Theology of 1 and 2 Thessalonians, Philemon, Philippians, and Galatians," in *Pauline Theology*, ed. Jouette M. Bassler (Philadelphia: Fortress, 1994), 1:245. See also James 2:1–9; favoritism may not be practiced in the new society.

84. On Onesimus, see the helpful essays in Matthew V. Johnson, James A. Noel, and Demetrius K. Williams, eds., *Onesimus Our Brother: Reading Religion, Race and Culture in Philemon* (Minneapolis: Fortress, 2012).

already experienced massive sociocultural change. He has been separated (v. 15) from his owner, Philemon. He has met and been dramatically influenced by Paul. He has become a Christ-believer. He has become very close to Paul in a new and newly shaped kinship relationship where Paul imagines and describes a familial parent-child relationship with him. While he was a "useless" slave, he is now a "useful" person to both Philemon and Paul. He has become a servant to Paul in the chains of the gospel, which must mean that he understands the gospel message and is interested in its proclamation and influence in the world. Onesimus would be conscious of the implicit freedom he now possessed as child of Paul and brother of Philemon. He may well have been conscious of the social implications of his new status in regard to his relationship with Philemon and the *ekklēsia* meeting in Philemon's house and with regard to his life and relationships in Roman, Asian, and polis communities. Onesimus is, as a person now "in Christ," a freeperson and "no longer" the slave of Philemon. It seems altogether likely that he knew Paul was composing the letter and was aware of its content and that Paul would have it sent to Philemon. The letter does not describe Onesimus's response or his emotions regarding all this, nor his understanding of his new social and cultural situation, but he must have been conscious of what had happened to him so far and simultaneously concerned about what would happen when Philemon received Paul's letter. He knew that he would be going to Philemon as a brother in Christ and as the metaphorical child of Paul. He may have known Philemon well enough to predict how he would be received, but, on the other hand, he might have been full of uncertainty and trepidation. We cannot know his precise circumstances and nothing about his intellectual or emotional understandings. The social formation being elicited by the letter has already been encountered and felt by Onesimus. The ethic for both Philemon and Onesimus in the new social situation is the gospel ethic of service in the chains of the gospel and partnership with Paul.

Partnership

Philemon is continuously challenged in his social and cultural space by Paul's letter. The challenges demand responses. Paul challenges him as a faithful and loving man to continue in those qualities. Paul challenges Philemon in the social and cultural context of the *ekklēsia* and persons he knows like Apphia and Archippus who are watching for his response. Onesimus will surely be hoping for a positive response. Paul challenges Philemon relative to the social and cultural settings of empire as it functions in Asia Minor. There is, in all of this, a kind of "push and shove"[85] that is familiar to humans in their interrelationships. A significant, possibly somewhat daunting, challenge to Philemon comes when Paul says, "If therefore you have me as partner, receive him as me" (v. 17). This immediately follows Paul's "much more" statement, which was clearly designed to pressure Philemon. Paul has been speaking to move Philemon in high-pressure and personal ways. Philemon already recognizes Paul as a coworker and one who loves him. He knows Paul has been praising him for his good works, particularly his ability to refresh the viscera of many. He by now recognizes the gospel and eternal connections of Paul's argumentation. He has heard Paul's familial language regarding Onesimus and the request that he himself receive Onesimus as a brother. Paul in fact will shortly call Philemon "brother" (v. 20). So by raising the point of partnership (κοινωνός) Paul sets up an intense personal "push and shove" rhetorical situation. As a Christ-believer and coworker in the gospel with Paul, Philemon will want to maintain the heretofore implicit but now explicit partnership. This places social pressure on Philemon. He has not, presumably, had misgivings about his "partnership" with Paul. Still, he is being strongly pushed to receive Onesimus happily against the social conventions he lives with in Asia Minor in favor of a continuing partnership with a currently imprisoned Christ-believer who is in contact with his separated slave.

Indebtedness

The possibility that Onesimus has a debt owing to Philemon provides a platform for Paul to insert another challenge-response topos into the discourse.[86] The conditional statement "but if he has wronged you or owes you anything" (v. 19) establishes a challenge to Philemon's social space and honor.[87] As was noted above, Paul might be aware of or at least suspect that the tension of debt overhangs the owner-slave relationship, but this is by no means clear or necessary to the situation. What he does is employ condi-

---

85. See Robbins, *Exploring*, 80.

86. On challenge-response, see Robbins, *Exploring*, 80–82.

87. On the meaning and usage of ὀφείλω and ἐλλόγα as commercial and rhetorical terms, see Martin, "Rhetorical Function," 321–37. The first-class conditional should not be read as "since" (Wallace, *Greek Grammar*, 690–91).

tional and commercial language in his rhetorical argument.[88] Paul uses the possibility of debt owed to Philemon in order to cross the boundary further into Philemon's personal space. An actual debt is not needed to make this rhetoric forceful. Paul intensifies the challenge by saying "charge it to me." In usual cultural conditions, when a debt is incurred the debtor, on the one hand, is honor bound to pay off the debt. On the other hand, the honor of the creditor requires that he be repaid and that he not ignore what is owed to him. Philemon is the allegedly harmed party (ἀδικέω, "to wrong, harm, injure, do wrong"). Paul challenges the situation of honor versus shame by injecting himself as a third party into a suggested creditor-debtor relationship and taking the debt on himself.[89] He reinforces the challenge with two statements: "I Paul, I write in my own hand, I will repay," and "not that I say that you owe yourself to me." Paul the prisoner of Christ and Caesar challenges Philemon the honorable householder and slave owner. The socially low challenges the socially high. The prisoner personally writes his intention to pay for a debt owing to a relatively powerful man.[90] Philemon is challenged financially by a prisoner who has (presumably) very little cash or cash flow. This is followed up with a directly personal social challenge that, rhetorically, says what it claims not to say ("not that I say that"). By claiming he does not say what he actually does say, Paul employs rhetoric that makes it difficult for Philemon to offer a riposte. The entire notion of indebtedness has been turned away from Onesimus and placed directly on Philemon. Philemon is now the debtor. This is, of course, intentional on Paul's part. His rhetoric aims to address any opposition Philemon might have to the idea. Paul has subtly placed Philemon's reputation emotionally on the line. Philemon can repay Paul only by accepting Onesimus in love as brother. The pressure put on him will push him toward acceding to Paul's request.

Obedience

"Confident of your obedience, I write to you knowing also that you will do even more than I say" (v. 21). This is a nice piece of social rhetoric that

---

88. On this, see Martin, "Rhetorical Function," 334–37. See above section on *argumentative texture*.

89. Thus Paul is a kind of literary Christ figure.

90. Martin, "Rhetorical Function," 335–36, claims this is an "appeal to pity," to Philemon's emotions, where Paul asks that Onesimus's debts be charged to him. Philemon may feel pity for Paul, who is willing to take on another's debt.

lays out a proleptic view of Philemon's reaction to the letter. It presumes that Philemon will receive Onesimus as Paul requests. Philemon is presumed to be "obedient." This statement might be perceived as an attack on Philemon's honor with Paul trying to push him around, or it might be perceived as having an embarrassing or humbling effect on him. It does have a pathos force to it, because it sets Philemon in the space of equality with a slave. As a slave is to be obedient to the owner and to recognize and practice subservience, so does Paul anticipate Philemon's obedience, not just to Paul's request but to the raising up of Onesimus to a social level equal to his own. The topos and action of obedience has the force of abolishing the owner-slave relationship between Philemon and Onesimus. Although Paul has been careful to say that he does not command Philemon to receive Onesimus as a brother, although he has been careful to argue his case judiciously, he still anticipates and expects and is persuaded of Philemon's obedience, his acquiescence, in the matter.

Sacred Texture

Step Two (Verses 8–10)

In this step Paul employs "in Christ" (v. 8) and "Christ Jesus" (v. 9) terminology to support the initial stage of his direct appeal to Philemon. His boldness ($\pi\alpha\rho\rho\eta\sigma\iota\alpha$, v. 8) to act by appealing to Philemon in the letter (vv. 9–10) is situated in his connection to Christ. He repeats the "prisoner of Christ Jesus" language, thereby reemphasizing his sacred and inviolable commitment to Christ. The sacred commitment is exemplified in Paul's emotional description of Onesimus as "my child, whom I have birthed in chains." The close, existential relationship between Paul and Onesimus has emerged entirely because of the holy connections.

Step Three (Verse 11)

While it is not explicit, the change in Onesimus from being "useless" to being "useful" is attributable to his "birth" as Paul's child, hence, implicitly, to his recently acquired belief in Christ Jesus. Onesimus is a member of the new society of believers. His life is changed.

Step Four (Verses 12–14)

This step delineates the ethical actions that spring out of Paul's sacred commitments regarding the situation at hand. Paul does not present Philemon with direct commands. He is also not presumptuous regarding Onesimus. He sends Onesimus back to Philemon rather than demanding he remain with Paul for gospel service. In other words, Paul does not serve his own needs, nor does he demand that Onesimus be permitted to remain to serve with him on Philemon's behalf (v. 13). Honest and sacred commitment means that Onesimus must be sent back to Philemon for voluntary consent. The irony, of course, is that Paul's not so subtle rhetoric places nearly irresistible pressure on Philemon to do "the good thing" (τὸ ἀγαθόν, v. 14). The recognition that Onesimus can function as a servant of the gospel with Paul on Philemon's behalf suggests that the action of God is the basis for all that is going on.

Step Five (Verses 15–16)

These lines are central to the **sacred texture**. The use of the divine passive "he was separated" (ἐχωρίσθη, v. 15) makes clear, in a subtle way, that Onesimus and Philemon are separated because God has acted and continues to act in order to bring about good. The world, in this case at least, is not operating according to human desires or in a materialistic way. It functions at the will of God, even in a tense and difficult situation that carries with it dramatic, perhaps daunting, social, cultural, and religious implications. The separation is envisioned to be temporary, "for a while." The temporary nature of the separation can be accepted and understood only on the level of faith, not of sight, since Philemon and Onesimus are geographically far apart as the letter is written. Similarly, the view toward reconciliation is presented as a matter of faith since it looks toward Philemon having Onesimus back forever, for the ages (αἰώνιον). The view toward having Onesimus back in the household and in the *ekklēsia* is, obviously to Paul, the beginning of a new sacred relationship: Onesimus will be "no longer a slave, but more than a slave, a beloved brother, especially to me, but so much more to you also in the flesh and in the Lord" (v. 16). The new sacred relationship that Paul envisions indicates the holy task set before Philemon: Onesimus is his brother in a double connection, being considered so in the flesh—in living, human reality—and in the Lord—in the holy union with Christ Jesus. These are relationships understood, once again, by faith. The community is fully established in the broadest possible terms. In the sacred environment cultural, social, economic, and other barriers are broken down and removed. The slave is not now a slave, but is a full member of the sacred assembly. Paul does not work out all the details of how this will function, but he does move Philemon, Onesimus, and the community along a particular holy trajectory.

Step Six (Verses 17–20)

Paul's employment of the word "partner" (κοινωνός, v. 17) recalls the personal and community language of step one, where Philemon is described as "beloved" and "coworker" and where Paul wishes that the "partnership" (κοινωνία, v. 6) of Philemon's faith might become effective among believers. This language of partnership is a **sacred texture**, because it impresses on Philemon the sense of unity that exists between himself and Paul and emphasizes their place and effectiveness together in the community. Onesimus is a member of this holy partnership as Paul's "child" and Philemon's "beloved brother" and, explicitly, because Paul says, "receive him as me." Paul extends the function of the partnership by demonstrating his own commitment to it: if Onesimus owes Philemon anything, Paul warrants to pay it. Philemon is drawn into the reality of the situation. Paul is not prepared to allow Philemon to avoid the partnership or avoid the issue with Onesimus. He reminds Philemon of a debt owing. Philemon owes his own life—presumably his life as a Christ-believer and member of the new society—to Paul (v. 20). Then the language of this sacred trajectory is extended back, in subtle rhetoric, from Philemon to Paul when Paul says, "Yes, brother, might I possibly have this benefit from you? Refresh my viscera in Christ!" (v. 20). The sacred locus "in Christ" presses the rhetoric home. Philemon cannot refuse. He is drawn in to practice the sacred life by refreshing Paul as he has previously refreshed others.

Rhetorical Force as Emergent Discourse

Life is no longer the same in the apocalyptically shaped new society that Paul, Philemon, Onesimus, and the *ekklēsia* inhabit. The middle of the letter emerges directly and powerfully into Philemon's Christ-believing, ecclesial, and sociocultural environments calling for striking changes to how he lives with other people. This section of the letter delivers a new wisdom for a new society that must, according to Paul, remove cultural and social boundaries between people while ignoring, indeed rejecting, both internal and external pressures to maintain them. Practicing the new wisdom is a sacred duty. The new life where there are no longer any slaves, where all are family members, and where prisoners of the state are partners with householders like Philemon is now the social ethic for Christ-believers. For Paul this is an unavoidable conclusion since he believes that all persons in Christ are "Abraham's offspring, heirs according to the promise" (Gal 3:29). Paul's rhetoric about all this is profoundly forceful and transformational.

Frame Four

As in the opening of the letter, several conceptual frames in the middle blend to move Philemon toward new social relationships in Christ.[91] Frame four displays Paul in a role more directly relevant to the presenting situation of the letter. He is the prisoner literally in chains but also in the metaphorical chains of the gospel who has, in a gospel sense, given birth to Onesimus his child (vv. 10, 13). Here are more directly "prison" and "parent" rhetorolects where Paul speaks from the spaces, roles, and voices of imprisonment and of begetting a child. It is in these spaces that Paul and Onesimus have met and in which Onesimus has become a Christ-believer. Paul is also, in this input frame, Philemon's "partner," a notion he uses to appeal to Philemon (v. 17). This rhetoric works on Paul's assumption that Philemon accepts the reality of the partnership in their faith and existence in Christ. The partnership of Paul and Philemon in the service of the gospel is suggested in verse 13, where Paul imagines that Onesimus could serve with him on Philemon's behalf. This partnership exists because of the apocalyptic work of God. It is a feature of Paul's request and argument: "receive him as [if he were] me, [your partner]." In this frame Paul presents himself as ready, if necessary, to pay for any debt owed by Onesimus to Philemon (vv. 18–19). Paul understands the new apocalyptically shaped reality in Christ and is therefore willing to do what he can to meet the needs of other believers. In other words, Paul is himself prepared in this way to refresh Philemon's viscera in a way not unlike what Philemon has done for the holy ones. Whether there is a real debt owed or whether Paul

---

91. See the discussion of "Rhetorical Force as Emergent Discourse" in The Opening, above, with the first three frames described there.

uses the possibility of debt in order to intensify his persuasive argument is not significant. That Paul is willing to pay is adequately compelling. In the closing section, Paul uses his expectation of Philemon's obedience as a subtle avoidance of command (cf. vv. 9–10). He could hardly anticipate this obedience if he did not know that Philemon had been deeply affected by the gospel and that Philemon would be extremely unlikely to refuse to accept Onesimus.

Frame Five

The fifth frame is occupied by Onesimus. He is a slave and, as such, at least with regard to Philemon, was formerly "useless." He has for some amount of time been separated from Philemon but now, having met Paul, has been affected by the gospel and become Paul's child; he is "useful." He is returning to Philemon, being sent by Paul. Onesimus has affected Paul deeply; he has become Paul's own viscera (v. 12), something similar to how Philemon has affected the holy ones. The connection between Onesimus and Paul is very intense. Onesimus is capable of being a servant with Paul "in the chains of the gospel" (v. 13). But he is imagined standing as an equal brother with Paul and Philemon in wisdom space. There is here an emergent slavery-freedom New Testament discourse and rhetorolect.

Frame Six

The sixth frame focuses in more closely on Philemon, emphasizing him as the slave owner to whom the appeal and direct argumentation are made. He hears Paul's priestly, intercessory rhetoric on behalf of Onesimus. He observes Paul as his partner and visualizes Paul signing his name to guarantee any thought of debt owed by Onesimus. He feels the pressure of Paul's rhetoric stating that he owes much, his new life as a Christ-believer, to Paul (vv. 17–19). He is also aware that the people of his household and the *ekklēsia* are watching and listening. He hears the appeal to provide a benefit to his "brother" Paul, and the imperative to refresh Paul's viscera (v. 20).

Frame Seven

The seventh frame importantly employs a number of dynamic, moving, topoi. These topoi function as an apocalyptic rhetorolect that indicates or is related to important developments and changes that are, in Paul's and

Philemon's perspectives, now present "in Christ."[92] These are rhetorically shaping topoi, because they are intended to bring about Philemon's social formation by evoking ideological change in him as a Christ-believer with regard to Onesimus. They function in the letter, because they are cultural frames that will be understood by Philemon in the Christ-believing culture in which he has lately been living.

Christ

Paul is a prisoner of Christ (vv. 1, 9), he recognizes the "Lord Jesus Christ" (vv. 3, 25), and he knows the importance of the locative rhetoric of the notion of being "in Christ" and "in the Lord" (vv. 6, 8, 16, 20, 23). Implicit in this Christ topos are Paul's convictions regarding the apocalyptic work of God in Jesus Christ. Christ is the one who, Paul believes, fulfills Israelite and scriptural expectation, who "died for our sins," was raised, and is now alive (e.g., 1 Cor 15:3–4). For Paul, for Philemon, and now for Onesimus, this means an apocalyptic change has been made to how the world is viewed. Being a prisoner of Roman civil authorities is apparently not worth mentioning directly, and being a prisoner of Christ Jesus is not dishonorable to Paul in any way. Philemon is presumed by Paul to understand this. Things are different now. In Christ prisoners and slaves, even if chained, are de facto free. In Christ slaves are not "useless" but are "useful" servants of the gospel. In Christ Philemon works hard to provide refreshment to other Christ-believers. These things are aspects of the rhetorical force and environment of the letter.

Ekklēsia

The assembly of Christ-believers located in Philemon's house is the apocalyptically shaped new community. Onesimus is to be part of this localized *ekklēsia* when he arrives. So also will Paul be part of it when he comes to occupy a room in Philemon's house (v. 22). Membership in the *ekklēsia* means that people recognize and believe in the apocalyptic action of God in Christ. They are participants.

---

92. By apocalyptic, I mean the rhetorolect and space that indicates or reveals that God has acted to bring about good in the world.

Love

Philemon's love (v. 5) and Paul's love (v. 9) demonstrate that apocalyptic and gospel change have affected them. Philemon loves the Lord Jesus and all the saints. He has done good for them. Paul, who could demand obedience, chooses to make his appeal through love so that Philemon would extend his love to Onesimus (v. 16). This love is foundational to the rhetorical force of the letter. It is the basis of action, the anticipated result of the argument, and the motive for action.

Refreshed Viscera

This rhetoricized terminology describes the wisdom work of Philemon's life. He has already engaged in refreshing the viscera of the holy ones (v. 7). He is called to do it again, (v. 20), but now with respect to the tension-filled situation with Onesimus. This intensifies the rhetorical force of Paul's appeal, because Onesimus is a slave who is separated from Philemon, his owner. Paul too, of course, feels the visceral force of his own relationship with Onesimus.

The Paradigmatic Stories: Joseph; Exodus; Deuteronomy; Slavery, Freedom, and Kinship

While these ancient and sacred texts are not mentioned explicitly in the letter, they are **intertextures** that form narrational and theological paradigms for Paul's approach to the separation and anticipated reconciliation of Philemon and Onesimus.[93] They are hidden, intertextural frames. The key feature of these stories is the faith understanding that God was at work—apocalyptically and often miraculously—to bring about good for people who were oppressed in slavery but were made free. When free they lived together in a restored brotherhood-kinship-family or wisdom situation. Joseph was sold as a slave by his brothers and was taken to Egypt. Eventually, Joseph was freed, elevated to a high and powerful position, and reconciled with his brothers as family. This good conclusion to the story is clearly attributed to the action of God (Gen 45:7–8; 50:20). In the Exodus narrative, the Hebrew slaves suffer under Egyptian oppression and God/Yahweh hears their cry for release (Exod 2:22–25; 3:7–9). With Moses as leader, the Hebrew slaves experience an apocalyptic, God-empowered release from slavery and movement across the waters of the

93. See above on **intertexture**.

Red Sea to freedom and the nation-building of a family, the descendants of Abraham, Isaac, and Jacob (Exod 4–20). Deuteronomy regularly refers to this great action of Yahweh; slaves are freed by Yahweh's "mighty hand and outstretched arm" (Deut 5:15; 6:20–21; 15:15; 16:12; 24:18, 22). God is always the apocalyptic supplier of freedom from slavery and continuing existence in kinship. Slaves are freed, and they become brothers (again). Those who are freed by Christ, says Paul, are not to fall back into slavery again. Nor should they employ their freedom to indulge the flesh. They should, ironically and perhaps at first glance counterintuitively, become slaves of each other (Gal 5:1, 13). This kind of slave is what Paul is as prisoner of Christ and parent of Onesimus; he is the servant, obliquely, of Philemon. Onesimus is now to be understood as the reconciled brother of Philemon. Philemon should do the right thing. This entire understanding demonstrates a focused rhetorical dialect of early Christianity. It is slavery-freedom-kinship rhetorolect. It is a discourse that describes freedom and reconciliation and kinship as central features of Paul's gospel and apocalyptic understanding. It is discourse that speaks of the new reality in Christ. The community of Christ-believers functions as a household of freed slaves, that is, of family-related persons who together, in Paul's slavery-freedom-kinship language, are "children of God" and offspring of Abraham (Gal 3:26, 29; 4:1–5) and, in his rhetoric, imagined as his own "children" (τέκνα μου, Gal 4:19), like Onesimus.

Eternity
This apocalyptic conception is inserted into the rhetoric when Paul says to Philemon, "Perhaps for this reason he was separated for a while, so that you might have him back forever" (v. 15). As Christ-believers, both Paul and Philemon have this apocalyptically shaped view toward eternal or everlasting (αἰώνιος)[94] existence. This eternal, reconciled state of Philemon and Onesimus is not existence as owner and slave, but is the kinship existence of brothers (v. 16). It is the existence of people whose life conditions have been directly altered by God. It is existence of eternity already in the present. The view to eternity presses on Philemon to remember and act on his commitments to Christ and the community.

---

94. The word αἰώνιος is placed in emphatic position in the clause.

Blended Space

The new blended space evoked by Paul's rhetoric is the new realm and new society of Christ, the gospel, the *ekklēsia*, and eternity. It is the new space of freedom and brotherhood. It is the space where people recognize that God has brought about apocalyptic newness and where people in it live in love and harmony with one another, practicing love and faithfulness to all others who share the space with them and engaging in acts of refreshment. It is the space where not only Paul and Philemon are brothers, where not only a sister like Apphia is described in family terms, but also where a "nonperson" like the slave Onesimus is also a brother. The culturally and socially conditioned and politically expected segregation of the ancient Mediterranean world cannot properly exist in this blended space. In this blended wisdom space, memories of formerly "useless" slaves are abolished, because in Christ they are now "useful" and engage in productive behaviors, as do others, like Philemon, who had not been slaves. If there are grievances due to past injuries or debts, they are set aside. This is the space where Paul and Philemon and now also Onesimus live as free, equal persons, and Onesimus is not treated or visualized as a slave. Slavery is abolished in the *ekklēsia* and the household of believers. This is the emergent structure of early Christianity as issues were faced and the apocalyptic work of God in Christ was brought to bear on the issues. This new society is not brought about because its human members are deserving, but because they are now ἐν Χριστῷ.

The direct object of concern, actually the direct *person* of concern, is not Onesimus; it is Philemon. Slavery, similarly, is not a direct object of concern. In the emergent blended space, the concern and the expectation is Philemon's reception of Onesimus. For Paul, popular culture and the social expectations of civil society are not guiding forces for Christ-believers. Things are different in the new society. This is what Philemon is to understand more fully than he had previously. Brotherhood, kinship, family, love, equality are now extended to slaves who are no longer slaves. This is the blended situation and the rhetorical force of the letter. This is how things are now in the wisdom, ecclesial, household space. This is what the blended slavery-freedom-kinship rhetorolect of early Christianity is about. The rhetorical force of the letter to Philemon brings about this new situation in the ancient Mediterranean.

The rhetorical turning point is the language describing the change in Onesimus. He has been birthed by Paul, who considers Onesimus to be his child (v. 10). His behavior now accords with his name (v. 11). He has become as Paul's own viscera (v. 12). He is competent to serve with Paul in "the chains of the gospel" (v. 13). All that has occurred between Philemon and Onesimus has been the work of God with a view toward eternity (v. 15). The turning point, then, is that Onesimus has become to Philemon a "brother ... in the Lord" and is to be imagined also as a brother "in the flesh" (v. 15). All this can only mean that Onesimus has become a believer in Christ Jesus, just like the other persons mentioned in the letter. This is an apocalyptic change that Paul, in his prophetic and priestly space relative to Philemon, aims to convey. In this blended space, the emotional connections are altered. Honor versus shame in the ancient community where slaves are always subordinate is replaced by the honor of being in Christ and where former slaves are brothers. Shame in the new society would be to maintain the traditions of slavery. This understanding, this blended rhetoric and space, comes, rather ironically, from persuasion given by a man experiencing the indignity of imprisonment. The rhetoric is meant to elicit an understanding in Philemon, a psychological moment when he gets it. He has been captured and drawn along by Paul to follow his rhetoric and to be moved to do what Paul calls him to do. The blended frame sets Philemon fully into the ideological space of the new society, where he can do the right thing in Christ precisely because it is the right and faithful thing to do.

The Closing, Philemon 21–25

Closing Texture

The shift to *closing texture* occurs at verse 21, where the argument of claims and expectations begins to move toward the conclusion of the rhetoric. The rhetoric of verse 20, "Yes, brother, might I possibly have this benefit from you in the Lord? Refresh my viscera in Christ!" repeats the rhetoric of verse 7, "because the viscera of the holy ones have been refreshed by you, brother," thereby bringing the thought back to Philemon's wonderful ability to refresh the viscera of people and forming an end point to the central argumentation. There is no direct linkage by means of a particle between verses 20 and 21. Paul begins his closing lines by stating that he is confident Philemon will do—literally out of his "obedience"—even more than what Paul wants. This statement of confidence works to close the rhetoric of the letter by punctuating Paul's expectations for Philemon's behavior. The closure is intensified by Paul's rather brazen suggestion that he will be coming to see Philemon and needs a place to stay (v. 22).

Progressive Texture

Four progressions draw the discourse to a conclusion.

1. Verse 21
   ²¹ πεποιθὼς τῇ ὑπακοῇ σου ἔγραψά σοι,
   εἰδὼς ὅτι καὶ ὑπὲρ ἃ λέγω ποιήσεις

   ²¹ Confident of your obedience, I write to you
   knowing that you will do even more than I say

This first concluding progression presents Paul's bold assertion of his certainty that Philemon will do the right thing, indeed that he will do more than Paul requests. This progression begins the conclusion to the letter, because Paul's argumentation for resolving the situation between Philemon and Onesimus has been completed.

2. Verse 22
    ²² ἅμα δὲ καὶ ἑτοίμαζέ μοι ξενίαν,
        ἐλπίζω γὰρ ὅτι διὰ τῶν προσευχῶν ὑμῶν χαρισθήσομαι ὑμῖν

    ²² But at the same time, prepare hospitality space for me,
        for I hope that because of your prayers I shall be restored to you

By means of the words ἅμα δὲ καὶ, "but at the same [time] also," Paul moves the entire discourse ahead by indicating his hope of coming and receiving hospitality from Philemon. This progression tells Philemon that he really cannot avoid accepting Onesimus as Paul has requested. He should expect a personal visit, a "restoration" of Paul in face-to-face presence.

3. Verses 23–24
    ²³ Ἀσπάζεταί σε Ἐπαφρᾶς ὁ συναιχμάλωτός μου ἐν Χριστῷ Ἰησοῦ,
        ²⁴ Μᾶρκος, Ἀρίσταρχος, Δημᾶς, Λουκᾶς, οἱ συνεργοί μου

    ²³ Epaphras my fellow prisoner in Christ Jesus greets you,
        ²⁴ as do Mark, Aristarchus, Demas, Luke, my coworkers.

Here is presented a greeting from Paul's coprisoner Epaphras, who may be known personally to Philemon (see Col 4:12). In a statement that relies on the singular verb indicating Epaphras's greeting, four additional coworkers send their acknowledgment to Philemon.

4. Verse 25
    ²⁵ Ἡ χάρις τοῦ κυρίου Ἰησοῦ Χριστοῦ μετὰ τοῦ πνεύματος ὑμῶν

    ²⁵ The grace of the Lord Jesus Christ be with your spirit.

This progression states the final and, like the prescript, verbless closing greeting. It employs the plural, thus including the addressees mentioned in verses 1–3.

This analysis of *progressive texture* shows once more how very focused the letter is on Philemon. It directly seeks his response to the situation that has arisen regarding Onesimus and with Paul relative to Onesimus.

Philemon is the object of concern, not Onesimus. Onesimus is to be the recipient of the proposed good actions of Philemon. Onesimus is, at best, the indirect object of concern, even if it is his separation from Philemon that has led to the composition of the letter. Nor, it may be important to say, is slavery, particularly slavery among Christ-believers, the object of concern, even if Paul was an abolitionist, as the letter seems to indicate. The progressive discourse is meant to bring about moral and social, indeed gospel change in Philemon. The letter is about Philemon's spiritual formation. The progressions also point us quite directly to *narrational texture*.

Narrational Texture

By step eight (v. 21), the narration of claims and expectations is moving toward conclusion. Narrating the sequence of his thinking and perhaps still writing with his own hand, Paul expresses his confidence in Philemon's positive response, actually described as "obedience" toward the story about Onesimus. The rhetorical force of the language is very strong in its proleptic direction. Paul anticipates Philemon's future behavior. The discourse fully expects Philemon to treat the slave Onesimus as if he were a family member who will do what Paul says. It is as if Paul were saying, "I'm sure you will do the right thing," thereby maintaining the intensity of pressure on Philemon.

Step nine (v. 22) voices a kind of addendum to the closing thought of verse 21. "But at the same time, prepare hospitality space for me, for I hope that because of your prayers I shall be restored to you." Paul the narrator, prisoner, old man, maintains a high level of hope. He plans to visit Philemon, suggesting that he wishes to have firsthand knowledge of how Onesimus the brother is treated after he returns to Philemon. Paul is close enough as a friend to Philemon to be confident he can make a request for a room and hospitality. The addendum adds to and complements the narrative. It indicates to all whom Paul knows that all of the people connected with Philemon (ὑμῶν, "you" plural) have been praying for him during his imprisonment. He believes that these prayers have been effective and that he will be released and will join Philemon and the *ekklēsia* in due course. The ethos of the entire letter, because it emphasizes the common work of Paul and Philemon, their partnership, and their common faith in and love for the Lord Jesus comes together here in expectation of Paul's arrival. It emphasizes the necessity for Philemon to heed Paul's request.

Step ten (vv. 23–25) ends the narration with greetings from several persons who may be thought to be at the periphery of the story, but are interested people who may well have helped prepare the letter or gathered materials for its production as Paul's coworkers (οἱ συνεργοί μου). They may be thought of as participants with Paul and persons who support his request concerning Onesimus, even if a step further removed from Philemon than Paul. Epaphras is singled out, although as "fellow prisoner" (συναιχμάλωτός) with Paul rather than the "prisoner" (δέσμιος) Paul calls himself. They are interested parties so have a relatively important role. Each one is named in the nominative case, so each is the subject of his own greeting. Their presence in the narration lends support and power to the rhetoric. The closing greeting, "The grace of the Lord Jesus Christ be with your Spirit," ends the letter but is not a passive or merely polite remark. It signals closure to the ideas and expectations of the narrative, but also indicates that more people are aware of the situation and are looking on than might have been thought at first glance. People are looking over Philemon's shoulder from a distance. Perhaps he is meant to be aware that these other friends are watching.

The *narrational texture* in Philemon provides a story that ends, but the ending is the beginning of an important future.[1] That is, even though the letter ends, life for Philemon, Onesimus, and Paul continues on in the new society where the slave is not a slave but a beloved brother, and more, a "partner" in the gospel with Paul and Philemon, and a "child" of Paul! This is the promise that the story of existence "in Christ" does not end with the Letter to Philemon, but imagines a continuing narrative where life is good. This is wisdom rhetorolect envisioning productive living as people move along in their lives.

Argumentative Texture

There is a shift in step ten, verses 21–22, to argumentation that assumes the anticipated results of the middle are by now certain. It is as if Paul has been persuaded by his own rhetorical argumentation and is sure that Philemon will properly receive Onesimus: "Confident of your obedience, I write to you knowing that you will do more than I say" (v. 21). The rationale for

---

1. On this notion, see Christopher Bryan, *Listening to the Bible: The Art of Faithful Biblical Interpretation* (Oxford: Oxford University Press, 2014), 99–101.

the argued assumption is based on Paul's confidence in Philemon. Despite his stated confidence, Paul goes on to offer a surprise: he is coming to see Philemon. "But at the same time, prepare hospitality space for me, for I hope that because of your prayers I shall be restored to you" (v. 22). While Paul has confidence in Philemon, he nevertheless aims to persuade him with one more argument that functions by indicating that he is coming to check on Philemon. To increase the social pressure Paul returns now to using plural pronouns in order to bring the *ekklēsia* directly into play. Paul will be watching how Philemon responds to the letter, and so will the members of the *ekklēsia*. The implied result of this argumentation is that Philemon should get ready for the visit not only by preparing for Paul's arrival but also by receiving Onesimus.

> Case: Paul is confident Onesimus will do the right thing. Still, he plans to visit Philemon and the *ekklēsia*.

> Rationale: Paul thinks that Philemon is persuaded by his overall argument. But checking up personally is likely to ensure Philemon's agreement and action with regard to Onesimus.

> Implied result: Philemon should prepare for Paul's visit mentally and by arranging for hospitality (food and lodging).

The concluding rhetoric (vv. 23–25) closes the letter with greetings from five explicitly named persons and a blessing from Paul. These words are standard epistolary features in New Testament letters, but nevertheless form their own *argumentative texture* and have rhetorical power. Paul returns to the prophetic and priestly spaces and rhetorolects with which he began in verses 1–3. The prophetic, proclamatory argument is subtle and implicit. Five presumably recognizable, named persons send their greetings to Philemon along with Paul. The implicit argument is that these persons, coworkers with Paul,[2] know of the situation facing Philemon regarding Onesimus and are interested observers. In this way they function as participants in the situation and in the argumentation. Epaphras is watching, as are Mark, Aristarchus, Demas, and Luke. It is as if they are saying, "We know about all this Philemon! We are hoping for the outcome Paul

---

2. Demas is described, later, as having abandoned Paul (2 Tim 4:10).

has set out for you!" The tension between Philemon and Onesimus is not a private matter. The expectations of partnership (v. 17) and community place strong pressure on Philemon. This argument effectively comes from Paul and all five others.

> Case: Onesimus is returning to Philemon, and Paul anticipates a reconciliation and brotherly relationship.
>
> Rationale: Caring people send their greetings. The subtle, implied rationale is that they are interested observers who are watching to see how Philemon receives Onesimus. This places pressure on Philemon.
>
> Anticipated result: Onesimus will be received as a beloved brother and member of the *ekklēsia* in Philemon's home.

The closing priestly rhetoric is intercessory. Paul calls for grace from the Lord Jesus Christ. This argues that there is gospel power and encouragement to do the right thing. It argues that the blessing of grace comes "from" the Lord Jesus himself (τοῦ κυρίου Ἰησοῦ Χριστοῦ). Grace is also implied for Onesimus and for all who are with Philemon. This argues for a present and future peaceful, peaceable, loving, and faithful reality where Paul, Philemon, Onesimus, and the *ekklēsia* exist and work in unity. This is a subtle argument for the envisioned situation of verse 16. It imagines the ecclesial space of wisdom, of the new society.[3]

> Case: There is good grace for Philemon, Onesimus, and all others connected with the situation indicated in the letter.
>
> Rationale: Such grace comes from the Lord Jesus Christ (Ἡ χάρις τοῦ κυρίου Ἰησοῦ Χριστοῦ).
>
> Anticipated result: Even though the current situation is tense, there will be a good outcome, a strengthened society and refreshed viscera with[4] "the spirit" of all concerned (μετὰ τοῦ πνεύματος ὑμῶν).

---

3. See the same wording in Phil 4:23.
4. Abiding with, abiding in.

Sensory-Aesthetic Texture

The *sensory-aesthetic texture* of the closing is observed in three steps:

Step eight (v. 21)
> ²¹ πεποιθὼς τῇ ὑπακοῇ σου ἔγραψά σοι,
> εἰδὼς ὅτι καὶ ὑπὲρ ἃ λέγω ποιήσεις

> ²¹ Confident of your obedience, I write to you
> knowing that you will do even more than I say

Step nine (v. 22)
> ²² ἅμα δὲ καὶ ἑτοίμαζέ μοι ξενίαν,
> ἐλπίζω γὰρ ὅτι διὰ τῶν προσευχῶν ὑμῶν χαρισθήσομαι ὑμῖν

> ²² But at the same time, prepare hospitality space for me,
> for I hope that because of your prayers I shall be restored to you

Step ten (vv. 23–25)
> ²³ Ἀσπάζεταί σε Ἐπαφρᾶς ὁ συναιχμάλωτός μου ἐν Χριστῷ Ἰησοῦ,
> ²⁴ Μᾶρκος, Ἀρίσταρχος, Δημᾶς, Λουκᾶς, οἱ συνεργοί μου.
> ²⁵ Ἡ χάρις τοῦ κυρίου Ἰησοῦ Χριστοῦ μετὰ τοῦ πνεύματος ὑμῶν.

> ²³ Epaphras my fellow prisoner in Christ Jesus greets you,
> ²⁴ as do Mark, Aristarchus, Demas, Luke, my coworkers.
> ²⁵ The grace of the Lord Jesus Christ be with your spirit.

In step eight, Paul comes to his conclusion with the perfect participle πεποιθώς, indicating that he has become confident in, remains confident in, and is trusting in Philemon's obedience (compliance) to his request. Paul comes now to what is already known to the senses if not yet seen in temporal reality. This is Paul's own sensory expression, his own viscera, regarding Philemon. He is internally and emotionally confident; in fact according to the participle's meaning, he depends on Philemon's reception of Onesimus. He is sure of it. This *sensory-aesthetic texturing* makes the expected reception of Onesimus a reality to the senses for Philemon and for readers and listeners. What is real to the senses will surely become real and physical and observable in concrete time and space. This is very pushy language; what Paul speaks Philemon will do. This is literarily, emotionally, and viscerally proleptic, that is, it speaks of the future as if it were present. There is a proleptic assurance of the future. Paul has faith in Philemon, his brother-partner. Paul is still very much physically engaged with this rhetoric in a sensory way, because he continues to use his hand to write (ἔγραψά σοι). He is persuaded by his own rhetoric and is certain that the future will be better than the present. The force of this texturing is enhanced and pressed home by the natural sensory balance and melopoeia of each line of thirteen syllables, by the -ώς sounds and endings of the initial participles, by the corresponding first-person-singular verbs in each line (ἔγραψά and λέγω), and by the final second-person-singular forms of each line (σοι and ποιήσεις). These features appeal to ears and eyes to evoke sensory connections.

Step nine provides what at first glance seems to be a rather soft ending that closes the moral argument of the letter. The hard evocation of the senses by the letter up until now seem to be ameliorated by Paul's request: "But at the same time, prepare hospitality space for me, for I hope that because of your prayers I shall be restored to you." But, on the other hand, this is not such a soft ending, because it contains a subtle sensory rhetoric that keeps the entire situation in front of Philemon's face and, with the reappearance of second-person-plural pronouns (ὑμῶν and ὑμῖν), before the faces of the church that meets in Philemon's house. As if he has not already said enough to affect and stir up Philemon's own viscera, Paul now states his intention and hope to come to see Philemon and take advantage of his hospitality. This step shouts out to Philemon: "And I'm coming to see you!" While Paul and Philemon are friends, this line suggests an awkward sensory and physical situation for Philemon. Not only has he been called to make sensory-aesthetic and social space for the slave Onesimus, he is now called to make physical space and provide hospitality for Paul, whose own release is anticipated. Paul projects his own bodily presence into the scene. The noun ξενία, used only here and in Acts 28:23 in the New Testament,[5] implies the notion of a guest room or lodging place but refers more directly to hospitality or the entertainment of guests. So Paul is requesting physical space and direct, personal interaction with Philemon and the church in his house. The implications could hardly be more sensory. Paul cannot be avoided by Philemon. This suggests, of course, that Onesimus cannot be avoided by Philemon either. The natural sensory response is for Philemon to prepare for what his coming visitor expects.

---

5. The cognate verb ξενίζω is used eleven times in the New Testament.

Paul is "in his face." The pressure on Philemon is intensified even more because Paul says, "for I hope that because of your prayers I will be restored to you." Philemon is apparently directly tied to Paul's forthcoming release from prison. It is Philemon, along with the assembly of believers in his house, who is connected by his own thoughts and mouth and speech in prayers for Paul's release. It is as if it is Philemon's own fault that Paul will soon be accepting his hospitality. While this should be a welcome sensory thought (a refreshing of the viscera?) for the *ekklēsia* and Philemon, it also intensifies the sensory pressure on Philemon to do the right thing. Provide for Paul the old man-prisoner the kind of hospitality you are asked to give to the slave Onesimus. The sensory view here is toward the future, toward the answer to prayers, and to reception and hospitality. It is about the expectation of good in coming days.

Step ten, the final closing rhetoric, is, from a sensory-aesthetic point of view, much more than a simple or standard closing greeting to a New Testament letter. The ears hear and the mind's eyes see that Paul is not alone in his requests of Philemon. All these people, perhaps more than them for all we know, are watching, paying attention from a distance. There is a much larger group than first indicated. There is, certainly, Philemon, Apphia, Archippus, and the *ekklēsia* in Philemon's house. There are Paul and Timothy. But here are the names of five more people, coworkers, faithful persons, whom, we assume, know the narrative, know the requests being made of Philemon, and perhaps know Onesimus. They are Paul's entourage. They send their own greetings to Philemon, so it is likely that he knows who they are. Like Philemon they are "in Christ Jesus" (ἐν Χριστῷ Ἰησοῦ). The grace of the Lord Jesus Christ will be with them as they wish it for Philemon. All this is very highly sensory. It touches on ideas and people recognizable to Philemon. There is simply no sensory, bodily relief for Philemon from Paul's requests. Too many people are watching. Epaphras, like Paul and with Paul, is a fellow prisoner (ὁ συναιχμάλωτός μου) for the sake of Christ. This means that prisoners are greeting Philemon from the location of their distress. They are more than mere greeters, more than simply other persons known. The sound effects enhance the sensory effect with the verbless chain of names with nominative -ς endings. The repetitive "my" (μου) following articular nouns (ὁ συναιχμάλωτός μου; οἱ συνεργοί μου) creates harmony. The plural pronoun "your" (ὑμῶν) creates a sensory collective of people with their own spirit. Philemon is pressured, but he can go away with confidence in the presence of God's grace and the good wishes of friends.

Intertexture

As with the opening, the obvious **intertexture** related to the closing are the endings of the Pauline letters, other New Testament letters, and other ancient Mediterranean letters. The wording of the closing greeting, "The grace of the Lord Jesus Christ be with your spirit" (v. 25, verbless in Greek), is paralleled exactly in Phil 4:23, with slightly shorter wording in Rom 16:20; 1 Cor 16:23; Col 4:18; 1 Thess 5:28; 1 Tim 6:21; and Titus 3:15; with somewhat longer versions in 2 Cor 13:13 ("the Grace") and Gal 6:18; and with a closely similar wording in 2 Thess 3:18 and 2 Tim 4:22. Paul employs his own, Christ-believing, standard closing greeting forms.

Confidence

Paul states that he is confident of Philemon's obedience, certainly with regard to his request—which he said earlier is not a command, though he now speaks of obedience—seen in verse 16. In other letters Paul has expressed confidence (πείθω/πείθομαι) in people (2 Cor 2:3), in God (Phil 1:6), and in the Lord Jesus (2 Thess 3:4) and in the notions that he will remain alive (Phil 1:25), that he will return to visit believers in Philippi (2:24), and that his imprisonment has served to build up the confidence of some believers (Phil 1:14). The author of Heb 2:13, drawing on Isa 8:17–18 LXX, portrays Christ as having confidence in God. In each case the confidence is warranted.[6] Paul is confident of Philemon's response here not because of his apostolic authority—which he does not mention in the letter—but because of his argumentation and his relationship with Philemon. Paul is confident that he will get what he wants and that Philemon will be properly generous to Onesimus, inviting him to brotherhood and all that implies. Although Philemon is in a socially superior position, he will be obedient to Paul. The superior can be obedient to the inferior. Intertexturally, 2 Sam 22:36 LXX describes God being obedient to David (καὶ ἡ ὑπακοή σου ἐπλήθυνέν με). Confidence of obedience is something in the air for Paul, a feature of his intertextural and cultural milieu.

---

6. As the perfect tense πεποιθώς in both passages indicates. See James D. G. Dunn, *The Epistles to the Colossians and to Philemon*, NIGTC (Grand Rapids: Eerdmans, 1996), 344.

Hospitality Space

Paul asks Philemon to provide him with "hospitality space" (v. 22). The noun ξενία refers to hospitality, reception, a room, lodging. The cognate verb ξενίζω means "I entertain." Because Paul here requests both reception on his return from prison and some living space, it is translated as "hospitality space." Acts 28:23 employs ξενία to describe Paul's lodging in Rome, where Jewish leaders came for discussion with him. His lodging clearly doubled as space where he could receive guests. Paul himself employs the cognate noun ξένος ("host")[7] in reference to Gaius (Rom 16:23). According to 2 Sam 8:2, 6 LXX, the defeated Moabites and Syrians (Arameans) provided ξενία for David, that is, they provided tribute, goods, and hospitality. According to 1 Macc 10:36, Jews enlisted in the Seleucid army were to receive the same "maintenance" (ξενία) received by other military personnel. After Egyptian forces invaded Syria (1 Macc 11:1–19), Jonathan of Judea provided the Egyptian king with many "gifts" (ξενία), indicating his hospitable reception. Similar meaning of ξενία is observed in 3 Macc 1:8; Sir 20:29; and Hos 10:6 LXX. Pseudo-Clementines 12.2 uses ξενία with lodging in mind. What Paul wants is living space, food, and household hospitality when he is "restored" to Philemon. This is very likely what Philemon already supplies for the *ekklēsia* that meets in his house (v. 2). Such hospitality is a feature of refreshing the viscera of people, something for which Philemon has a reputation (v. 7). It is clear that Philemon can offer such hospitality in his home. It is, then, part of Paul's expectation of his "partner" Philemon.

Restoration

Paul anticipates his release from imprisonment and restoration to Philemon (v. 22). On this expectation, he requests the "hospitality space." The term used for "restoration" is χαρίζομαι, which means "to show favor," "give freely," "grant," "forgive," and "gratify." The semantic ideas extend to "release" (Acts 3:14) and "hand over" (Acts 25:11). The *Bibliotheca historia* of Diodorus Siculus 13.59.3 (60–30 BCE) speaks of the restoration by Hannibal of captured possessions and kinspeople to Empedion. Paul uses

---

7. In most places where this noun is used it means "strange" (adj.), "stranger," or "foreigner" (noun). See BDAG 548; LSJ 1189.

χαρίζομαι to mean "give freely," "freely give," or "grant" in Rom 8:32; 1 Cor 2:12; Gal 3:18; Phil 1:29; Phil 2:9; and Col 2:13. Paul expects that he will be granted release and restoration to the home of Philemon. Philemon, through his prayers, has a significant, perhaps determinative role in this restoration. Paul anticipates his release from imprisonment and, rather generously, integrates Philemon into it.

Personal Greetings

Some of the characters named in the closing greeting are seen in other Pauline letters, notably Col 4:7–17. Epaphras is mentioned in Col 1:7 and 4:12–13. The descriptor of Epaphras as "my fellow soldier in Christ" suggests that he is imprisoned like Paul. Συναιχμάλωτός, more literally indicating the military notion "prisoner of war," is used elsewhere in the New Testament only in Col 4:10 and Rom 16:7.[8] While Epaphras can be a shortened form of the name Epaphroditus (Phil 2:25; 4:18), there is no direct evidence, intertextural or otherwise, for thinking that the names refer to the same person. Mark is likely the same person appearing in Acts 12:12, 25; 15:37, 39 and was at least at some time a source of conflict for Paul. Colossians 4:10 refers to him as a cousin of Barnabas.[9] Aristarchus appears here and in Acts 19:29; 20:4; 27:2; and Col 4:10. He is described in Acts as being from Thessalonica in Macedonia and, in Col 4:10 as a "fellow prisoner" (again συναιχμάλωτός) with Paul. Demas is noted in Col 4:10, but in 2 Tim 4:11 he is described as someone who has deserted Paul. Luke, whose name occurs only three times in the New Testament (Phlm 24; Col 4:14; 2 Tim 4:11), is described as a loved and faithful coworker with Paul.

Intertexture in the letter functions interactively to produce powerful argumentative, rhetorical, and ideological effects on Philemon. Paul has laid out the intertextural topoi in order to make his persuasive argumentation flow dynamically in the direction he wishes to move Philemon to take. The analysis of **intertexture** provides us with information about things from outside the text known implicitly by Paul that inform his views. Philemon will recognize some of these things explicitly and some implicitly. Philemon will be affected by them rhetorically and emotion-

---

8. See above n. 6 in Repetitive Texture and n. 25 in The Middle.

9. This relationship might offer some level of explanation for the separation of Paul and Barnabas according to Acts 15:36–41. Paul and Mark apparently reunited at a later time.

ally. The analysis provides contexts for assessing the change from slavery to brotherhood that Paul calls Philemon to put into practice. It demonstrates the movement toward productive wisdom living in the new society of which Paul, Philemon, and Onesimus are members. Much pressure is placed on Philemon to take on Paul's critical point of view that brotherhood, kinship, and partnership define relationships in Christ.

Social and Cultural Texture

New Space: A Room

In the closing, Paul makes his final social request. He asks for new space, in this case an actual physical space, a room, presumably in Philemon's house, where the *ekklēsia* meets and where it might be gathered when the letter is read or heard by Philemon.[10] Brash old Paul has yet one more persuasive shot to take. He hopes and anticipates that he will see Philemon face-to-face in Philemon's space. This is a kind of social invasion. The prisoner wants the more socially powerful property owner to receive him—not only the slave—into his home. The one who offers to pay for what the slave might owe the owner asks for a room and hospitality, for space, hence something of value, in order to operate in the owner's own social realm. Paul adds, in a brilliant rhetorical move, that his anticipated release from imprisonment and restoration to Philemon is the result of good works in the form of the prayers of the *ekklēsia*. This sets more emotional pressure on Philemon. His own close associates are by their faithful efforts bringing Paul and perhaps Onesimus directly to Philemon. Paul here plays a strongly authoritative social role over Philemon even as he appears to have no authority at all.

Dyadic Social Features

Individual persons often have their sense of self-perception and their social and cultural behaviors identified and defined through their interrelationships with other persons. "Dyadic personality" is what is observed when one's self-perception is shaped by the expectations and reactions

---

10. Note here that while Paul uses the second-person-singular verb ἑτοίμαζέ to address Philemon, he returns to use of the second-person-plural pronouns ὑμῶν and ὑμῖν, indicating that the entire *ekklēsia* is once again in sight.

of another person with respect to how they perceive him or her.[11] Some-times a person needs another person in order to know who she or he is. Similarly, a "dyadic contract" is established when there is implicit agree-ment binding pairs of persons together.[12] Implicit dyadic contracts pres-sure people to reciprocate, to "pay back," for things given to them. Such paying back is a way of maintaining honor in a society.[13] These implicit, unwritten relationships can be powerfully influential in cultures and societies when they relate to things like commerce, marriage, property transactions, and religious sensibilities.[14] Social and cultural expecta-tions move people to action. Philemon is in a variety of ways identified and defined by his dyadic relationship to or contrast to others: he is the beloved coworker of Paul and Timothy; he is closely connected to Apphia, Archippus, and the *ekklēsia* that meets in his own house; he has an owner-slave dyadic relationship to Onesimus; we know who Philemon is because of his dyadic personality as one who has faith and love toward the Lord Jesus and all the holy ones. He has an implicit dyadic contract with One-simus as slave owner and possible creditor in some fashion. He has an implicit dyadic contract in a partnership with Paul, which Paul makes at least partially explicit. There are, then, expectations and pressures that the letter places on Philemon's mind. People on what might be imagined as the "less equal" low side of the dyads, namely, Paul the prisoner and Onesimus the slave, and on the "more equal"[15] high side of the dyads, namely, the people of the *ekklēsia* (and perhaps Paul), are likely to push Philemon to reciprocation, toward the social formation indicated by and in the gospel. The dyadic interrelationships pressure Philemon. Do they move him to act? We can hope so, but we have only Paul's "half" of the communication and do not know what wisdom formation and behaviors actually occurred.

---

11. See Vernon K. Robbins, *Exploring the Texture of Texts: A Guide to Socio-rhe-torical Interpretation* (Valley Forge, PA: Trinity Press International, 1996), 77–78.

12. See ibid., 79.

13. So, for example, when people have been invited and given, say, dinner at the home of friends or acquaintances, they may feel obligated to invite their hosts to dinner at their own home.

14. See ibid., 79.

15. I recognize I am using the odd terms "less equal" and "more equal." But they help convey an idea despite the incongruency.

Final Cultural Categories: What Social and Cultural Conditions Are Evoked and Created?

All the people playing roles in the rhetoric of the Letter to Philemon live in the dominant culture and rhetoric[16] of the eastern provinces of the Roman Empire. This means they are well aware of the presence of slavery, its practices, and its implications. They are also well aware of the new dominant culture and rhetoric of Christ Jesus, the gospel, the church, and eternity. It is this new dominant culture, the existence of which Paul presupposes (since he addresses Philemon as a believer), to which he calls Philemon to an even fuller practice than Philemon has engaged in previously. Presentation of the dominant cultural condition reminds Philemon of the faithful society of which he is already part. It is a contracultural or oppositional cultural rhetoric, because it calls for, it effectively commands, receiving the much lower status and separated Onesimus as a beloved brother. It calls for the de facto manumission of a slave. The rhetoric has the effect of creating the proper wisdom conditions, mindset, and social behavior of the new society.

Sacred Texture

Step Seven (Verse 21)

Paul has been demonstrating his fulfillment of the ethical commitment he has as a prisoner of Christ Jesus. In this step, he indicates his confidence that Philemon, too, will be obedient, indeed will do more than Paul asks. In the sacred, gospel, and *ekklēsia* context, Philemon can be counted on to do the right thing.

Step Eight (Verse 22)

Now Philemon is called to an additional and unexpected task. Paul, because he is rhetorically astute, knows that Philemon will feel the pressure to "obey," so he intensifies the force by claiming that Philemon's own prayers, which Paul presumes Philemon is offering on his behalf, will result in him coming to see Philemon. Paul requests Philemon to prepare

---

16. See ibid., 86–88.

hospitality space for him. Paul is implying that he is coming to check up on the sacred space and the sacred activity. So if Philemon is not praying for Paul, he is now pressured to begin, and he should expect that Paul will find some way to check up on the situation between himself and Onesimus. Philemon, to be sure, will be acting to refresh Paul's viscera by preparing the hospitality space.

Step Nine (Verses 23–25)

The closing step emphasizes the sacred texturing and ties it together. The greetings from the background characters—Epaphras, Mark, Aristarchus, Demas, and Luke—are all given "in Christ Jesus," just like the opening statement about Paul as prisoner of Christ Jesus. The closing benediction, corresponding to the opening greeting, warmly calls for grace on the spirit[17] of all concerned from the Lord Jesus Christ. The entire literary, rhetorical, and community environment is viewed as being in a sacred space.

There is a sacred argument in the **sacred texture**.

> You, Philemon, live in the sacred environment of Christ-believers. Live it out, therefore, do the right thing regarding Onesimus, because you now exist in the sacred environment. Live the reality of the new existence in the new society.

This sacred argument depends on the faith understanding that God and Christ Jesus are real characters in the narration. Neither God nor Jesus Christ speak in Philemon. Their existence and involvement is mostly implicit (except for God's role in the divine passive "he has been separated" in verse 15). God's action is anticipated even though it is unexplained. But the letter would not have been written nor the events of the situation narrated if God had not already and continuously been active. The sacred is therefore foundational to the letter. God is implicitly the source and sustainer of all the good accomplished and anticipated. Grace comes from God and Jesus Christ. God is the Father, and Jesus is the Lord of all of them. All things have a view toward eternity (v. 15). In Christ, in the Lord Jesus, there are new sacred connections. Philemon and the *ekklēsia* com-

---

17. Humans have a "spirit" (v. 25). This is the enlivening, life-sustaining human spirit, not the Holy Spirit. Mentioning it increases attention on the sacred as fundamental to the ideology of the discourse.

munity live and owe their allegiances not to the local, urban, and Roman sociocultural contexts, but to the context of Christ the Lord. Philemon is requested to behave correctly within this holy context. It is presented as the desire of God. Onesimus must be given all the care and consideration that others have already received in this same context.

Rhetorical Force as Emergent Discourse

The closing places final rhetorical pressure on Philemon as a leader in the emergent Christ-believing new society. Paul continues and completes his use of carefully crafted, emergent Christian language to shape Philemon's understanding and practice of relationship with Onesimus in the new society. Paul's rhetoric has forced Philemon and all listeners to consider that the usual ways of life must be examined, because things are more complex in the new society in Christ than they seem to be in the seemingly ordinary, culturally conditioned Mediterranean communities. Life in the new society of the *ekklēsia* is much more important than getting along in the societies outside it. Paul is prepared to hold Philemon responsible to the emerging morality by his own physical presence in Philemon's home and by pointing out that a number of fellow Christ-believers are watching to see what Philemon will do regarding Onesimus. In his emergent discourse Paul is creating a new wisdom of social relationships. People simply must not be oppressed and socially stratified in the *ekklēsia*.

Ideological Texture

Ideological texture considers "the social, cultural, and individual location[s] and perspective[s] of writers and readers."[1] Ideologies have to do with the beliefs, values, assumptions, philosophies, points of view, notions of right and wrong, justifications of positions whether well argued or not, doctrines, systems, politics, and power structures that affect people and things in the cultures in which they live. Ideologies have to do with how people see and understand the spatial and mental worlds in which they live. They direct and influence the expectations people have for what are perceived to be normative social organization, social behavior, and social interaction. People do not need to be immediately conscious of ideologies for them to be effective. People in cultures anticipate that they and others will behave socially in particular ideological ways or within generally understood boundaries. This makes ideologies powerful sociocultural or religious/theological constructs. Yet ideologies change because humans encounter or develop new or different ways of seeing life and material or spiritual reality and, consequently, desire or sometimes promote or even force ideological and sociocultural change.[2]

Texts (or the use of language at all, spoken, written, visualized, or implied) present themselves as rhetoric and so create ideologies. The ideologies created by the rhetoric are understood intellectually and psychologically when one "gets it."[3] These ideologies are not single and isolated,

---

1. Vernon K. Robbins, *Exploring the Texture of Texts: A Guide to Socio-rhetorical Interpretation* (Valley Forge, PA: Trinity Press International, 1996), 95. To "writers and readers" we can add "listeners" and even "visualizers."

2. On **ideological texture,** see ibid., 95–119.

3. Rhetoric often elicits what Ezra Pound called a "flash of understanding," "an affective psychological event" (Pound, "How to Read," in *Literary Essays of Ezra Pound,* ed. T. S. Eliot [London: Faber & Faber, 1954], 25–26; Roy R. Jeal, "Melody, Imagery, and Memory in the Moral Persuasion of Paul," in *Rhetoric, Ethic and Moral Persuasion*

but function in complex and frequently interactive or at least simultane-
ous ways. Ideologies created by textures and rhetographs are not value
neutral. They are meant to have argumentative power and outcomes. They
are meant to be effective in the lives of audience members. There are multiple ideological accounts to be considered. Examining the **ideological texture** of the Letter to Philemon in its ancient Mediterranean environment
is a complex undertaking, because it anticipates that the people connected
with the texts have varying and opposing points of view. Paul was working
from an ideology and aiming to move Philemon toward that ideology. He
employed the power of words in order to be socially formative. The letter
presents ideologies of new spaces of mind and behavior. These are wisdom
spaces where members of the new society live in loving, faithful, and productive ways.

My Ideology

It is fair for me, as author of this commentary, to offer some brief thoughts
about my own ideology.[4] I study and write as a biblical scholar who has a
deeply embedded theological orientation and a commitment as a Christian believer. I approach my own discipline of biblical studies critically and
rationally, yet simultaneously theologically, rhetorically, artistically, imagi-
natively, and confessionally. I think that it is right to do it in these ways. As
such, while I am ideologically committed to scholarship and to studying
New Testament texts for their own sake, I am also ideologically committed
to investigating what biblical texts *do* to people, *how* they evoke thoughts
and beliefs in human minds, and *how* they move people to behavior. I
am committed to good education that assists and encourages learners
to become critically knowledgeable persons who have a discerning perspective on life so that good can be done in the world and so that God
is respected and praised. This, in sociorhetorical terms, is a wisdom perspective where life is lived faithfully and productively in the world, in the
household, and in the church; where people aim to live the life of heaven
already in the present time. This means that I must "live" with the texts
and ideas and rhetorical force of the materials with which I work. I must
become part of the implicit narratives and metanarratives of the material

---

in Biblical Discourse, ed. Thomas H. Olbricht and Anders Eriksson, ESEC 11 [London:
T&T Clark, 2005], 162–63.
    4. See Robbins, *Exploring*, 96–98.

so that they are in my σπλάγχνα, my viscera. I study and learn the material first for the sake of learning and for the sake of what the biblical texts do to me, for what they make me to be. Then I am positioned to convey interpretation to others. My sociorhetorically informed ideology envisions something of the rhetorical force or rhetorical goal of the Letter to Philemon, namely, freedom for Onesimus, the end of slavery as a social construct and a cultural reality, and the kinship (brotherhood) of all in Christ.

Overall Ideological Texture

The overall ideology of Philemon is a wisdom, household, ecclesial worldview set within the ancient Mediterranean Roman context that envisions and promotes the new social order of the gospel. It is focused in the ecclesial environment in Philemon's house and, because of Paul's location (with Onesimus and perhaps others, vv. 10, 23), the place of his imprisonment (vv. 1–2, 9).[5] According to this new way of seeing the Mediterranean world, there are no distinctions among people. All persons—including and especially those who are imagined to be socially inferior like slaves and prisoners—are free family members, and Onesimus is explicitly to be regarded as Philemon's "beloved brother." Slaves are no longer slaves, and they dine with those who were owners and those who formerly ignored and mistreated them. The letter in this way throws Mediterranean people ideologically off center, undoubtedly Philemon in particular, but also Onesimus and the *ekklēsia* that meets in Philemon's house. This is a new ideological understanding that challenges and alters the generally accepted way of the world. It is important to Paul to push people to an off-centered position, because he understands the gospel to be countercultural and anticultural. The gospel is countercultural in the sense that it aims to alter some cultural and ideological understandings. It is anticultural in the sense that it stands against some cultural and ideological norms. It is by being moved ideologically off center that positive forward movement occurs. It does not matter that Onesimus the (former) slave and Philemon the (former) slave owner are separated. What does matter is that Onesimus has become a Christ-believer and is now linked to Paul in a (fictive) kinship, parent-child relationship (v. 10). Onesimus has become a servant of the gospel with Paul (v. 13). Paul implicitly claims

---

5. See ibid., 110–15, "Spheres of Ideology."

that perceived natural and hierarchical distinctions between and among people are invalid and may not be ideological positions for Christ-believers.[6] For Paul and for Philemon, Christ Jesus and the gospel are ideologically transcendent. There are now changed social and cultural expectations. This new ideology, however, creates questions and new situations vis-à-vis the ideologies with which Philemon, Paul, and the *ekklēsia* have been living. Christ-believers are called to a wisdom position that is out of synchronization with Mediterranean ideology. Paul does not indicate concern for the pressures and expectations of the ideological environment. He has his own allegiances that he is concerned to convey to his audiences. These ideologies are discussed in what follows.

Paul's Christ Jesus Ideology

Paul is the ideological change-maker in the letter by means of the rhetorical force of his language. For him, Christ Jesus is the ideological center of life. He is a "prisoner of Christ" (vv. 1, 9); he honors Jesus Christ as "Lord" (vv. 3, 5, 25);[7] he speaks of himself and others as being "in Christ" (vv. 8, 20, 23); and good is practiced with a view toward those who are in Christ (εἰς Χριστόν, v. 6). Paul is committed to faith in Christ Jesus and to those who are Christ-believers, including women (e.g., sister Apphia, v. 2) and slaves. His commitment extends to fictive kinship relations and language in the ideological "brother" (nominative ἀδελφός, v. 1; vocative ἀδελφέ, vv. 7, 20). This Christ ideology means that Paul is bound to the notion of the Christ-believing community, the *ekklēsia*, and to receiving all who are members of it. They are all understood in family relationship, as beloved brothers and sisters, in some cases as metaphorical parents and children (v. 10), without regard to social status or connections (cf. Col 3:11). Christ-believers are people whose actions are directed outward toward the good of others and who provide refreshment for the viscera of other Christ-believers (vv. 5–7, 20).

---

6. This is reminiscent of the narration of Acts 10, where new ideologies of food and ethnic relations are presented.

7. Paul characteristically refers to "Christ Jesus," but when he prefixes the word "Lord" he reverses his usage to "Jesus Christ" or simply "Jesus."

Paul's Prisoner Ideology

Though an actual prisoner, Paul views himself ideologically as a "prisoner of Christ" (vv. 1, 9, cf. vv. 13, 23). He declares this imprisonment openly in the letter. Being incarcerated does not in itself stop Paul from his service to Christ, because he recognizes a power higher than the civil power to which he is bound. His prisoner ideology stands against and, at least on his personal level, subverts Mediterranean ideology. Paul does not refer to himself as a prisoner of Caesar, of Rome, of the empire, or of local authorities.[8] Being a prisoner of Christ Jesus means that his work is tied ideologically to Christ, not to the more culturally acceptable and honorable ideology of being tied to Caesar and empire. Paul does not suffer from a sense of social dishonor or shame; indeed he implicitly refuses it. Paul knows that the absolutist emperor, living in his own household space, and the empire in its absolutist civic space do not directly care about Paul or the people connected with the letter. The emperor and the empire through their various agents will charge, imprison, and kill to continue their absolutist agenda. Paul knows that Christ Jesus does care for him, and he is therefore willing to be Christ's prisoner and refer to Jesus as Lord, rather than Caesar as Lord.

Ideology of the Gospel

Although the word "gospel" is employed only once in Philemon ("so that he might serve me on your behalf in the chains of the gospel," v. 13), the ideology implied is important. Paul rhetoricizes the gospel as something to which he and Philemon and Onesimus are bound or chained (δεσμός). Clearly Paul refers to the gospel, or good news of Christ Jesus, which he proclaimed and which Philemon and Onesimus have heard and believed. The gospel has affected the lives of all three persons (and clearly the others mentioned in the letter), and Paul anticipates that the proclamation will continue, now, he hopes, with the service of Onesimus. It is likely in this gospel connection, where Onesimus is imagined to serve with Paul on behalf of Philemon, that Paul aims to draw Philemon along with the notion of partnership ("If therefore you have me as partner, receive him as me," v. 17). Onesimus, in Paul's mind at least, is to

---

8. On the location of his imprisonment see the introduction to this commentary.

be Philemon's representative in the gospel partnership. For Philemon to receive Onesimus as a brother would be, figuratively speaking, to receive his gospel partner Paul. The ideology of the gospel implies that there is work to be done and all parties to the letter should be participants.

Ideology of Love and Faith

Love and faith[9] are central ideological notions that necessarily play a role in the **ideological texture**. Love (forms of ἀγάπη, vv. 1, 5, 7, 9, 16) and faith (vv. 5, 6) function as a kind of ideological bond that ties all persons together. It is clear that all persons named in the letter have faith in God and Christ Jesus. Love is the quality that moves people like Philemon to action for the good of others. The mindset of faith and love, then, is a fundamental feature leading toward the desired result of Paul's discourse.

Ideology of Eternity

Paul has a view beyond the present and, indeed, beyond his expectation that Philemon will receive Onesimus as a beloved brother. His view of the relationship has an eternal (αἰώνιος) perspective extending beyond the time of the return of Onesimus ("For perhaps this is why he was separated from you for a while, so that you might have him back forever," v. 15). In other words, according to Paul's ideology, what people see here and now where there are tensions between and among people is not how it shall always be. Paul believes in eternity, in "forever," and uses the notion to support his persuasion of Philemon to do the right thing.

Ideology of Abolitionism

Abolitionism is a modern term, but it is understood to refer to the ideology and associated movements to end slavery. While the history of the reception of the Letter to Philemon indicates that it has, in various times and circumstances, been understood both to support and oppose slavery, the sections above on **intertexture** and **social and cultural texture** demonstrate that Onesimus can no longer be visualized or treated as a

---

9. The terms appear in this order in verse 5 rather than the more frequent order "faith and love."

slave. Oppressed, marginalized, separated, and enslaved people have been reconciled in Christ and must be understood and treated accordingly in the *ekklēsia* community and by individual Christ-believers. Philemon can no longer treat Onesimus as a slave, because Onesimus has been freed in Christ. Philemon is to treat Onesimus as a "beloved brother," hence, implicitly and necessarily, *not* as a slave. Just as Joseph and his brothers were reconciled, so also must Philemon and Onesimus be reconciled. The formerly "useless" Onesimus is now "useful" and is a brother "in the Lord." Paul holds to an ideology of abolitionism, indeed to a theology of abolitionism, that demands, in fact provides, freedom for slaves. Philemon, now the brother of Onesimus, can no longer be imagined or rhetoricized as a slave owner. He is a person who has a reputation for refreshing the viscera of the holy ones, so he must now also refresh Onesimus. In the new society, which Paul considers to transcend Roman and Asian societies, those who were slaves are family members. This, to Paul, is the ideology of the *ekklēsia*. It is the ideology of the freedom of the gospel that Paul discusses in Gal 5 and Rom 6. It is the ideology of reconciliation that brings together Jews and gentiles, males and females, and slaves and free. It is the ideology of outsiders made to be insiders where the promises of God for reconciliation are fulfilled even in (relatively) minor characters like Philemon and Onesimus in some locale, perhaps Colossae, in the eastern provinces. The ideology of abolitionism contrasts sharply with Mediterranean ideology, which took slavery for granted and, from a practical point of view, considered slaves as nonpersons who deserved to be slaves. It amounts to an anti-imperial movement and stands opposed to the Aristotelian philosophy of slavery.[10] Philemon may have felt significant pressure to conform to the cultural and ideological understandings of slavery that he lived with. But at the same time, he felt the force of Paul's rhetoric, which did not permit him to reject the now useful Onesimus.

The **ideological texture** of Philemon suggests beliefs and views of the world and culture for audiences from Philemon and the Christ-believers who met in his house to people like us. It makes the letter theologically, rhetorically, and pragmatically important. While many have claimed that Philemon is short and *without* theology, in reality it is short and *full* of theology.

---

10. See on **intertexture**.

Rhetorical Force as Emergent Discourse

This profound letter is a small piece of the emergent discourse of early Christianity that is presented in the New Testament. It enters the socio-cultural, ideological, and religious world of the ancient Mediterranean, where society was highly and visibly stratified and people were expected to recognize and remain in their social levels and roles.[1] Paul the apostle thought deeply and shaped his language in order to express the new messianic faith understandings that were entering this world that he and other believers like Philemon inhabited. He was profoundly affected by his apocalyptic and gospel convictions about Jesus as the Messiah who fulfilled the expectations of Israel and brought about the reconciliation of all people (Jews and gentiles, slaves and free, males and females, Gal 3:28) and hope for the renewal and restoration of the creation (Rom 8:18–23). Out of all this he interpreted the new condition and new reality of life ἐν Χριστῷ as he went along. Paul did not work, speak, and write letters using a set of a fully developed, monolithic beliefs, doctrines, behaviors, and language that would suit any situation. Rather, he came to understand and write letters as his thinking and the demands and implications of life in Christ and in the *ekklēsia* called for applications to emerging circumstances such as the separation of Philemon and Onesimus and his own contact with Onesimus. This is the emergent nature of the Letter to Philemon. This is Paul "on the ground" addressing a new and very real situation requiring careful interpretation of the new faith and its multifaceted implications.

---

1. There was a distinct social hierarchy in the empire where social class and a patronage system (patron-client) was employed to maintain orderly, if segregated, relations. On this, see Richard P. Saller, *Personal Patronage under the Early Empire* (Cambridge: Cambridge University Press, 1982). See also Philip A. Harland, *Associations, Synagogues, and Congregations: Claiming a Place in Ancient Mediterranean Society* (Minneapolis: Fortress, 2003), 26–28. See the section above on **social and cultural texture** in "The Middle, Philemon 8–20."

The messianic faith entered a tough world for slaves, preachers, and faithful persons. Despite the recommendations of people like Seneca (*Ep.* 47),[2] slaves were effectively "nonpersons" of extremely low social status without power or prestige.[3] Rome ruled by force, and slaves were expected to do whatever they were directed to do, as beings who deserved to be the slaves they were. Preachers of the new messianic faith could find themselves in social and legal difficulty, even imprisonment, like Paul was experiencing when the Letter to Philemon was composed. Paul claims to have been imprisoned a number of times (2 Cor 11:23; Phil 1:12–14). Culturally speaking, old things were considered to be better than new things, so the proclamation of a new faith, or a new angle on an old one, was subject to question, debate, and rejection.[4] Religions of provincial or conquered peoples were tolerated by Rome, provided they did not stand against Roman religion or the government and customs of the empire itself.[5] The household, like Roman social structure more generally, was hierarchical. Leadership by the male head of family (the paterfamilias) was always assumed, with decreasing status through household members to women, children, and slaves. Altering the structures or allowing children or slaves to be undisciplined would very likely lead to social shame.[6] The point is that sociocultural expectations in the Roman Empire were rigid, and change was resisted. These conditions were not seen as things to change or overcome, but as things to accept as the normal and natural way life and society is ordered.

Paul entered this environment with his gospel proclamation. In other letters probably written during the same period of years as was Philemon (approximately 54 to 58 CE, perhaps to 60 CE at latest), he does not clearly indicate whether he had come to a complete view, as a believer in Jesus Christ, of slavery as a Mediterranean phenomenon. He has much to say about the enslavement of sin and freedom from it (Rom 6:16–22; Gal 5:1),

---

2. See above on **intertexture**.

3. Though there are examples of slaves who became influential.

4. Wisdom was perceived to lay with the people and ideas of the past, so the emerging messianic faith was often suspect (cf. Seneca, *Ep.* 90.44). On old being appreciated more than new, see Paul J. Achtemeier, Joel B. Green, and Marianne Meye Thompson, *Introducing the New Testament: Its Literature and Theology* (Grand Rapids: Eerdmans, 2001), 284.

5. See ibid., 285–87.

6. For discussion, see ibid., 287–88.

a corresponding but opposite enslavement to righteousness and to God (Rom 6:18, 22; 1 Cor 7:22), and the decision, by persons freed from the power of the law and sin, to become slaves to each other (Gal 5:13–14). Paul refers to himself as δοῦλος, a slave of Christ Jesus (Rom 1:1; Gal 1:10; see also Titus 1:1). However, when he addresses the existence of Christ-believers who are slaves in Corinth (1 Cor 7:21[–23]), his language is difficult to comprehend clearly. Does he mean there that slaves who become believers should remain enslaved? Does he mean that they should seek freedom? Or does he in fact mean that believers should continue conscientiously in their calling by God to faith in any situation in which they find themselves?[7] Certainly many early Christians were slaves. But in these letters Paul does not indicate or imply that slave owners should manumit their slaves because they are together familial members of the Christ-believing community. But when Paul comes into direct contact with the slave Onesimus, who becomes a believer and whom Paul knows is owned by his "partner" and "coworker" Philemon, he encounters and addresses a real life situation apparently not faced (or at least not mentioned) when the other letters were composed. What emerges is a new and particular ideology and request that transcends and in fact stands against the expectations of Mediterranean people. Philemon, the Christ-believing slave owner, should receive, accept, and treat Onesimus "no longer as a slave, but more than a slave, a beloved brother" (v. 16). There is here an inclusive and explicit vision of social relationships relative to slaves. There is a new society where the stratified and hierarchical arrangement of Mediterranean and Greco-Roman societies is resisted and replaced. In the new society slaves are no longer slaves, they are family members. This is the emerging, gospel view that Paul aims to impress on Philemon's mind. The slavery discourse that describes freedom from the slavery to sin and law in other letters from Paul is extended to the relationship between owner and slave and to the life of the localized believing community.

Why did Paul not explicitly request that Philemon manumit Onesimus? The absence of a clear and literal request for manumission has frequently been noted, persuading some interpreters to believe that Paul

---

7. As claimed by S. Scott Bartchy, *Mallon Chresai: First-Century Slavery and the Interpretation of 1 Corinthians 7:21*, SBLDS 11 (Missoula, MT: Scholars Press, 1973; repr., Eugene, OR: Wipf & Stock, 2003). For a description of views, see Markus Barth and Helmut Blanke, *The Letter to Philemon*, ECC (Grand Rapids: Eerdmans, 2000), 191–200.

did not stand against slavery. Some, in the history of interpretation, have thought that Paul, by not making an explicit statement against it, supported the institution of slavery. Others suggest that Paul was not explicit, because he and other authors of New Testament documents[8] were not willing "to announce a full frontal assault on the institution of slavery ... a social revolution that the church could not contemplate."[9] The answer to these views is that Paul *does* say it, *subtly, obliquely,* yet *clearly* enough in his rhetorical shaping of language. Onesimus is not a slave; he is a brother. Paul does not command Philemon, though he claims he could do so righteously (v. 8). His approach, in contrast to the brute force and social expectations of empire, is to seek voluntary consent. Still, he calls Philemon to resist social and cultural expectations and pressures regarding slavery. This is new religious discourse in the empire and in the church. While freedom from slavery might be only implicit and more theologically oriented in other Pauline letters, it is in Philemon developed more fully around a specific human situation. In this letter a Christ-believing slave is owned by someone who is also a believer. Paul has been moved to inform the owner, Philemon, that the inequality and oppression of slavery has no place in the new society. Among its members the fundamental relationship is familial. It is incongruous for "brothers" to be simultaneously to one another owners and slaves. It would be frivolous to imagine that Paul had in mind, in this letter, to mount a full and public attack against slavery. It would be some time before the letter would receive a wider circulation. The social inversion within the *ekklēsia* nevertheless produces an emergent structure in Mediterranean discourse and society, initiating a powerful developing notion that would inevitably be noticed in the larger public community.

Paul makes his appeal against slavery in a personal message to Philemon, knowing that others are looking on and listening in. Although there are a number of these onlookers, they are all insiders who are connected with Paul or with Philemon in some way. Paul employs manipulative but gentle rhetoric and the social topoi of love, partnership, brotherhood,

---

8. See, e.g., 1 Pet 2:18–25.

9. David A. deSilva, *Honor, Patronage, Kinship and Purity: Unlocking New Testament Culture* (Downers Grove, IL: InterVarsity Press, 2000), 235. Yet many New Testament texts indicate a strong rhetoric of resistance to social, cultural, and imperial customs and institutions. The real king is Jesus not Caesar. Paul terms himself a prisoner of Christ, not Caesar (Phlm 1).

eternity, and refreshment of the viscera to make his point and his appeal to Philemon. This rhetoric is forceful as new Christian discourse that contrasts with usual wordings intended to give directions and instructions. Love is central to Paul's approach. He subtly juxtaposes Philemon's love for the Lord Jesus and all the holy ones (vv. 5, 7) and his own appeal through love (vv. 8–9) with his "child" (v. 10) Onesimus, who is a slave (v. 16). In this visible and palpable context of love, Paul works to move Philemon to extend love to his slave. In stark contrast to socially expected relationships with slaves, love (ἀγάπη) is to be extended to Onesimus. Closely associated with love are the relational notions of "partnership" (κοινωνία, v. 6; κοινωνός, v. 17) and "viscera" (σπλάγχνα, vv. 7, 12, 20). Philemon is already well known for his refreshment of the viscera of Christ-believers (v. 7). Onesimus has become Paul's own viscera, hence deeply emotionally connected to Paul (v. 12). Paul and Philemon are "partners," coworkers in the gospel and the care of fellow believers. Paul calls on his partner Philemon to refresh his viscera by receiving Onesimus in the same way Philemon receives Paul himself (vv. 17, 20). Onesimus is presented by Paul in this manner as someone who is *equal* to himself and Philemon in every way. The topos of "eternity" (αἰώνιος, "eternal") is also rhetorically significant, because it extends the anticipated brotherly relationship between Philemon and Onesimus beyond the present temporal plane to everlasting existence.

Paul has produced an emergent rhetorical discourse that is not found in the same ways in other Mediterranean or New Testament contexts. The topoi of love, partnership, viscera, and eternity are inward, emotional, pathos, and sacred things understood by Christ-believers, yet contextually new to them and to the ancient Mediterranean setting. Paul has himself been moved to these understandings through his own encounters with the apocalyptic gospel and his more recent relationship with Onesimus, who is a dramatically different man than he was previously. Formerly he was "useless," but now he is "useful" and a fellow believer with Paul and Philemon. Now he, too, can do good things for the sake of the gospel (vv. 11, 13). The belief and behavioral changes in Onesimus must surely make for a turning point in Paul's thinking. In this new and different sacred, ideological, and emotional context people are brothers and sisters, family members, together. This family is the new society, the *ekklēsia*, some members of which already gather in Philemon's home. The mental locus of this new context is "in Christ" and "in the Lord" (vv. 6, 8, 16, 20, 23) with God as Father (v. 3). God is the Father by whom grace and peace are provided, not the *Pater Patriae* Caesar.[10] Paul does not, like Seneca, for example,[11] simply offer criticism about how owners (and others) treat slaves. He envisions and calls for actualized familial relations, based on his apocalyptic conception of the new, transformed reality of eternity already in the present time.

Philemon very likely found Paul's letter to present an imposing challenge. People living in the polis and empire were not accustomed to receiving slaves in the way Paul requests. The dramatic changes that reception of a slave as a brother imply could have been very uncomfortable due to the potential for questioning and conflict. Still, Paul calls for the new society to include persons envisioned to be socially unacceptable. Recognizing that things have changed, he calls for familial existence and resistance to social pressures regardless of what people think. Paul calls for the reality of one body of diverse yet interrelated and interconnected parts (cf. 1 Cor 12:12–27). This one and unified body is an emerging community that is receiving instruction and being made real precisely through this piece of early Christian literature. Philemon is an emergent text, and the *ekklēsia* is an emerging body in the ancient Mediterranean context. Paul makes a bold and brilliant social move. His rhetoric aims to bring the slave owner Philemon on side in the matter regarding Onesimus, not to command obedience. Perhaps not all who were called to receive former slaves as brothers could (or would) grasp the idea. Some households remain in dysfunction. It is not our task here to inquire into that psychology. Paul's rhetoric requires a mature view, a view past the more juvenile and earthly concerns to maintain power and status by force. Paul asks for maturity and a mature spirit.

The rhetorical force in this emergent structure is found in the new story line, the new narrative of life where, rather than the emperor and the brutality of empire, the Lord Jesus Christ, the gospel, love, and faith shown in the refreshment of people, reconciliation, freedom, equality, and brotherhood are the central motifs. This narrative transcends the present in its view to eternity. The rhetorical force of the text is aimed directly at Philemon, to bring about, in him, a new disposition of mind that is socially formative. The rhetoric is meant to move Philemon to put his love and faith into full practical application. Its rhetoric moves people to fullness

---

10. Nero, the emperor when the letter was written, was one of the emperors who was declared *Pater Patriae*, "father of the fatherland," by the Roman Senate.

11. See above on **intertexture**.

of inclusive community ἐν Χριστῷ. This is a morality new to the Roman world of the Mediterranean basin.

The rhetography, the rhetorolects, and the textures of the Letter to Philemon present a very complex interplay of images, language, and ideas that overlap and interweave with each other. This interplay functions to bring socially separated and potentially antagonistic characters together. Paul compellingly plays a very strong role over Philemon even as he portrays himself as an elderly prisoner under the authority of Christ. Paul lays out and manipulates the visual scene. It seems clear that, in the end, he will get what he wants. Philemon, along with his house-church friends and along with readers of the letter like ourselves, is driven to visualize Paul traveling to Philemon's house and staying there in the lodging provided and to visualize brother Onesimus there at the same time.

The new social space brought about by the blending of images, textures, and spaces challenges and aims at reforming Mediterranean understanding and practice. In this new space the old social roles of owner and slave are no longer discernible. Now brothers are seen, living in a newly created social and faith space where tensions of a former time are removed.[12] Philemon's anticipated change of behavior is not brought about by sudden enforced change, or by apostolic order, but by persuasion. He is *moved* into new space where a new kind of future is envisioned. The letter to Philemon presents a visual microcosm of a major aspect of Paul's work "on the ground": bringing socially diverse and antagonistic peoples together.

We might be surprised at the highly manipulative rhetoric of the letter. Paul might be seen as calculating and unfairly shrewd. He pushes Philemon into a corner. It might seem odd that such a personal communication was placed in the New Testament canon. Clearly, however, it received a wider notice, and it has a distinctive place in the Pauline corpus of letters. Its innovative, socially striking forcefulness prompts the minds of its audiences to envision its characters and activities, but also to see beyond the immediate picture of Paul, Philemon, Onesimus, and the others to the larger theological scene of the new caring community in actual operation. The new society is a loving company of believers who look after each other. In this way the letter turns out to be not so personal and local after all. Placing it in the New Testament canon was a wise move. It is crucial

---

12. A great sadness, of course, is that Christians and the church, despite the good they have done, have often not—perhaps rarely—lived up to the life of this space.

for understanding Paul's thinking. His rhetoric is about drawing disparate people together. This is integral to his theology. Though short and often only at the periphery of the interest of readers of the New Testament, indeed often overlooked, it turns out to be a key to understanding Paul and his letters. It demonstrates something of his understanding of what Christ Jesus has brought about in the world. It demonstrates his grasp of the scope of the church, of community, of fellowship, and Christian partnership and affinity. It tells us much about Paul's rhetorical and intellectual ability. All of this is suggestive about why the letter was preserved and canonized. Paul is a teacher. He wants the churches and the people in them to do the right things and be productive and inclusive. This is Paul's Christ-believing character, his life, his viscera.

Bibliography

Achtemeier, Paul J., Joel B. Green, and Marianne Meye Thompson. *Introducing the New Testament: Its Literature and Theology*. Grand Rapids: Eerdmans, 2001.

"Ancient Writing Materials: Wax Tablets." University of Michigan Library website. http://www.lib.umich.edu/papyrus-collection/ancient-writing -materials-wax-tablets.

Andreau, Jean. *Banking and Business in the Roman World*. Cambridge: Cambridge University Press, 1999.

———. "Personal Endebtment and Debt Forgiveness in the Roman Empire." Committee for the Abolition of Third World Debt Website. 17 December 2012. http://cadtm.org/Personal-endebtment-and-debt.

Aristotle. *Art of Rhetoric*. Translated by J. H. Freese. LCL 193. Cambridge: Harvard University Press, 1926.

———. *Nichomachean Ethics*. Translated by H. Rackham. LCL 73. Cambridge: Harvard University Press, 1926.

———. *On the Soul; Parva Naturalia; On Breath*. Translated by W. S. Hett. LCL 288. Cambridge: Harvard University Press, 1957.

———. *Politics*. Translated by H. Rackham. LCL 264. Cambridge: Harvard University Press, 1932.

———. *Rhetorica ad Alexandrum*. Translated by H. Rackham. LCL 317. Cambridge: Harvard University Press, 1937.

Arzt-Grabner, Peter. "How to Deal with Onesimus? Paul's Solution within the Frame of Ancient Legal and Documentary Sources." Pages 113–42 in *Philemon in Perspective: Interpreting Pauline Letter*. Edited by D. François Tolmie. Berlin: de Gruyter, 2010.

Barclay, John M. G. *Colossians and Philemon*. NTG. Sheffield: Sheffield Academic, 1997.

Bartchy, S. Scott. "The Epistle to Philemon." *ABD* 5:307–8.

———. *Mallon Chresai: First-Century Slavery and the Interpretation of 1 Corinthians 7:21*. SBLDS 11. Missoula, MT: Scholars Press, 1973. Repr., Eugene, OR: Wipf & Stock, 2003.

Barth, Markus, and Helmut Blanke. *The Letter to Philemon*. ECC. Grand Rapids: Eerdmans, 2000.

Bauernfeind, Otto. "Ἀναπαύω." *TDNT* 1:250–51.

Bjerkelund, C. J. *Parakalō, Form, Funktion und Sinn der parakalō-Sätze in den paulinischen Briefen*. Oslo: Universitetsforlaget, 1967.

Brown, Raymond E. *An Introduction to the New Testament*. New York: Doubleday, 1997.

Bruce, F. F. "Colossian Problems Part One: Jews and Christians in the Lycus Valley." *BSac* 141 (1984): 3–15.

Bryan, Christopher. *Listening to the Bible: The Art of Faithful Biblical Interpretation*. Oxford: Oxford University Press, 2014.

Byron, John. "The Epistle to Philemon: Paul's Strategy for Forging the Ties of Kinship." Pages 205–16 in *Jesus and Paul: Global Perspectives in Honor of James D. G. Dunn for His 70th Birthday*. Edited by B. J. Oropeza, C. K. Robertson, and Douglas C. Mohrmann. London: T&T Clark, 2010.

Bultmann, Rudolf. "Ἀναγινώσκω, ἀνάγνωσις." *TDNT* 1:343–44.

Cahill, Thomas. *Sailing the Wine-Dark Sea: Why the Greeks Matter*. New York: Doubleday, 2003.

Callahan, Allen Dwight. *Embassy of Onesimus: The Letter of Paul to Philemon*. Valley Forge, PA: Trinity Press International, 1997.

Canavan, Rosemary. *Clothing in the Body of Christ at Colossae*. WUNT 334. Tübingen: Mohr Siebeck, 2012.

Cicero. *Rhetorica ad Herennium*. Translated by Harry Caplan. LCL 403. Cambridge: Harvard University Press, 1954.

Deissmann, Adolf. *Light from the Ancient East: The New Testament Illustrated by Recently Discovered Texts of the Graeco-Roman World*. London: Hodder & Stoughton, 1910.

DeSilva, David A. *Honor, Patronage, Kinship and Purity: Unlocking New Testament Culture*. Downers Grove, IL: InterVarsity Press, 2000.

———. "The Invention and Argumentative Function of Priestly Discourse in the Epistle to the Hebrews." *BBR* 16 (2006): 295–323.

———. "Seeing Things John's Way: Rhetography and Conceptual Blending in Revelation 14:6–13." *BBR* 18 (2008): 271–98.

———. "A Sociorhetorical Interpretation of Revelation 14:6–13: A Call to Act Justly toward the Just and Judging God." *BBR* 9 (1999): 65–117.

Dinesen, Isak [Karen Blixen, pseud.]. "Echoes From the Hills." Pages 119–20 in *Shadows on the Grass*. Chicago: University of Chicago Press, 1960.

Doty, William G. *Letters in Primitive Christianity*. Philadelphia: Fortress, 1973.

Dunn, James D. G. *The Epistles to the Colossians and to Philemon*. NIGTC. Grand Rapids: Eerdmans, 1996.

Elliott, Neil. *The Arrogance of Nations: Reading Romans in the Shadow of Empire*. Minneapolis: Fortress, 2010.

Elliott, Neil, and Mark Reasoner, eds. *Documents and Images for the Study of Paul*. Minneapolis: Fortress, 2011.

Felder, Cain Hope. "The Letter to Philemon." *NIB* 11:883–905.

Fitzmyer, Joseph A. *The Letter to Philemon: A New Translation with Introduction and Commentary*. AB 34C. New York: Doubleday, 2000.

Glancy, Jennifer. *Slavery in Early Christianity*. Minneapolis: Fortress, 2006.

Harland, Philip A. *Associations, Synagogues, and Congregations: Claiming a Place in Ancient Mediterranean Society*. Minneapolis: Fortress, 2003.

Harrill, J. Albert. *Slaves in the New Testament: Literary, Social and Moral Dimensions*. Minneapolis: Fortress, 2006.

Hays, Richard B. "Crucified with Christ: A Synthesis of the Theology of 1 and 2 Thessalonians, Philemon, Philippians, and Galatians." Pages 227–46 in vol. 1 of *Pauline Theology*. Edited by Jouette M. Bassler. Philadelphia: Fortress, 1994.

Head, Peter M. "Onesimus and the Letter to Philemon: New Light on the Role of the Letter Carrier." *RBECS*. 31 May 2012. http://rbecs.org/2012/05/31/peter-m-head-letter-carrier/.

Houlden, J. Leslie. *Paul's Letters from Prison: Philippians, Colossians, Philemon, Ephesians*. London: Penguin, 1970.

Hurtado, Larry W. "Oral Fixation and New Testament Studies? 'Orality,' 'Performance' and Reading Texts in Early Christianity." *NTS* 60 (2014): 321–40.

Jeal, Roy R. "Blending Two Arts: Rhetorical Words, Rhetorical Pictures and Social Formation in the Letter to Philemon." *Sino-Christian Studies* 5 (2008): 9–38.

———. "Clothes Make the (Wo)Man." *Scriptura* 90 (2005): 685–99.

———. *Integrating Theology and Ethics in Ephesians: The Ethos of Communication*. Lewiston, NY: Mellen, 2000.

———. "Melody, Imagery, and Memory in the Moral Persuasion of Paul." Pages 160–78 in *Rhetoric, Ethic and Moral Persuasion in Biblical Dis-*

course. Edited by Thomas H. Olbricht and Anders Eriksson. ESEC 11. London: T&T Clark, 2005.

———. "Rhetorical Argumentation in Ephesians." Pages 310–24 in *Rhetorical Argumentation in Biblical Texts.* Edited by Anders Eriksson, Thomas H. Olbricht, and Walter Übelacker. ESEC 8. Harrisburg, PA: Trinity Press International, 2002.

———. "Visual Interpretation: Blending Rhetorical Arts in Colossians 2:6–3:4." In *Biblical Rhetography through Visual Exegesis of Text and Image.* Edited by Vernon K. Robbins, Walter S. Melion, and Roy R. Jeal. ESEC. Atlanta: SBL Press, forthcoming.

Johnson, Luke Timothy. *The Writings of the New Testament: An Interpretation.* Rev. ed. Minneapolis: Fortress, 1999.

Johnson, Matthew V., James A. Noel, and Demetrius K. Williams, eds. *Onesimus Our Brother: Reading Religion, Race, and Culture in Philemon.* Minneapolis: Fortress, 2012.

Josephus. *Jewish Antiquities.* Translated by Ralph Marcus. Vol. 3. LCL 281. Cambridge: Harvard University Press, 1934.

———. *Life of Josephus. Against Apion.* Translated by Henry St. J. Thackeray. LCL 186. Cambridge: Harvard University Press, 1926.

Kahneman, Daniel. *Thinking Fast and Slow.* New York: Farrar, Straus, & Giroux, 2011.

Kennedy, George A., trans. *Progymnasmata: Greek Textbooks of Prose Composition and Rhetoric.* Atlanta: Society of Biblical Literature, 2003.

Kittel, Gerhard. "Αἰχμάλωτός." *TDNT* 1:195–97.

Kittel, Gerhard, and Gerhard Friedrich, eds. *Theological Dictionary of the New Testament.* Translated by Geoffrey W. Bromiley. 10 vols. Grand Rapids: Eerdmans, 1964–1976.

Knox, John. *Philemon among the Letters of Paul.* 1935. Repr., New York: Abingdon, 1959.

Köster, Helmut. "Σπλάγχνον." *TDNT* 7:548–59.

Kreitzer, Larry J. *Philemon.* Readings: A New Biblical Commentary. Sheffield: Sheffield Phoenix, 2008.

Lampe, G. W. H. *A Patristic Greek Lexicon.* Oxford: Clarendon, 1961.

Lampe, Peter. "Kleine 'Sklavenflucht' des Onesimus." *ZNW* 76 (1985): 135–37.

Lanham, Richard A. *A Handlist of Rhetorical Terms.* Berkeley: University of California Press, 1968.

Lausberg, Heinrich. *Handbook of Literary Rhetoric: A Foundation for Liter-*

ary Study. Edited by David E. Orton and R. Dean Anderson. Leiden: Brill, 1998.

Lee, Margaret Ellen, and Bernard Brandon Scott. *Sound Mapping the New Testament*. Salem, OR: Polebridge, 2009.

Lee, Max. "More Pastoral Reflections on the Life of a Slave and Paul's Letter to Philemon." In *Paul Redux: The Gospel of Jesus Christ in the Greco-Roman World* (weblog). 26 February 2014. http://paulredux. blogspot.com/2014/02/more-pastoral-reflections-on-life-of.html.

Malherbe, Abraham J. *Ancient Epistolary Theorists*. Atlanta: Scholars Press, 1988.

Malina, Bruce J. *The New Testament World: Insights From Cultural Anthropology*. 3rd ed. Louisville: Westminster John Knox, 2001.

Martin, Clarice J. "The Rhetorical Function of Commercial Language in Paul's Letter to Philemon (Verse 18)." Pages 321–37 in *Persuasive Artistry: Studies in New Testament Rhetoric in Honor of George A. Kennedy*. Edited by Duane F. Watson. Sheffield: JSOT Press, 1991.

Martin, Dale B. *Slavery as Salvation: The Metaphor of Slavery in Pauline Christianity*. New Haven: Yale University Press, 1990.

McManus, Barbara F. "Social Class and Public Display." *VROMA: A Virtual Community for Teaching and Learning Classics*. 2009. http://www. vroma.org/~bmcmanus/socialclass.html.

Michaelis, Wilhelm. "Θεωρέω." *TDNT* 5:315–18.

Moo, Douglas J. *The Letters to the Colossians and Philemon*. PNTC. Grand Rapids: Eerdmans, 2008.

Moulton, J. H., and G. Milligan. *Vocabulary of the Greek New Testament*. London: Hodder & Stoughton, 1914. Repr. Grand Rapids: Baker, 1995.

Mullins, Terrence Y. "Formulas in New Testament Epistles." *JBL* 91 (1972): 380–90.

Murphy-O'Connor, Jerome. *Paul: A Critical Life*. Oxford: Oxford University Press, 1998.

Nordling, John G. "*Onesimus Fugitivus*: A Defense of the Runaway Slave Hypothesis in Philemon." *JSNT* 41 (1991): 97–119.

———. *Philemon*. ConC. Saint Louis: Concordia, 2004.

O'Gorman, Ned. "Aristotle's *Phantasia* in the *Rhetoric*: *Lexis*, Appearance, and the Epideictic Function of Discourse." *Philosophy and Rhetoric* 38 (2005): 16–40.

Pao, David W. *Colossians and Philemon*. ZECNT. Grand Rapids: Zondervan, 2012.

Pearson, Brook W. R. "Assumptions in the Criticism and Translation of Philemon." Pages 253–80 in *Translating the Bible: Problems and Prospects*. Edited by Stanley E. Porter and Richard S. Hess. Sheffield: Sheffield Academic, 1999.

Petersen, Norman R. *Rediscovering Paul: Philemon and the Sociology of Paul's Narrative World*. Philadelphia: Fortress, 1985.

Philo. *On the Creation. Allegorical Interpretation of Genesis 2 and 3*. Translated by F. H. Colson. LCL 226. Cambridge: Harvard University Press, 1929.

Plato. *Laws*. Translated by R. G. Bury. 2 vols. LCL 187 and 192. Cambridge: Harvard University Press, 1926.

Pliny the Younger. *Letters*. Translated by Betty Radice. 2 vols. LCL 55 and 59. Cambridge: Harvard University Press, 1969.

Pound, Ezra. "How to Read." Pages 15–40 in *Literary Essays of Ezra Pound*. Edited by T. S. Eliot. London: Faber & Faber, 1954.

———. *How to Read*. New York: Haskell House, 1971.

Rapske, Brian. *The Book of Acts and Paul in Roman Custody*. Vol. 3 of *The Book of Acts in its First Century Setting*. Edited by Bruce W. Winter. Grand Rapids: Eerdmans, 1994.

———. "The Prisoner Paul in the Eyes of Onesimus." *NTS* 37 (1991): 187–203.

Richards, E. R. *The Secretary in the Letters of Paul*. Tübingen: Mohr Siebeck, 1991.

Robbins, Vernon K. "The Dialectical Nature of Early Christian Discourse." *Scriptura* 59 (1996): 353–62.

———. *Exploring the Texture of Texts: A Guide to Socio-rhetorical Interpretation*. Valley Forge, PA: Trinity Press International, 1996.

———. *The Invention of Christian Discourse*. Vol. 1. Dorset, UK: Deo, 2009.

———. *The Invention of Christian Discourse*. Vol. 2. SBL Press, forthcoming.

———. "Rhetography: A New Way of Seeing the Familiar Text." Pages 81–106 in *Words Well Spoken: George Kennedy's Rhetoric of the New Testament*. Edited by C. Clifton Black and Duane F. Watson. Waco, TX: Baylor University Press, 2008.

———. "Socio-rhetorical Interpretation." Pages 192–219 in *The Blackwell Companion to the New Testament*. Edited by David E. Aune. Oxford: Blackwell, 2010.

———. *The Tapestry of Early Christian Discourse: Rhetoric, Society and Ideology*. London: Routledge, 1996.

Saller, Richard P. *Personal Patronage under the Early Empire.* Cambridge: Cambridge University Press, 1982.

Saramago, José. *The Cave.* Translated by Margaret Jull Costa. Orlando: Harcourt, 2002.

Seneca. *Epistles.* Translated by Richard M. Gummere. 3 vols. LCL 75. Cambridge: Harvard University Press, 1917.

Spicq, Ceslas. *Theological Lexicon of the New Testament.* Peabody, MA: Hendrickson, 1994.

Stowers, Stanley. *Letter Writing in Greco-Roman Antiquity.* Philadelphia: Westminster, 1986.

Sumney, Jerry L. "Writing in 'The Image' of Scripture: The Form and Function of References to Scripture in Colossians." Pages 185–229 in *Paul and Scripture: Extending the Conversation.* Edited by Christopher D. Stanley. Atlanta: Society of Biblical Literature, 2012.

Thompson, Marianne Meye. *Colossians and Philemon.* Two Horizons Commentary. Grand Rapids: Eerdmans, 2005.

Visser, Margaret. *Beyond Fate.* 2002 Massey Lectures. Toronto: House of Anansi, 2003.

———. *The Geometry of Love: Space, Time, Mystery, and Meaning in an Ordinary Church.* Toronto: HarperPerennial, 2000.

Wallace, Daniel B. *Greek Grammar beyond the Basics: An Exegetical Syntax of the New Testament.* Grand Rapids: Zondervan, 1996.

———. *Scribal Methods and Materials.* The Center for the Study of New Testament Manuscripts. iTunesU. https://itunes.apple.com/us/itunes-u/scribal-methods-materials/id446658178.

Wansink, Craig S. "Philemon." Pages 263–67 in *The Oxford Bible Commentary: The Pauline Epistles.* Edited by John Muddiman and John Barton. Oxford: Oxford University Press, 2010.

Weima, Jeffrey A. D. "Paul's Persuasive Prose: An Epistolary Analysis of the Letter to Philemon." Pages 29–60 in *Philemon in Perspective: Interpreting a Pauline Letter.* Edited by D. François Tolmie. Berlin: de Gruyter, 2010.

Wessels, G. François. "The Letter to Philemon in the Context of Slavery in Early Christianity." Pages 143–68 in *Philemon in Perspective: Interpreting a Pauline Letter.* Edited by D. François Tolmie. Berlin: de Gruyter, 2010.

Westermann, William L. *The Slave Systems of Greek and Roman Antiquity.* Philadelphia: American Philosophical Society, 1955.

White, John L. "Ancient Greek Letters." Pages 85–105 in *Greco-Roman*

Literature and the New Testament. Edited by David E. Aune. Atlanta: Scholars Press, 1988.

White, John L. *Light from Ancient Letters*. Philadelphia: Fortress, 1986.

Wilson, Robert McL. *A Critical and Exegetical Commentary on Colossians and Philemon*. ICC. London: Bloomsbury, 2014.

Winter, Sara C. "Paul's Letter to Philemon." *NTS* 33 (1987): 1–15.

Wright, N. T. "Return of the Runaway?" Pages 3–74 in *Paul and the Faithfulness of God*. Minneapolis: Fortress, 2013.

Ancient Sources Index

Modern Authors Index

Subject Index

abolition(ism), abolitionist, 2, 127–28, 162, 179, 200–201

amicus domini. See friend of the master

anacoluthon, 99, 110–11

anticipated result, 31–32, 42, 67, 70–72, 88, 110–13, 115–16, 119–20, 173, 180, 182, 189

apocalyptic, xii, xiii, xxvii, 6, 33, 49–50, 95–96, 112–15, 155, 169, 170–76, 203, 207–08

appeal, request, urging, 1, 20, 24, 27, 31–33, 60–62, 69, 70–71, 73–74, 77, 86, 90–91, 94, 99–100, 101–2, 105–9 115, 119, 122–31, 132–34, 136, 137, 156, 160, 167, 170–73, 179, 183–85, 205–7

Apphia, 21, 22, 29, 33, 39–41, 66, 69, 70, 75, 78, 86, 89, 93, 95–96, 106, 164, 175, 185, 190

Archippus, 19–22, 25, 29, 33, 39–41, 66, 69, 70, 75, 78, 86, 89, 93, 95–96, 106, 164, 185, 190

argumentation, 13, 18, 20, 31–32, 36, 41–43, 45–46, 59–61, 64–65, 70–72, 86, 88, 99–100, 104, 106–20, 123, 135, 170–71, 173, 177, 180–82, 184, 186, 192, 196

Aristarchus, 16, 18, 21, 28, 40, 54, 56, 178, 181, 183, 188, 192

Asia Minor, Asian, 31, 84, 161, 164–65, 201

assembly, xviii, 1, 6, 8, 14, 19, 21–23, 25, 27, 29, 32–34, 40–41, 43–45, 48–49, 53, 68, 70–71, 76, 78, 81, 83–86, 88–96, 106, 114, 116, 118, 131, 133– 35, 139, 144, 153, 155–57, 160–62, 164, 168–69, 171–72, 175, 179, 181–82, 185, 187, 189–93, 196–98, 201, 203, 206–10

audience, 20–22

aural reception, 9, 13, 17–18, 20, 36, 46, 73, 76–78, 80, 119, 123, 126, 128–29, 131–32, 184–85

author, 16–18

beloved brother. *See* brother

blending, 1, 9, 11, 45, 46, 209

brother, 1, 8, 23–24, 26, 31–32, 42–43, 49–53, 61, 68, 70, 74, 80, 86, 99, 105, 108–10, 114–16, 118–20, 124, 127– 28, 131, 144, 152–57, 160–69, 171, 173–76, 180, 182, 197, 198, 200, 201, 205–6, 208–09

brotherhood, 2, 23, 44, 61, 78, 80, 85, 88–89, 95, 106, 108–9, 114, 119, 124, 127–28, 131, 138–39, 148, 153–57, 164, 173–75, 186, 189, 197, 198, 206. *See also* family

Caesarea Maritima, 26, 30

canonicity, 2, 22–23, 209

captatio benevolentiae, 102, 109

chiasmus, chiastic structure, 74–77

child, 1, 24, 31, 44–45, 47, 49, 50, 88, 101–3, 106–7, 111–12, 116, 120, 124, 127, 131, 134, 157, 164, 167, 169–71, 175–76, 180, 187, 207

Christ. *See* Jesus Christ, Christ Jesus

church. *See* assembly; *ekklēsia*; new society

circumstances. *See* occasion

cognitive ease, cognitive strain, 100

CPSIA information can be obtained at www.ICGtesting.com
Printed in the USA
LVOW11s1630291015

460296LV00003B/606/P